RELENTLESS

BILL DANIELS
AND
THE TRIUMPH OF CABLE TV

RELENTLESS

BILL DANIELS
AND
THE TRIUMPH OF CABLE TV

BY STEPHEN SINGULAR

ISBN 0-9670128-1-3

Produced by James Charlton Associates
Designed by CMYK Design Inc.

Photos courtesy of The Bill Daniels Estate

Acknowledgments

The author and trustees of The Bill Daniels Estate gratefully acknowledge and thank these people for their extraordinary assistance:

Gretchen Bunn, for her invaluable research that included interviews with more than 250 individuals.

Bob Russo, for his vision and determination to honor Bill's life and legacy through this text and priceless photographs.

John Saeman, for his tireless efforts to ensure the accuracy and integrity of this biography.

Introduction

If one were to ask me to name someone who exemplified the dynamism of America in the twentieth century, I'd be hard-pressed to come up with a better model than my old friend, Bill Daniels.

He was a child of the Depression who came to manhood in the crucible of World War II. He was a legendary fighter pilot who survived the first kamikaze attack of the Pacific war, was a team member of the prototype for the Blue Angels, and served his country in the Korean campaign as well.

When he returned to civilian life in the early 1950s, he embarked on a visionary and adventurous career that ultimately impacted the way the world communicates. He was not only the father of cable television, but one of the first to see that cable had the potential to create programming alternatives to the limited world of the three broadcast networks.

Along the way he played a pivotal role in the way America, and the world, would learn about the news, watch sports, and even talk on their cell phones. His path crossed many of the legends of his era, from Muhammad Ali to Ted Turner to Ronald Reagan.

Bill made and lost and remade fortunes. As an entrepreneur he took great risks, and those who believed in him benefited enormously.

He loved politics, and he loved the Republican Party. But even more, he loved the give-and-take of political discourse. Bill had friends on both sides of the aisle and respected his opponents as much as he respected his allies. He was a gentleman in a game where a lot of people didn't always play by the rules.

Bill was no saint—some of his escapades were legendary. But when he passed away, over a thousand people journeyed to Denver to pay him homage. Not just the rich and famous, but people whose lives had been touched by his generosity, his kindness, his concern for others.

Winston Churchill once said, "You make a living by what you earn, you make a life by what you give." By Churchill's standards, Bill made quite a life.

He used his great fortune to transform educational institutions, like the pathbreaking Daniels School of Business at the University of Denver, the first major graduate business program in the country to make ethics the center point of its curriculum. He established the Daniels Fund, a foundation that nourishes the potential of students from low-income backgrounds and provides them with the support and funding to attend four-year colleges around the country. His former home now serves as the official residence for the mayor of Denver.

To the Bush family, he was a great and loyal friend, who was there during the good and the bad times. To his country, he was a great patriot and warrior. And to all who met him, he was larger than life. He was a true Point of Light, and I feel fortunate to have known him.

George H. W. Bush

Prologue

Fall was the very best time for a drive through the Rocky Mountain West. As you came up from New Mexico into southern Colorado, the piercing autumn sunlight seemed to crack open everything and let the color out. Stands of aspen made golden flames on the hillsides, and evergreens grew on the snow-patched faces of the Sangre de Cristo range. Red-tailed hawks soared overhead as herds of pronghorn antelope grazed alongside the highway. Long rides across vast western landscapes provided perfect opportunities to reflect on the past and to think about the future. The man behind the wheel this afternoon was in just such a pensive mood. Early that morning he'd pulled out of Hobbs, New Mexico, and was heading north to Casper, Wyoming, where he was about to start a new job and a new life. Thirty-two years old, uncertain and anxious to get on with things, Bill Daniels couldn't help wondering what lay ahead. He only hoped to find a little more challenge and excitement in Casper than he'd left behind in Hobbs.

Daniels had a taste for action and adventure, even danger. During the past decade he'd satisfied some of these urges by fighting in World War II and then Korea. In 1941 he'd turned down an appointment to the U.S. Naval Academy in order to sign up as a Navy fighter pilot. A few weeks before he completed flight school, the Japanese bombed Pearl Harbor and the United States went to war. Daniels was first stationed in North Africa before shipping out to the South Pacific. In aerial combat he destroyed eleven enemy planes and earned the Navy Cross, the Air Medal, and the Distinguished Flying Cross. Near the end of the war, he was awarded the Bronze Star for heroism after a kamikaze plane smashed into his ship, the U.S.S. *Intrepid*, and Daniels risked his life while carrying shipmates to safety. Five years later, when the Korean War started, he was reactivated for combat duty. When that conflict ended, he was ready for more risks and led the first flight demonstration of the Blue Angels flying team.

The young man was quite familiar with daring and with death. He liked facing the unknown and coming out of it with new experience and knowledge.

He loved beating the odds. The two wars had changed him or unleashed parts of himself that had been untapped. Combat had shown him that he could lay everything on the line and survive. He was stronger and smarter and more capable than he realized. Throughout his adult life he'd felt badly because he hadn't gone to college and taken a degree as so many others had, but he found you could learn things when fighting for your life that you couldn't learn in a classroom. Maybe he didn't need that diploma, after all. And maybe he didn't need to live in fear of failure—or to be concerned with the judgments of others. Such things were trivial after what he'd been through. He'd survived for a reason, it seemed, but he was approaching middle age and he really hadn't discovered what that reason was. On the other hand, he'd never stopped looking, which was why he'd packed his car and gotten out of Hobbs.

He knew one thing for sure. He didn't want to repeat his father's life—a prospect that hung in the back of his mind and haunted him. Bob Daniels had died a few years earlier at age fifty-four, worn out by the emotional and financial strains of hustling for a living and raising four children during the Depression. He'd known gloom and alcoholism, and had died too young. His son was determined to avoid that fate, but what would fulfill him and make him happy? That was the question he couldn't answer. War affected you strangely. Since leaving the service and going back home to New Mexico, he'd had difficulty finding anything as stimulating or satisfying as aerial combat over enemy skies.

Two wars had made him look older than he was and somehow a more finished product as a man. He was not a large figure: just under five feet seven inches and right below 150 pounds. He was handsome in a tough, square-faced, military, and Irish kind of way. A little cockiness played across his face and around his solid jaw. He had a full head of dark hair, striking blue eyes, and a prominent nose. It started down from his forehead in one direction, then veered off in another, and then wound up pointing slightly to his left. It had once been straighter and much more predictable. A number of years ago, when he was a student and cadet at the New Mexico Military Institute in Roswell, he'd taken up boxing. He was not only a good fighter but thoroughly enjoyed getting in the ring and letting his fists fly at his opponent. Not every punch landed but the ones that did made an impression. He'd also taken enough shots to get his nose permanently flattened and then broken. Two years in a row he'd been the New Mexico Golden Gloves champion. The promising middleweight might have won more titles if he hadn't splintered his hand on another boxer's head. This ended his pugilistic career, but he retained the air of someone who knew how to handle himself if called out or threatened. He still looked as scrappy as he was.

His fighting escapades had begun as a boy when defending his little brother, Jack, who was four years younger. "When we were kids," Jack Daniels recalled many years later, "I'd pick a fight and Bill would jump in and try to take it over from me. He'd pop the guy before it got very far along. I guess you'd call that getting in the first lick. He was absolutely fearless. The bigger the guy—or the more of them—the better he liked it. If there were four of them and two of us, I could count on him to take three of them himself."

The brothers were always close but competitive, and after their father died, both of them took over his oil field insurance business following World War II. When Bill went away to Korea and then returned again in the early 1950s, things had changed. He remembered it this way: "I came back to Hobbs and said, 'Move over, Jack, I'm home.' He said, 'Move over, my ass. You've been gone and I'm running the business now.'"

Bill angrily rejected this response, but then asked himself if he'd come through two wars in order to come back to Hobbs and sell insurance for the rest of his life. After he calmed down and Jack offered to buy out his interest in the business, he took the money and packed his bags, ready to leave behind this small, isolated town in the southeastern corner of the state. If the French countryside had its *mistral,* which was said to blow across the land and drive people to madness, Hobbs was subject to the hot, dry, dusty wind that came out of West Texas and swept through eastern New Mexico, bending trees and stirring up dirt, making some locals feel overwhelmed and edgy—if not crazed with the desire to move on. With some cash in his pocket, Daniels was traveling north to the rough-and-tumble oil town of Casper to open his own insurance business. It would be good to get away from Hobbs. He'd show Jack what he could do up there.

"There were other worlds to conquer," Bill once said, "instead of staying there in Hobbs. I told Jack, 'See you later, pal. I'm going up to the Rocky Mountain area.'"

For decades, people had been traveling around the American West looking for something different, going from place to place in search of a better life. Daniels was following in their footsteps, but with a modern twist. He wasn't just seeking a new town or a new job, but a new idea and a new set of possibilities. He didn't know what it was, but he knew it was waiting for him and he knew he'd find it.

When he reached the outskirts of Denver, the sun had fallen behind the mountains, and it was dark by the time he pulled up in front of one of his favorite haunts in the Mile High City. Murphy's Bar was an institution on South Broadway, a hangout for both locals and those just passing through. Daniels liked the corned beef sandwiches and the atmosphere inside the tavern. It was friendly and informal, a place where he could relax and meet other people as unpretentious as himself. He always looked forward to stopping here because there was a welcome feeling at Murphy's.

He entered the tavern and made his way to the bar, where he sat down and ordered a beer and the corned beef. While making small talk with the bartender, he noticed something behind the bar out of the corner of his eye. It was a moving picture on a small glass screen encased in a metal and plastic box. The image was flickering in black-and-white and sound was coming out of the box. Daniels looked more closely and made out two men standing in a ring, boxing. His love of fighting instantly emerged, and he stared at the picture, captivated, as the words poured out of the box and described the action. He put down his beer, unable to look away from the screen. He'd never seen anything like this before.

He still followed the fight game and remembered that it was Wednesday. On Wednesday evenings fights were held at Madison Square Garden in New York City. He wondered where the men on the screen were fighting and how their pictures had gotten into this box. And where did the sound come from? He asked the bartender about the talking contraption, and the man told him that it was a television.

"Television?" Daniels said.

He kept staring at it, his blue eyes growing brighter and more intensely curious. He'd heard of TV before but had never actually seen one operate.

He asked the bartender what event they were watching, and the man told him it was indeed the Wednesday night fights from Madison Square Garden. The pictures on the screen were live, the man explained. People in Murphy's were able to see the match as it unfolded nearly two thousand miles to the east. Daniels shook his head in disbelief. None of this seemed possible. As he gazed at the set, he experienced a revelation.

"I knew we had something here," he recalled more than three decades later, "but I wasn't smart enough to know what it was. I did know that it was good and was the single greatest development of my lifetime."

He finished his sandwich and left the bar, still thinking about what he'd seen. He went up to Casper and settled into his new job, but he couldn't forget watching that fight in Murphy's Bar. He had to find another TV set. Casper had no television, so he couldn't view anything there, but when the weekend came, he drove several hours back to Denver to catch the Friday night fights. He was drawn to the boxing, but he was pulled much more deeply by the magic of sitting in a tavern in Colorado and viewing something that was taking place in Manhattan. He wondered if the people in Casper and other small western towns, which offered virtually no forms of entertainment, might be interested in TV. He thought they would be. On his long rides to and from Murphy's, he started asking himself questions and devising a plan, certain that if you could get a television signal from New York City to Denver, there had to be a way to get it from Denver to Casper, only a few hundred miles to the north.

He began talking to people about making this happen. During these conversations he kept hearing about something that existed in Pennsylvania and a few other parts of the nation, but had not yet spread to the Rocky Mountain West. Called cable TV, it had the capacity to bring television programs from major cities to small towns that did not have their own TV stations. Daniels had a hundred and then a thousand inquiries about how this was done, and he began calling around the country to get some answers. He began spending less time on his oil insurance business and more time trying to learn how to bring cable up to Casper. He began putting together a strategy and a group of people to get this done. At the time, he just wanted to bring the fights to Casper so he could stop making all those trips to Denver.

He and his partners were also interested in creating a business around cable TV, but beyond that Daniels didn't know exactly where this venture was leading him. He ran on gut instinct, and that first night in Murphy's his gut had told him that he'd just caught a glimpse of the communications future. He couldn't have known that he was jumping into a much larger endeavor or that it would take him from one corner of America to another in his efforts to bring television to people everywhere. He couldn't have realized that he was in the process of creating a new industry or that it would become the most significant media business of the last half of the twentieth century. He couldn't have guessed that more than anything else, this industry was going to need a special person to play a special role—a scrappy and tireless individual who was never afraid of entering a fight against long odds. If cable was ever going to succeed against all the powers aligned against it, somebody needed to do just that.

In 1952 Daniels had no idea of the size of the adventure he was undertaking. He could not have imagined that by the end of the century cable television would change America's relationship with politics, economics, warfare, religion, sports, entertainment, and the news business. He could not have dreamed that cable would forever change how we looked at our world or that he himself would put together the deals leading to the formation of seven of the nation's ten largest cable enterprises. Daniels could not have conceived that the companies he owned or helped shape would provide jobs for more than a hundred thousand people. In the early fifties, there was no such thing as a cable broker, so how could he have known that he would eventually manage $2 billion worth of cable deals a year?

Back then there was something else he could never have imagined—that his casual weekend trips to Denver to watch boxing matches would become part of the legend behind a global revolution in communications technology. It would never have occurred to him, as he drove across those open western landscapes while making his way back to Murphy's, that he would one day be known as the father of cable television. No one else could have played the role he did—when someone had to play it.

The man and the mission were the same.

BILL DANIELS' VALUES

HONESTY

INTEGRITY

PRINCIPLED

FAIRNESS

HUMANENESS

COURTEOUSNESS

RESPECTFULNESS

RELIABILITY

PUNCTUALITY

ACCOUNTABILITY

LOYALTY

ENTHUSIASM

ORGANIZATION

MANNERS

COMMUNITY-MINDEDNESS

SOCIAL AWARENESS

SOCIAL RESPONSIBILITY

COMMITMENT TO EXCELLENCE

Toddler Bill Daniels sits on his mother Adele's lap.

The Daniels children, including Dorothy, Bobette, Bill, and Jack, pose for the camera.

One

Bill Daniels' great-grandmother Sara Ferguson was born in Castlebar, Ireland, in 1836. The Fergusons were Catholics, and under the Penal Laws enacted by the British Parliament at that time, the rights of Irish Catholics were all but eliminated. Their land was divided and then divided up again, until the average size of a farm fell below fifteen acres. That was enough to survive on until 1845, when a severe blight struck the potato crop and wiped out the core staple that ended up on countless dinner tables. When the Great Famine swept through Ireland and many farming tenants could not meet the rent, they were evicted by absentee English landlords. Others had their homes destroyed by armed land agents employed by aristocrats. The shipping ports were filled with Irish cattle for export—cattle that could have been eaten by the native population to avoid starvation—but the English refused to take any measures that would lower their profits.

Roughly a million Irish died from hunger and disease. Another million, many of them mothers with young children, left their homeland to sail across the Atlantic in "floating coffins" that were afflicted with the plague. As they made their way to the United States or Canada, tens of thousands died before reaching land. A U.S. newspaper described one of these vessels as a "filthy, foul and feverish pen" filled with "ghastly and corpse-like" passengers. Many of the young women who survived were immediately drawn into prostitution.

In 1847, by the time she was eleven, Sara Ferguson had lost her mother to typhoid, and Irish death records indicate that her father had died as well. Relatives stepped in to raise her and two years later the girl set sail from Liverpool on the British ship *Euphemia* for a six-week trip to America. One of her fellow travelers was another Irish refugee, William McTigue, a middle-aged man from Castlebar, and during the journey McTigue paid a lot of attention to Sara. When the *Euphemia* arrived in New Orleans, he suggested that she go with him to St. Louis. He had kin there who sheltered Irish immigrants until they could find work and a place to live. After reaching St. Louis, McTigue announced that he was going to marry Sara, who'd just turned fourteen. They were soon wed and had what Bill Daniels' own mother, Adele, would much later characterize as "a most unhappy marriage."

In 1860 Adele's mother, Mary, was born to the couple in St. Louis. She was educated at a convent and wanted to be a nun, but her father had died and she had to go to work to support Sara. Mary, an attractive young woman with a lovely singing voice, found a job selling hats at Barr's Department Store in St. Louis; her best customers were the ladies of the evening, who would spend as much as $20 on hats adorned with plumes and ribbons. Despite the earnings Mary brought in, she and her mother needed more income, so they rented an upstairs room to a young medical student at nearby Washington University. William Mumford Davis had earlier attended a junior college in Kirksville, Missouri, where he'd boarded with John Pershing, who would go on to become the legendary General "Black Jack" Pershing, commander-in-chief of the American Expeditionary Forces in World War I.

While living at the McTigue residence, William Davis rarely had a chance to see Mary, but every time he did, he tried to think of a way to see her again. His room had only a bowl and a pitcher of water for sponge baths or shaving. Sara always kept the pitcher full of fresh water for her tenant. One evening after returning from school, Davis heard voices downstairs in the kitchen and decided to take action. He opened his bedroom window and threw out all the water in the pitcher. Then he walked down the stairs and into the kitchen, where he "ran into" the mother and daughter. After Sara was forced to introduce him properly to Mary, Davis sheepishly asked the older woman if he could have more water. Sara instantly understood his ruse but chose to keep quiet. He was, after all, studying to be a doctor and seemed like a polite, if conniving, young man. Before long, Davis had mustered the courage to ask Mary out for a buggy ride, and Sara agreed to this as long as it took place on a Sunday afternoon. The romance had officially begun, but his proposal and their marriage had to wait until he'd graduated from medical school.

The young couple eventually moved to Dawn, Missouri, a town of three hundred people with no other doctor within thirty miles. Sara accompanied the newlyweds to Dawn and moved in with them. Davis and his bride joined the local Protestant church (he was not Catholic) and they both sang in the choir, an activity they enjoyed and something that added a touch of music and aesthetic pleasure to their lives. In 1889 their first child, Beulah Mae, was born, and in 1891 a second daughter, Georgina Ruth, came along. Three years after that, Adele arrived.

Decades later, Adele wrote this about her own birth: "In 1894, the final blow, I was born Adele-Marie. My grandmother cried for three days, saying, 'All this again and another girl!' Surprisingly enough, they kept me!"

Another daughter was soon born, and Mary was extremely busy raising four girls. But she was also tired of living in a small community. She wanted her daughters to be exposed to more people and more cultural activities. Her husband had a brother in Omaha, but before the family could move to Nebraska, they had to find a replacement for Dr. Davis in Dawn. Mary advertised his practice in the *American Medical Journal* and found someone willing to take over his job. They all boarded a train for Omaha, where they took up residence in a large corner house. A fifth daughter, Alta Isabele, was born there. For many years Dr. Davis served the community in South Omaha, which was filled with immigrants who labored in the local slaughterhouses. When his patients couldn't afford to pay him in cash, they settled their account by giving him pigs or chickens. The Davises might not have been rich, but they were never hungry.

In the early 1640s, James Daniels sailed from Essex County, England, to the Massachusetts colony with a large group of Puritans. Several generations later Robert C. Daniels was born in Queens County, New York, in 1801. He became a skilled woodworker in Westfield Township, on the shores of Lake Erie near Buffalo. He constructed gristmills and sawmills built to meet the increased demand for goods created by the completion of the Erie Canal. He and his wife, Nancy Hannah, raised nine children on the upstate New York frontier, making their own furniture and clothing. When the Civil War started in 1861, Westfield was committed to the side of the Union and the end of slavery. Many of its citizens were involved in the Underground Railroad, which sheltered blacks on their way north to Canada. One of the Daniels children, nineteen-year-old William, fought for General Sherman's armies during the battles at Chickasaw Bayou and Vicksburg. William received a serious gunshot wound but survived the war and married Sarah Browder of Hopkinton, Iowa.

William's son, Robert E. Daniels, was born in Iowa in 1869. When he was twenty-two, Robert married Lily May Yates and two years later their own son, Robert W. Daniels, was born in Denver. The family soon moved to Council Bluffs, Iowa, and Robert W.—always known as Bob—grew up working in his father's grocery store and dreaming of attending the University of Iowa, where he would study law and afterward become a prominent attorney. When his father died at forty-two, Bob's hopes for a law degree perished as well and he had to take over the grocery store. His ambitions were unfulfilled and he was never entirely able to put his disappointment behind him. He wanted more than the grocery business could offer, but what choices did he have? If he couldn't have the job he desired, he was determined to make up for that in his personal life, by marrying the girl of his dreams.

One day a young woman came into the grocery store and began chatting with Daniels. She told him about attending a recent dance at Creighton University in Omaha, which was right across the border from Council Bluffs. At the dance she'd made the acquaintance of a vivacious school teacher with blond hair and big round blue eyes (the boys she'd grown up with had nicknamed her twice; they'd called her "Pepper" because of her boundless energy and "Dreamy" because of the faraway expression in her eyes). The way the woman in the grocery store described her fired Daniels' attention. He immediately began asking questions about her and didn't stop. What was her name? Where did she live? Where did she teach? Was she single? How could he meet her?

Her name was Adele Marie Davis, and she'd received a teaching certificate from the University of Nebraska, where she'd also majored in music. She taught first grade in the Omaha public school system. The woman who'd told Daniels about the young teacher agreed to introduce him to Adele. He instantly took up the offer and began courting her by streetcar, proposing during the first week. Adele said yes, and the couple was married in Omaha on October 23, 1915.

Adele quit her teaching job and became pregnant. Bobette was born in 1917 in Council Bluffs, and two years later Adele gave birth to Dorothy, who was mentally disabled and would spend the rest of her life living with her mother. In 1920 Bob got the chance to represent a wholesale candy firm named Woodward & Company in Greeley, Colorado, so the family moved west to the town named after Horace Greeley. On July 1, 1920, their third child arrived. Because Robert William Daniels III was born on the first day of the month, when all the family bills had to be paid, they decided to call this child "Bill." His first three years were spent in Greeley, but then Woodward & Company was sold and the family moved back to Council Bluffs, where Bob went into the insurance business. They lived in Bob's mother's home because it was big enough to hold everyone and had no mortgage. Adele's birthday was on Halloween and on October 31, 1923, she gave birth to her last child, John Wilson Daniels, who would also get a nickname that would be the source of humor throughout his long life. Everyone introduced him as "Jack Daniels" and then most people couldn't help but smile.

In 1926, in addition to mothering four children, Adele pursued her lifelong interest in the arts by acting in a production at the Omaha Community Playhouse. She was on the bill with a young thespian named Henry Fonda, who was making his stage debut in Omaha (another young Nebraska actor named Marlon Brando would also get his start at the Playhouse). A decade after this performance, Adele and one of her sisters visited Fonda in Hollywood, where they also met Jimmy Stewart and several other rising stars. Adele was at home around artists and actors. She had a commanding presence and a style, strength, and flair that were palpable. In a different time and place, she might have had a successful career in the dramatic arts, but as with her husband, many of her deeper or less conventional ambitions would never be realized. She spent decades staying home and taking care of her disabled daughter.

In later years, whenever Bill Daniels spoke about his parents, his father remained a rather shadowy figure, a source of discomfort and pain, a man who'd lived with too much disappointment and died too young. But when he brought up his mother—and he brought her up throughout his life at all times and in all circumstances—she was as vivid as if she were sitting in the room with him. He wasn't the only person who remembered her that way.

"Adele was very theatrical," says Peach Daniels, who married Jack. "She was the queen and we all knew it. They were from Missouri and she had a lot of *southerner* in her. A southern belle attitude. One time Jack was sitting at the dinner table with the family. Adele asked him whom he was taking to the prom, and he said he was taking Opal. Adele said he was not taking Opal because she was common, and she said, 'You're going to take Liddy.' He said, 'I am not. I am going to marry Opal.' And at that, Adele picked up her glass of water and threw it in his face. And his father said, 'Apologize to your mother right now!'"

When Bill was nine, the Depression hit America. By then he'd already gone to work. At eight, the youngster had begun selling the *Saturday Evening Post* door to door. He had a dozen customers and delivered the publication each week, gradually expanding his route by peddling *Liberty Magazine*. He earned two cents for each copy sold. His dad, in order to supplement the family income, operated peanut machines around Omaha. With his hard-won cash, Bill dropped a penny in the machines and got a handful of peanuts. He soon had a newspaper route and then began delivering groceries for a local market. When the Depression became truly severe, he and his younger brother gathered firewood in the hills around Council Bluffs in order to keep their furnace warm. Adele made hand lotion and sold it in the neighborhood. Bob, like his father-in-law doctor in South Omaha before him, was soon exchanging life insurance policies for chickens and eggs.

"When the real Depression hit," Jack says, "we had a real nice house in Omaha, and I remember Mom and Dad sitting in the living room with tears running down their faces, wondering what they were going to do, where we would live. We were in a rented house, but Dad couldn't make enough money to pay the rent. My grandma in Council Bluffs—Monga, we called her—was a precious lady and she had a house her husband had built for her. He died of cancer when he was forty-five. This was my dad's dad. He had a lip sore created from smoking a pipe, and it developed into cancer and of course back then they didn't do much about it. It went through his whole body.

"So we went to live with her and that was hard on Mother and Dad. They hated to impose on her. It was hard on Monga, because she valued her privacy, to have us move in at that point and there were four kids. We lived with her from about 1931 till 1937."

At twelve, Bill got an old bicycle and began selling ice cream on the streets. His best customers were garage mechanics, who were sweating through the midwestern summers of the 1930s. Bill bought a nickel's worth of ice cream in a Dixie cup and sold it for a dime, making a hundred percent profit. At fifteen, he became an all-night short-order cook in a hamburger stand. He worked till the small hours of the morning and then got up and went to school. He wasn't a great student because he was interested in many things other than books. One was girls and another was athletics. He played basketball, football, base-ball, and developed a lifelong passion for sports—pursuing this passion would become one of the most expensive indulgences of his adulthood. As a teenager he also liked the fine art of fighting. If any person or group of kids picked on him or his brother, they were going to meet up with Bill's fists, and it made no difference how big the opponents were. He didn't weigh the odds of winning or losing before raising his hands. He wasn't deterred by fear. He just came out swinging.

"He was a cloud of lightning," Jack says, describing his brother's pugilistic style. "It didn't matter who was taking him on. He just whaled away."

By his teenage years, Bill saw himself not only as a breadwinner in the family, but also a disciplinarian. If Jack got out of line, Bill threatened to whale on him too. The older boy wasn't large, and most people would not have described him as particularly talented or gifted, except perhaps with his fists. But he exuded confidence and carried himself like a leader even back then.

Two

In 1937 Bill's father decided to move the family to Hobbs, New Mexico. Bob Daniels had an opportunity to run a statewide insurance agency from there, so he left Council Bluffs first, with his wife and children soon to follow. Adele and the kids took the train from Omaha to Denver and then drove down to Hobbs. In better times it had been an oil boomtown, but those days had long since disappeared. The streets were unpaved and there were only wooden sidewalks where Adele expected to see paved streets. Many businesses had closed their doors. Trees were few, and when the Daniels family first entered Hobbs, the wind was kicking up dust clouds and blowing them everywhere, leaving dirt on every surface. The place looked and felt bleak, hollow, emptied out, almost uncivilized, which was not acceptable. If Adele was going to live here and raise her children, she would have to do something to improve the surroundings.

She and Bob began entertaining the locals with their singing and her piano playing, but her involvement would eventually go beyond that. She organized the Little Theatre Club and directed several productions, including *The Drunkard* and *Lady Windermere's Fan*, in which she starred. She found ways in Hobbs to give vent to some of her pent-up acting ambitions, and she encouraged others to express themselves on the stage.

The Daniels parents were not impressed with the educational system in Hobbs and felt that their oldest son should not stay in the town for his last two years of high school. They were worried about his fighting and his penchant for stirring things up when he got bored. And the more scrapes he got into, the more this might affect his younger brother. They were concerned with both of their sons.

"Later in life," Jack says, "Bill and I agreed that we could have very easily ended up in jail. We needed some discipline, and Bill in particular. I just don't think that Dad and Mother thought they could control him."

Against Bill's will, his parents enrolled him in the New Mexico Military Institute in Roswell. The NMMI specialized in using discipline to transform rebellious young men into obedient students. One afternoon Bill's father took him to the bus station in Hobbs, handed him a cardboard suitcase, slapped him on the back for good luck, and sent him away. The bus made its way north alongside the Pecos River and came to a stop in Roswell. The young man stepped out, ready for action.

Decades later, Daniels characterized his arrival at the NMMI this way: "I thought I was the toughest son of a bitch who ever came down the pike. But boy, did I find out in a hurry that I wasn't."

At the institute, his attraction to sports led to a connection with NMMI athletic coach Babe Godfrey, the first adult who helped Daniels channel his natural aggression into something more than random fistfights. Godfrey taught self-control, commitment, and teamwork—how to respect others and rely on them to get more done. Babe preached the gospel of never quitting.

Bill's height did not stop him from leading the 1938–39 NMMI basketball team to an undefeated season. He was the team captain.

It didn't matter how difficult the challenge was or how far behind you were in a game—you kept clawing and coming back. Losing was not a disgrace, but giving up before the contest was over was not an option. Godfrey instilled in his players the notion that being tough wasn't enough. You also had to be calculating and intelligent, and your game was far more complete when you used your inner strength as well as your muscles. His lessons went beyond sports.

In all things, he encouraged the cadets to act like well-rounded gentlemen and Daniels began to follow his advice. He was not only a standout athlete at NMMI but wrote for the yearbook, headed several committees, and attended all the balls and cotillions. If he was known as an eager dancer, he was also known for being obsessively neat, always cleaning the floor and the sink of his room, constantly straightening his closet and shining his shoes. Nothing around him could be out of place. Disorder was despised. He expected those he was living with to keep their desks and private spaces as spotless as he did, and if they weren't doing that, he wasn't shy about reminding them of their sloppiness.

"We were at the academy during the Depression and had very little money," says Morris Porter, Daniels' roommate at the school. "We had our allowance, which was maybe a dollar a week. But I remember Bill ordering a $22 raincoat through a catalog, and I asked him where he was going to get the money to pay for it. He said, 'I saved it, I got it.' Anyway, the coat came, but he wouldn't wear it until school was over. But he saw the coat and he was going to have it. I think that was the way he was throughout life. When he wanted something, he went after it."

The young Daniels was a striking combination of pristine housekeeping and a relentless firebrand in competition. In the late 1930s, the U.S. Army came out with a jeep that was, according to Coach Godfrey, "an indestructible mini-tank that was small, sturdy, tough and, being four-wheel driven, could go anywhere." Bill Daniels, Godfrey said, "was always good for sixty minutes [in football games], a good guard at 147 pounds…good for forty minutes always in basketball, always good for three rounds in the Golden Gloves, unless to the discomfiture of his opponent, it went for fewer rounds."

Because of Daniels' strength and adaptability, plus the way he performed in the sporting arena, Godfrey nicknamed him "Jeep," a handle that stuck with him among his NMMI buddies for the remainder of his life. During his first year there, he lettered in football and basketball. The next year he repeated this feat and led his basketball team to an undefeated season. For two straight years at the institute, Jeep won Golden Gloves boxing titles. Godfrey, who retired a colonel, made a great impact on the young man, and they would stay friends over the ensuing decades until Babe died. When Daniels eventually donated $5 million to NMMI, he cited Godfrey as one of the inspirations for his generosity. He could also have credited him with instilling in his players the fundamental idea of never walking away from a worthy challenge, no matter what odds you were facing, because that quality more than any other had led to Daniels' overwhelming success later in life.

That success remained a long way off. Jeep paid for his education at the institute by spending his summers laying oil field pipeline and working as a roughneck. In 1941, despite his lack of affection for the classroom or the study hall, he graduated in the top half of his class. He was also a leading contender in another more dubious category—getting the most demerits in his troop. During his first year at NMMI, he received twenty-two of them, but by his final year that number had swelled to eighty-five. In defiance of the rules, he and two roommates each pitched in $5 and bought a 1928 Chrysler convertible so they could have some wheels on the weekends. Daniels liked to drive fast, and some nights they sneaked out of Roswell with the tires burning, heading south for the fleshpots of Juarez, Mexico.

"We had a sergeant that everyone disliked," says Ray Corliss, who attended NMMI with Daniels. "He had been hit in the mouth quite a bit and he lisped. One night we took him to Juarez. He always wore a hat because he was ashamed of his bald head. We got him drunk that night, and Jeep and I wanted to get a fly with black wings tattooed on his bald spot. We had the tattoo lady all pulled out of bed, but then the other guys chickened out and wouldn't let us do it, but it was a pretty good idea."

Another evening Daniels and a cadet named Pat Patterson slipped out of the institute to visit Daniels' girlfriend in Hobbs, Martha Murray, the daughter of Jim Murray, who was New Mexico's lieutenant governor. The old Chrysler wasn't up to the trip.

"They were on their way back to Roswell," recalls Jack Daniels, "when they blew the motor out of the car. I'm at home and Bill comes to the back window and taps on the window and tells me to get the keys out of Dad's pocket. He said, 'You need to take me back to school.' It was about three or four o'clock in the morning. We get Dad's car out and take off for Roswell. I picked up a friend of mine to go with me, and he was smart enough to put some clothes on. I just put on slippers and a robe. We're about twenty miles out of Roswell and we blow the engine out of my dad's car!

"Bill said that he and the others would hitchhike because they had to make roll call. He said they would send somebody out to get us. It was cold. They took off hitchhiking, and someone stopped and picked them up. Bill called the Buick place and they sent out a wrecker. Here I am at eight in the morning down at the Buick showroom in my bathrobe and slippers."

Daniels and his friend were caught and charged with AP: Absent without Permission. They were sentenced to walking many extra tours of duty to pay for their sins. The walking tours were tedious but did nothing to cool Daniels' passion for the young woman back in Hobbs. She was pretty, she was funny, and Daniels was in full pursuit. In 1946, after serving in World War II, he would return to Hobbs to go to work in his father's insurance business and to wed Martha Murray. They would remain together for five years and have no children. Following their separation, she would go on to marry a Daniels cousin, and she would forever be cordially known within the family as "Aunt Martha." Bill's interaction with her established a lifelong pattern for him when it came to dealing with the opposite sex. He would never father a child or be able to settle down inside the confines of matrimony.

"He just loved different women," Jack says, "and he had a short attention span. Once he learned to do all this and not marry them, he was a helluva lot better off."

That learning process wouldn't fully kick in until many more years had passed—and he had several more ex-wives.

Jeep approached romance the same way he had approached combat and would later approach business—charge fearlessly into the action and then retreat, or if not retreat, at least reconnoiter and move on to the next thing. He could fall in love in a matter of minutes, if not seconds.

"Immediately after the war," says Ray Corliss, "I met a girl at the University of Missouri, and we were married on October 20, 1945, in Kansas City. Here comes Jeep flying into town and we had to get him to the wedding. My mother-in-law wouldn't let him wear his leather military jacket. We got him in a dress Navy uniform and the sleeves were too long for him. After the wedding, Jeep drove our getaway car, which caused my wife to already start giving me hell. We went down to the Plaza area of Kansas City, and Jeep fell in love with the maid of honor, a tall, beautiful girl. When they parted that day, Jeep said to her, 'I gotta have something to remember you by.' She fished a falsie out of her dress and autographed it, 'To my darling Jeep.' That was pretty racy for those days.

"We all knew Jeep was far from dumb. We all knew he had energy and the nerve of a burglar, but we had no idea we were living with a genius. When he got older and successful, he became a great note writer. He was the only man I ever knew who would say 'I love you' in a note. That was really touching. The average man would be so insecure he wouldn't wear a pink shirt or say 'I love you' to another man. Coming out of Jeep, that was quite wonderful.

"He always had a broad spectrum of interests. He had an ego the size of the Ritz, and he was no bottle of milk, no saintly thing. We're talking about a hell of a man. What people who really knew him remember about him is not his success but the incredible heart and soul and thought and warmth he put into things. He was original in his usefulness and deeply thoughtful for a guy that had a rough side and many lumps. He was a leader in every regard."

Daniels regarded the aftermath of romance like the natural-born salesman he was. Now that he'd closed the deal, what should he do next? How could he keep the romance going? How could he not keep from wanting to try something new? Throughout his life he seemed to be happy in all ways but one.

"Bill told me many times that his only failure was that he couldn't stay married," recalls Morris Porter, from NMMI. "I think one reason he could never stay in a marriage was he was in love with his mother and could never find a woman who measured up to her. Adele stayed in that little house in Hobbs all her life. He tried to buy her this and that, but she always said no."

Whenever Daniels met someone new, he instantly told his mother about the woman and shared his enthusiasm for what he thought might be a lasting relationship. Adele listened patiently and waited for the inevitable ending. After attending a couple of Bill's weddings, she stopped going to them. When someone asked her why, Adele said that she'd grown weary of watching her son's cheeks get pockmarked from all the rice that had been thrown in his face.

Following his graduation from NMMI, Daniels had an appointment to the Naval Academy, but he rejected it so he could enter the V-7 program in the U.S. Navy. Instead of having to wait three to four years to get his wings and join the war, he became a navy pilot in eleven months, graduating from the V-7 program two weeks after the Japanese attack on Pearl Harbor. In February 1942, he joined an active fighter squadron in Norfolk, Virginia, and flew in the American invasion of North Africa, operating off a small aircraft carrier called the *Sangamon*. He soon traveled through the Panama Canal and straight to the South Pacific and the Solomon Islands, the stage for some of the fiercest battles of the war.

He soon developed a great reputation—as both a fighter and a dancer. One evening he attended a gala party at the Hawaii beach home of tobacco heiress Doris Duke. With a war going on, soldiers were sometimes treated as very important persons.

"Jeep and I arrived to be treated as honored guests, with about ten leis draped around our necks and a perfect mai-tai in hand," recalls fellow pilot Major Donal Broesamle, who also served in the South Pacific in the Seventh Fighter Command. "The festivities commenced to get under way full bore! A Navy bus arrived with twenty-five young ladies, all of whom were very, very thrilled to dance and even to listen to some war stories. They were the pick of the crop and really made the party swing. There was a Hawaiian combo playing the lovely songs of the islands, with native girls in tea-leaf ankle skirts to dance the hula and so forth. After dinner they had a local disc jockey play Benny Goodman, Artie Shaw, and Glenn Miller for dancing under the stars, either barefoot or on the manicured lawns or on a koa-wood dance floor. And this is where one Jeep Daniels, fearless fighter pilot, earned the lifelong adulation of pilots and ground crew alike.

"Among the young ladies, mostly high school and college kids from the 'better families,' there happened to be an older woman—maybe twenty-four or even twenty-five—and Jeep zeroed in on her in two seconds flat, when I was dancing with her. She had confided to me that she was a professional dancer who performed at various officers clubs on the occasion of some hero getting a promotion or to celebrate the awarding of a medal. I relayed this bit of intelligence to the Jeep, and before you could say, 'Bob's your uncle,' they were

Lieutenant Bill Daniels receiving the Bronze Star in 1944 for heroism in action in saving the lives of naval personnel after the aircraft carrier Intrepid *was struck by bombs off Luzon in the Philippines.*

twirling across the koa-wood to Benny Goodman and his band's rendering of 'Stompin' at the Savoy.'

"When I say they were twirling, I mean jitterbugging. Unbeknownst to me, Jeep could jitterbug like Mickey Rooney, maybe better. He had one little move that always brought a full round of applause. He would spin her around so her pleated skirt would rise up and expose her delightful tush. Then as he would reach out with his left hand to catch her, he would turn his head away, looking off over his opposite shoulder. That brought a standing O!

"The band went through a medley of Benny, Duke, Count, and some Charlie Barnett. A few of the boys joined in, but the other young ladies couldn't quite match the pro or Jeep's moves. His training as a Golden Gloves boxer had given him the footwork drill and timing that rivaled the best. This older woman, I should note, had what was referred to as 'A Built.' Legs clear up to her rib cage as well as other remarkable attributes. It's possible that Jeep could have come close to falling in love."

After a while the dancing stopped, and Major Broesamle lost sight of his friend and fellow pilot.

"I figured that Jeep was in good hands and safe from permanent damage," he says. "A couple of hours later, the bus to take the young ladies back to the USO place had arrived and we all saw them off, but still no Jeep in sight. I went over to the gunnery sergeant and said, 'Have you seen Mr. Daniels?' 'Sir,' he said, 'I think he left with the young lady. The one he was dancing with arrived in her own car and offered to drop Mr. Daniels off at his quarters.' Well, this really puzzled me. I couldn't understand what had come over him to leave but guessed he had possibly downed a little excess 'medicine.' I went off to bed thinking he would probably find his way. I never saw the man again until two days later."

When he encountered Daniels, he asked what had happened to him two nights before.

"I don't want to talk about it," Jeep said.

"Well, where did you go?" the major inquired.

"I don't remember," Jeep replied.

That was the end of the conversation, and Major Broesamle never did learn anything more about what had transpired that evening. He also never forgot what he'd seen on the dance floor.

Light moments at dances were necessary breaks in the wartime action, considering what Daniels and the other men were facing the rest of the time. One morning Major Broesamle received a call from Daniels requesting that he come to his ship, the *Intrepid*, at eight A.M. the following day. The *Intrepid* was docked at Pier 2 on Pearl Harbor, and when the major showed up, he was greeted by an armed military guard.

"Major," said the guard, "you may go aboard, but I caution you that what you will see you will not take with you when you come ashore. Is that clear?"

"Aye, aye, sir," the major told him

As he boarded the *Intrepid*, he thought that it looked fine.

"I followed Jeep up the ladder onto the hangar deck," the major recalls. "My God, this hangar deck looked like the inside of a wood- or coal-burning stove! Everywhere one looked was black soot and debris with the heavy odor of burned oil and aviation gas. At least a dozen aircraft, or what remained of them, were scattered about, many with engines that had simply dropped off onto the deck. Bulkheads had been sprung and there was a gaping hole in the deck that had been roped off to keep you from falling through. At that point Jeep had said nothing, just let me look with wonder at this carnage. Because I had flown off the *Saratoga* at the time of the Battle of Midway and later off a smaller carrier at the Saipan invasion, I knew that this hangar deck was three inches of high-tensile steel.

"Then Jeep began to explain, 'Bro, have you heard about the kamikaze attacks?' I had not, but I was about to from one who had survived the first in the war.

"The *Intrepid* and its escort ships had been fighting off—along with its fighter aircraft—this air raid for some time when the kamikazes showed up. Many of them attempted to crash onto the *Intrepid's* flight deck but were driven off or shot down. But eventually the first one crashed aboard with a more than thousand-pound armor-piercing bomb. It and the aircraft's engine went through the hangar deck and one or two more decks and then the bomb exploded. Flames shot up and ignited the fuel being pumped into the planes and then ignited the planes. Jeep told me how the firemen were trying to get all this under control, but finally the heat was so intense that many of their hoses began to burn. And then the second kamikaze hit!

"Carnage below was already beyond my belief, and it now only got much worse. Some men were trapped by heavy smoke and intense heat and were about to expire. One of the chief petty officers told me later that Mr. Daniels had gone down into this compartment, asked how many were there, then had them hold hands and he'd lead them up and out. When they got up to the deck above, he counted noses—there were still some down there. He and one of the petty officers went back down and led the rest to safe ground. This guy was one who had made it on the first trip out. He thought Mr. Daniels was quite something. Me too. He should have been decorated—maybe he was, but he never mentioned it to me. No question, there were many instances of this heroic action. It is this sort of thing that helped save this ship and others to follow.

"Jeep gave me a tour to the point that my mind could not deduce how so much damage—caused by fuel explosions and ammo cooking off and exploding while men were fighting these fires—was finally contained many days later. Jeep explained that the navy did not want the Japs to know the extent of the success they were having with these kamikaze attacks, which is why I was ordered to keep my experience to myself and my mouth shut tightly.

"An hour or so later we went ashore and got in my jeep and headed for the officers' club at the submarine base to have a couple drinks and some lunch. As usual, I went to the door to my left. Lieutenant Commander Daniels stopped me and said, 'This is our door, we are now what you army clowns call field grade.'

"Oh boy! There were tables with tablecloths, napkins, Filipino waiters, bonded bourbon. Good scotch…and all like that. Jeep had sniffed it out, but it was all new to me. One of the perks of rank—and we loved the hell out of it."

Paul Thayer, who would go on to become deputy secretary of defense, flew in the Pacific with Daniels: "We became good friends very quickly and we went through quite a few combat missions together. Bill got a rush out of air-to-air combat. He was very aggressive, which good fighter pilots have to be. He didn't back away from anything and never gave me any indication that he was ever concerned about going on a mission and not coming back. We all grew up in a hurry. We all played hard and flew hard. Some of the pilots that you didn't think would make it became amazing fighter pilots, and the ones you thought

Bill Daniels flew many World War II fighter missions in the struggle for supremacy in the Pacific.

would burn up the skies just fizzled. Bill was the performer."

Frank Elkins also flew missions with Daniels during the war.

"Jeep was my wingman for several months," he says. "In November 1942 we flew together through Operation Torch near Casablanca in French Morocco. Our squadron was then temporarily land-based at Fighter Strip No. 2 on Guadalcanal. On April 13, 1943, the U.S. carrier air group was assigned the mission of attacking the Japanese airfield at Vila on the island of New Georgia in the Solomon Island group. Our Gremlin Wildcat fighters were designated as F4's and were the escorts for the bomber and torpedo planes.

"I successfully released mine, but Jeep's wing tank only partially released and got caught up in the center hub attachment. The tank had crossed sideways nearly perpendicular to the slip string, and most of the tank lodged against the Wildcat's retracted right wheel. This prevented him from being able to lower his wheels, and the drag of the tank was pulling the plane down, causing the plane to lose a lot of power and to use excessive fuel. Jeep tried to shake the tank loose by diving and pulling Gs, but to no avail. The situation had become a little desperate since we were a hundred twenty-five nautical miles from base, low on altitude and over a Jap airfield.

"The remainder of the group proceeded back to base, and had Jeep or I been attacked, we would have been able to do little to defend ourselves. As a last resort, and knowing that he could not make it back to base on his remaining fuel, I decided to try and knock the tank off. I flew under his right wing in an attempt to dislodge it with my left wing tip. I was unsuccessful, but I did manage to straighten the tank enough for Jeep to get his wheels down and reduce power to reduce fuel. Fortunately, we were able to return to base with Jeep having only five minutes of fuel remaining.

"On June 22, 1943, also in the Solomon Islands, we were aboard the USS *Vagabond,* which was the carrier we operated from. Jeep was meeting the second section of my flight on a scramble to intercept an incoming Japanese attack force. We never made contact and upon landing back aboard, Jeep's arresting tailhook pulled out, causing his Wildcat to hit the cable barrier. This wiped out its landing gear and ended up putting the plane on its nose. Upon reaching Jeep and asking if he was hurt, he replied, 'Hell no, I've had worse hits in the ring.'"

*   *   *

Daniels was a swashbuckling figure in his uniform, smoking cigarettes and getting ready to board his craft for his next mission. He conjured up images of
William Holden and John Wayne, with more than a passing resemblance to the
former. If his war experience was filled with a lot of booze, bravado, and
romance, it also held deadly seriousness and a life-altering vow. Although he
almost never talked about combat following the war, the trauma changed him
forever. He came home with two new missions: he wanted to do something
significant with his life and to give back to the world that he had been allowed
to stay in. He also developed a different relationship with the word no. From
now on, it would not be in his vocabulary. Whether he was searching for a new
job, pursuing a new woman, or trying to start a new industry against all the
odds, he had already seen the worst that life had to offer, and he would not be
discouraged or defeated by the resistance of people who did not have his
courage or vision.

He knew that making mistakes was insignificant—as long as you were
willing to get back up again. Failure was to be expected; it was the recovery that
was the critical part of the equation. He not only taught this to the people
he worked with throughout his life but had to practice it himself over and
over again.

Three

A fter a year-long tour of duty in the Solomons, Daniels flew home to the States and became a director for a Georgia school for young pilots preparing for combat. He soon joined a night fighter squadron, the VFN-101, which operated off carriers in the Pacific. Two-thirds of the men in his squadron were either seriously injured or killed, but he repeatedly engaged in combat without being harmed. He continued flying night missions against the Japanese until May 1945, a few months before the enemy surrendered.

Sometimes, when he was on leave in the States, he paid highly memorable visits to Hobbs, where he'd kept alive his romance with Martha Murray. "He would do cross-country flights in a small plane," says his brother, "like when he was in Corpus Christi or Long Beach or at some naval station. He would come home and drop off for a day or two and buzz the town. Right at the end of the street where we lived was this stone house, which was occupied by an old Greek gentleman named Johnny. Bill would fly down our street, and by the time he got to our house, he would be blowing the trees apart. He would fly like he was going right into Johnny's house, but just when he got there, he'd pull up. Johnny tried to report him to somebody, but nobody would take the report. One day Bill flew his plane at the local airport. He took that sucker over the field—about fifty feet off the ground—and barrel-rolled it! A stunt pilot would hardly do that."

"Bill wasn't big in stature," says longtime Hobbs friend Ben Alexander, "but his balls would look good on a six-hundred-pound gorilla."

When Jeep returned to Hobbs after the war, his father wanted him to get more education and even offered to send him to the renowned Wharton School of Business in Philadelphia. Daniels said no thanks. He briefly thought about studying medicine but what stood between the war-hardened veteran becoming a doctor was about a decade's worth of endlessly studying subjects that had always intimidated and mystified him. Deep down, he really had only one ambition.

"I wanted," he once said of his post–World War II years, "to get out into the business world and make some dough."

He and Martha were wed and Daniels started working in his father's business. Before long he was feeling cramped both at the office and at home. He and Jack were naturally competitive, which created tension on the job, and Bill was already restless inside his marriage.

"The Murray family was very prominent in Hobbs," Jack says, "and Bill had a hard time putting up with them. He just couldn't settle down. When he was still married to Martha, he took up with a gal named Jeri Brown."

Daniels had met the petite dark-haired woman while in training at a naval air station in Texas. After the war she moved to Hobbs, where she ran a magazine shop across from the insurance business known throughout the area as Bob Daniels and Sons. Jack couldn't help noticing that his brother was regularly crossing the street and spending time in the shop.

There were other problems building inside the small insurance business. Now that Bill was working around his father, he saw what others before him had seen.

"My dad was an alcoholic," he said in an interview with The Cable Center in Denver. "He had diabetes. He had a heart problem. My mother kind of kept the office together while my dad had his various periods of sickness. My return from the service was a big help to both of them. Although I knew nothing about the business, I learned rather quickly and we did okay as a family. Then my brother joined us a year later. He was also in the navy, on a destroyer."

Two years after Bill returned from World War II, his father died on June 1, 1948. The end was tough for everyone.

"My father had gone up to the Mayo Clinic [in Minnesota] for an impacted bowel," says Jack, "and he wound up having a heart attack there. They sent him home and said he needed to stay in bed for three months. My dad came home and someone told him that a shot of whiskey a day would help him. Well, he figured if a shot a day would help, a pint or a fifth would take care of everything.

"So he drank a lot and then he became addicted to barbiturates. Neither Bill nor I handled it very well. We were mad at him but didn't understand. We wanted him off the barbiturates. We sent him to treatment a time or two and had some help from local people doing that. He knew he was on a short stretch, and he was just going to do whatever the hell he wanted to do. He'd say, 'Listen, you little pip-squeaks, stay out of my business.'"

In later years, people often commented that Bill Daniels was never comfortable talking about himself in public settings. He was known for being endlessly curious about others, including the children in his presence. He would ask them twenty questions about themselves and a hundred and twenty before he would open up and speak about what he was really thinking or experiencing inside. Some of his friends thought this was because of the trauma that he and all young soldiers had lived through during World War II. They'd seen a lot of horrible things and hadn't known what to do with the feelings this had generated within them, so they'd just learned to keep still and not dwell on the horrors they'd witnessed. It was the only way for some of them to get through the war or to keep going back into combat. After the war, went this argument, they'd applied the same set of disciplines to any other emotional problems—just don't talk about them. But others felt that the source of Jeep's refusal to open up was much closer to home.

"If you think about Bill being so private and protective of himself," says Peach Daniels, "I think it came from the anger of losing his dad too soon and not getting to know him. During the war he was off fighting, and then not long after he came back, Bob was dead."

In 1950, two years after his father's death, the Korean War began and Bill was again called up. He joined another night fighter squadron and returned to the action. The government told him they would need him for two years, and precisely twenty-four months later, he was discharged and flew home, his military service finally behind him. Things had changed in his time away from Hobbs. He'd been replaced in the family business by his younger brother, who was running the office and making money. Bill was unhappily married to Martha and still seeing Jeri Brown. He wanted something new, something different and more exciting, but what? In every part

LT COMD. R.W. DANIELS JR.
ON
FIRST SHORE LEAVE IN
KOREA

In 1950 Lieutenant Commander Bill Daniels enjoys a humorous pose on his first shore leave in Korea.

of his life, conflict was growing, and he realized that there was no easy way to resolve it. Then something happened that brought matters to a head.

"We had several cars for my dad's insurance agency," says Jack. "The cars had big letters on the sides that said 'Bob Daniels and Sons' so everyone knew they belonged to the company. I knew that Bill was seeing this other gal, Jeri, and I knew that he was taking one of the cars out to her house and parking it right in front. One night I drove out there and knocked on the door. She opened it and I said, 'Is Bill there?' He came up behind her and said, 'Yeah, I'm here. What do you want?' I said, 'Move the car, man. You're at least as smart as that.' He said, 'Why don't you mind your own business?'

"He and Jeri came out onto the porch and I knew it was trouble. He took a swing at me and I ducked. He missed me and hit her right on the nose and decked her. I took off running and didn't stop for about three blocks. The next day at work I told him that Jeri wasn't worth one piece of his little finger. Well, that was exactly the wrong thing to say. Within two weeks he was making plans to leave Hobbs with her and to move up north. That was the end of our working together."

Jack bought out Bill for $35,000, and the older brother packed his bags for Wyoming. Although Bill never lived in Hobbs again, he would return often to see his family and friends, and especially his beloved mother, Adele. They would all gather at George's, a favorite restaurant, where a specialty was celebrating birthdays that fell on Halloween (as did several in the Daniels family). Wilma Voorhies was a fixture at George's, having been a waitress there for many years, providing service and fun to the Daniels clan. Bill had a lifelong soft spot for waitresses—realizing just how hard they worked—and particularly for this one. Decades after meeting Wilma, he would remember her with cards at Christmas. But one Christmas stands out. Two years before he died, she opened her customary holiday card and a check for $10,000 fell out. The card said that the taxes on this gift had been paid, and she could expect a tax-free check for this amount each year until her death.

"I got a call from Wilma one day," says Ben Alexander, whose Halloween birthday was one of those celebrated at George's. "She said that Bill had sent her a letter and she read it to me. He thanked her for treating him and his friends so well at George's over the years. Enclosed was a check for ten thousand dollars. As Wilma read this, she started crying on the phone. She was truly grateful to Bill Daniels."

When Jeep left Hobbs for Casper in 1952, he needed every nickel he could find. Jeri had three kids and insisted on having two things before he even thought about opening up an insurance business in Wyoming. She had to have a new washer and dryer, or she wasn't going. Bill bought Jeri the appliances and then hung out his shingle in the new town. He began to hustle as he'd never hustled before, scraping together a few clients and putting in fifty, sixty, seventy hours a week to stay ahead of the bills. When he wasn't looking for new contacts in Casper, he was driving to other towns around Wyoming and trying to broaden his customer base.

Jeri didn't like the fact that he was a workaholic and gone so much of the time, and she was not shy about delivering her point of view. She was, in fact, as feisty as her husband. One time they were cruising down the road in his convertible (no matter how strapped he was for cash, Daniels always had a good American-made car), and they got into an argument. It escalated until she reached over and hit him on the head with a whiskey bottle. There were a lot of hard feelings on both sides, but they soon made up and tried to go forward. The couple was married in 1952 but divorced only three years later. Jeri didn't want any alimony for herself or for her children, but she spent the rest of her life using Daniels for her last name. Long after she and Bill had drifted apart, he stayed close to her kids and regularly sent them gifts. When Jeri died in 1997, he paid for her funeral.

Despite the tumult in his personal affairs, Daniels was learning a lot of valuable things in Casper. He was gradually coming to understand that falling in love was one thing but being successfully married was something else entirely. Maybe he should think about it for a while longer before rushing into matrimony again—or maybe he just hadn't met the right woman. Maybe he wasn't as conventional as his parents had been when it came to domestic stability, and maybe there were alternatives in adult relationships that he hadn't yet discovered.

On the work front, he was still haunted by what he'd seen that night in Murphy's Bar in Denver. He wanted to know everything he could about this novelty called television, and he wanted to watch it some more. Across the country, countless other people felt exactly the same way he did.

Four

In 1948 Tuckerman Arkansas, located about ninety miles northwest of Memphis, was a town of two thousand people. James Y. "Jimmy" Davidson owned Tuckerman's only appliance store, and he also ran a radio repair shop, which allowed him to indulge in and expand his knowledge of electronics. Like Bill Daniels, he'd been shaped by the Depression and had served in the navy in World War II. He was a born entrepreneur, always looking for new opportunities and adventures on the job. In November 1947, when he learned that a Memphis radio station had received a license from the federal government to build and run a television station, he became excited about the possibilities opening up in the communications business. As with many other people across America and beyond its borders, he didn't want merely to see television but to bring it to his hometown.

Cable TV had first surfaced in the United Kingdom in the years before World War II. Several apartment buildings had been wired to one community antenna that was receiving the new TV shows coming from the British Broadcasting Company. Around the United States, a tiny group of inventors in small towns were trying to figure out how to pick up the signals from just-created TV stations in bigger cities. Jimmy Davidson was one of the most energetic and relentless. In Tuckerman, he placed a hundred-foot-high tower atop the two-story building next to his appliance store. He was soon picking up the test patterns coming out of Memphis on WMCT-TV. Sometimes he watched films or slide shows. Before long he'd run a stretch of cable from the tower into his store, attaching the wire to all of the TV sets he was trying to sell. This worked fine, but he wasn't sure if his next innovation would. He strung a cable from the tower to a home near his store, hooking it to the line that held up the town's only traffic light. To his amazement, the wire carried WMCT into the home. Cable TV had arrived in Tuckerman, and word of this quickly spread up and down Main Street and throughout the town. The locals could not be stopped from coming to this house and sitting in the living room and staring at test patterns. Soon they were watching black-and-white pictures. It struck them as miraculous that images could pass almost a hundred miles through the air and end up in an electronic box in somebody's home. A new age of entertainment had been born.

On November 13, 1948, people in Tuckerman watched a live telecast of a football game featuring the University of Tennessee versus the University of Mississippi. For the occasion, Davidson had wired a set and put it in the American Legion hall. The reception was at times flawed, but the game drew a standing-room-only crowd at the appliance store and the Legion hall. Televised sports were now a reality. Davidson was suddenly overwhelmed with requests to bring cable TV into other homes and communities. The concept soon spread to many small Arkansas towns, which began receiving TV signals from more than a hundred miles away in Memphis.

Similar events were taking place in outposts around the nation. In Astoria, Oregon, Ed Parsons, an engineer and the owner of a local radio station, had first encountered television at a broadcasters convention in Chicago in 1947. He attended the event with his wife, and after watching her first TV program, she decided that she had to have one of the sets. Buying one wasn't a problem, so he ordered a nine-inch model for his home. The cost was more than $1,000, which was bad enough, but there were no TV stations anywhere near Astoria. Parsons thought the whole venture was a waste of time and money, but his wife was convinced that Ed was intelligent and creative enough in the field of electronics to figure out a way to make the thing work. When KRSC, a radio station in Seattle, decided to build a TV outlet the next year, Parsons attempted to bring its test patterns into his set in Astoria. His experiments weren't successful until he discovered that the best place to pick up the signals was not in his residence but across the street from his apartment, on top of the Astoria Hotel. He built an amplifier and a converter (which eliminated the interference) and used coaxial cable to bring the signal from the hotel to his home.

Coaxial cable has been compared to a pipe that carries water. It was made of a copper wire surrounded by a layer of insulation. Both the wire and the insulation were then covered with a sheath of woven copper or aluminum, and all of this was wrapped in plastic. The woven copper kept the signals from leaking out and is interference from seeping in. Coaxial cable is unaffected by weather and capable of transmitting more information than standard telephone wire. Coaxial would be modified and improved over the years, but would remain essentially the same product throughout the early growth of cable TV.

On Thanksgiving Day of 1948, when KRSC-TV began its first broadcast from Seattle, the Parsons sat in their apartment and watched the program. They were not alone. All over town people had heard about this magical new invention and stormed into their home in the hope of seeing something from a faraway city appear on the tiny screen in the Parsons' living room. The set quickly became so popular that it disrupted the couple's lives. Ed went to the manager of the Astoria Hotel and suggested that he put a TV in the lobby. The manager agreed to this idea, but before long the lobby was so filled with non-paying locals sitting around watching television that it was bad for business. Parsons then moved the set to a nearby music store and ran the cable from the hotel over there. Within a few days, the police had to break up the crowds that were gathering inside and outside the store—all kinds of people loitering on the sidewalk just to catch a glimpse of the phenomenon. Parsons was getting exasperated, but then the police chief hit on the solution: wire the local bars and have people go there for TV watching. This was an immediate sensation, and the Astoria taverns were soon overrun with viewers.

Even that didn't satisfy the growing demand. People throughout Astoria wanted TV in their own homes, so Parsons began hanging wires from one end of town to the other. It cost $125 to hook up a TV set in Astoria, but money was no object. People were determined to get the signals no matter the price, and the service swept across the village, making it one of America's first cable communities. This news spread far beyond the town, and Parsons was inundated with questions about how to bring cable to other places located far from a major city.

You can, as the adage goes, have the best idea in the world, but if people aren't ready to embrace it, then its quality really doesn't make much difference. The reverse of this is equally true: if something is in very high demand, its quality is not always the most important thing—just get the product delivered

Bill Daniels realized the potential for cable TV in the early 1950s. His vision would help change American viewing habits.

and perhaps the quality can be improved over time. In post–World War II America, people were not simply interested in this new thing called television, they were starved for it. The emotional trauma left by the war and the Great Depression before it was immeasurable. Terrible memories cannot be quantified. In the 1930s, millions of people had known dirt poverty, and a decade later millions of young men had been sent off to fight in a war that all Americans knew was going to cost tens of thousands of lives. The numbers of the dead don't take into consideration the effect their dying left behind or the mental scars on those who fought in the war and survived. In the aftermath of the war, the world would never again be the same. When peacetime came and average folks had a few dollars to spend, they were looking for something different and new. They wanted to relax and to laugh and to escape at least for a little while—they wanted to be entertained.

TV, more than anything else, filled this vast appetite for amusement. In 1948 about 100,000 American homes had television. A decade later, 42,000,000 residences had plugged in the electronic box. People began to interact daily or weekly with real people on television and with fictional TV characters, who took root in their minds and emotions and became in some ways as real as the people next door. Human beings were now spending a significant portion of their time watching other humans through a piece of glass. In the lives on television, people were better-looking and funnier, and all of their problems were solved in thirty minutes or an hour. It was a change unlike any the world had yet seen.

Five

While cable was getting its start in small towns in Arkansas and Oregon, the real foundation of the business was being laid in Pennsylvania. The Keystone State was close to several major TV markets—Philadelphia, Pittsburgh, and New York City—and this made it the logical place for the first real growth in the industry. Once TV set retailers in Pennsylvania realized that there was a market for viewing television programs broadcast from these three big cities, they had to figure out a way to get the signals into the villages around their state. About seventy-five miles northwest of Philadelphia, John Walson ran an appliance store in Mahanoy City. He ran an antenna wire into his shop to pick up TV programs from Philadelphia and show people how the system worked. Before long customers were insisting that he string more wire around town so they could buy a TV and bring this new form of entertainment into their residences. He put up the wire and began charging $2 a month for the service. By 1957 he had 14,250 subscribers.

Over in Pottsville, roughly ninety miles northwest of Philadelphia, another appliance store operator named Martin Malarkey got his first exposure to cable TV in 1949, when he stayed at the Waldorf-Astoria Hotel in New York City. Inside his hotel room a ten-inch TV set put out a very good picture. When he asked a hotel engineer how this was possible, the man told him that he'd put a master antenna system into the Waldorf-Astoria which connected all 500 rooms to a large antenna on the roof. Malarkey went back to Pottsville and decided that if the hotel engineer could wire all the rooms, he could do the same thing in his small town. He contacted the RCA Corporation, and they sent several technical people out to Pottsville to see how to make this possible. The RCA crew picked up TV signals from Philadelphia and ran them from a cable down into the town via one big antenna. Many people in Pottsville wanted to hook up to this service, so Malarkey charged them $150 apiece for a connection fee and $3.75 a month. Within a year he had nearly a thousand customers. He employed his business savvy to convince the management of Pennsylvania Power & Light Company to let him string his wires from their utility poles. Then he borrowed all the money he could to expand his system into other areas of Pennsylvania as quickly as possible. Malarkey's reputation as a cable pioneer filtered up and down the East Coast and to the rest of the United States.

Before long, the Internal Revenue Service was on his doorstep, eager to put an 8 percent excise tax on the dollars Malarkey was getting from subscribers. The entrepreneur resisted the tax and promised to fight it legally. He would eventually take on the feds and their levies in court—and win. This was not the last time the government would try to corral the cable business or put damaging restrictions on it, but merely the first. The battles over cable's survival would only grow fiercer and nastier. The little industry that was springing up in small towns across the nation would be forced to take on some of the greatest powers in America—telephone companies, broadcasting networks, and Hollywood filmmakers—powers that were determined to squash it before it could became strong enough to compete with them. Sensing this possibility early on, Malarkey contacted other cable operators in the autumn of 1951 and asked them to come meet with him in the Necho Allen Hotel in Pottsville. Nine other men showed up and together they pledged $1,000 apiece and formed cable's first trade association, the National Community Television Council. Malarkey became the NCTC's first president. Strat Smith, a lawyer who'd previously worked with the Federal Communications Commission, joined up and convinced the NCTC to change the organization's name to the National Community Television Association. The NCTA would eventually evolve into the industry's premier trade and lobbying group.

Cable TV's success was spreading, but so was resistance to it. The major TV networks in New York felt that this upstart business was taking their product and distributing it without regard for how it had been produced. The networks had begun TV with a monopoly on the system and intended to keep it that way. They had an ally in the Federal Communications Commission, created in 1934 in order to govern communications in the United States. The FCC's initial task had been to divide up the limited-frequency spectrum to the latest

American craze: radio. Someone had to keep radio stations from broadcasting over one another and generating mass static and interference. After World War II, the FCC had a new challenge—how to regulate this upcoming medium known as television. Was TV just a novelty that would pass away in a few years, as some prognosticators were saying, or was it here to stay?

In 1945, when the feds first addressed this question, only half a dozen TV stations in America were operating and all were black-and-white. After much consideration, the FCC decided to give television enough of the spectrum in the Very High Frequency (VHF) range to allow for six more stations. Those stations with the same channel number had to be at least 150 miles apart, and those with different numbers had to be separated by 75 miles. With this ruling in place, TV began to take off. By 1948 there were 109 stations operating or about to debut in the United States, and many new regulatory challenges came with this growth. TV signals bounced around a lot and caused interference in stations several hundred miles distant. As engineers struggled to solve this problem, another bigger one surfaced. Instead of offering just black-and-white images, stations could now broadcast color pictures. This set off a new round of difficulties.

TV signals could be broadcast in numerous ways, and the FCC needed to decide the best method, which would become the industry standard. In the fall of 1948, confronted with all of these novel issues, the commission chose to stop licensing new stations until it could resolve the matters. The freeze lasted nearly four years. TV station owners and builders were upset, and so were many communities and potential viewers (the freeze kept Bill Daniels from seeing television until the fall of 1952). In many areas the public had been promised this wonderful invention called television, and now they had to wait. They protested, but that did nothing to push forward the FCC's schedule. Yet while the spread of *new* broadcasting outlets was stalled, TV as a whole was not. A group of entrepreneurs and engineers, like those in Arkansas and Oregon and Pennsylvania, were inventing cable TV across America and taking it to small towns and rural locations. In 1952, when the freeze was finally lifted, almost 14,000 U.S. homes were receiving TV signals via coaxial cable.

Word traveled around the country that the person with the most knowledge in the fledgling cable field was Martin Malarkey. Two thousand miles to the west, in Casper, Wyoming, Bill Daniels heard about Malarkey and decided that he had to meet him. Daniels had been seeking advice about building a cable system in the Rocky Mountain region, but nobody in his part of the country knew much about it. Daniels called Malarkey to set up an appointment, ready to jump on a plane. Malarkey said that a visit to his office would cost him, besides the price of a flight to Pennsylvania and lodging, $500 for one day's advice. Was he willing to lay out that kind of cash for a face-to-face session? Daniels, using the style and the speed that would characterize his entire career in cable, would have paid more and did not hesitate in heading east.

After discovering cable TV in Murphy's Bar, the young man had not been able to stop thinking about it. Despite working at his oil insurance business, he'd commuted steadily back and forth to Denver. Every chance he got, he returned to Murphy's for a corned beef sandwich, a beer, and the opportunity to watch television again. The only station in Denver at that time was a local station, Channel 2, which had no affiliation with the major networks. Daniels was not at all scientifically inclined and did not understand, in a technical sense, how TV actually worked, but he believed that if you could get these pictures from New York to Denver in less than a second, there had to be a way to get this new invention up to Casper. When he first encountered television, he'd never heard of cable or its possibilities. During his excursions throughout Colorado and Wyoming, he questioned many people about getting TV to locales outside the major cities—badgering engineers and electrical technicians in particular—but nothing happened.

He went back to Casper and kept selling oil insurance. He was good at it, he was making some money and meeting some well-heeled oilmen, but he wasn't satisfied. This was, after all, exactly what he'd been doing down in Hobbs and what he'd be doing right now if he'd stayed in New Mexico with his brother, Jack. He could make a go of it in the insurance business because he knew how to get people to buy things. He might even get rich, but he wasn't excited by the prospect of this career. He wasn't passionate about it. He didn't see how it could lead to other things, bigger things, unpredictable things, but he did see that it could lead him where it had led his father, and that was to drinking and death at age fifty-four. And that was one place he did not want his life to go.

Imagine what he could do, Daniels sometimes told himself, if he could sell something that he really believed in, something with a real future, something that was more fun than the insurance business. Imagine the money and opportunities he could generate, not just for himself but for others. Imagine the possibilities that must be out there, if he could just connect with them. He was deeply hungry for something different, something that he knew was around him, if he could only find it. It was in his nature to dig for information from almost everyone he met, so he kept asking people questions and looking for the answers.

One day he saw an article in Denver's *Rocky Mountain News* about cable television, which was bringing programming to places that lay outside the reach of big-city TV signals. Apparently you could use a wire named coaxial cable to carry the signals hundreds of miles over the countryside. Daniels was riveted by this story and had to learn more about the subject. He immediately called several of the people mentioned in the article. After gathering some information, he knew what to do next. In the early 1950s, Casper didn't offer many things, but it had one undeniable asset: a small group of oilmen with money in their pockets, an entrepreneurial spirit, a sense of adventure, and an eye for the next opportunity to increase their net worth.

Daniels lost no time in approaching them and asking each man to put up $5,000 for a local cable TV system. He spoke to Earl Lyle, Jeff Hawkes, Winston Cox, and Harold Barnes. He told them about watching the Wednesday night fights in Denver and how exciting that had been. He told them that people in Casper would love to be able to watch TV, just as much as he did. He told them that television was here to stay and would have an unlimited future. At the time there was no TV in Wyoming at all, not one set, so this was not an easy sell. It took Daniels a while to explain what cable was and why he was convinced that it would work in Casper, but he was so enthusiastic about cable and so persuasive that no one turned him down. He talked to more people and had soon raised nearly $50,000. As the head of this group, Daniels approached the local bank and gave them the same pitch. They didn't know anything about cable TV, either, but they knew an entrepreneur when they saw one. Daniels quickly borrowed the difference between what he'd already come up with and $250,000. With this money behind him, he couldn't go forward without more expertise. He needed information, so he called Martin Malarkey out in Pennsylvania. Dressed in cowboy boots and a cowboy-cut suit, he flew out to Pottsville and paid Malarkey $500 for one day of listening carefully to every word he said.

With a little direction and some cash, Daniels knew that his next challenge was to find people with the technical knowledge that he lacked. He really had no idea how cable worked, only that it was an idea that he was ready to expand into a business. One of his Casper connections, Earl Lyle, told him about two brothers down in Texas, Richard and Gene Schneider, who were ex-GIs and trained engineers. Like Daniels, they'd come home from the war searching for something new and different, something they hadn't been able to find so far in the Lone Star State. When Daniels phoned and asked if they wanted to throw themselves into the upstart cable TV business up north, they were initially cautious but found his salesmanship hard to counter. In fact, he was impossible to ignore. They'd already visited Casper, they told him, and liked the area.

They were willing to give the idea a try and soon began traveling around Texas looking for cable systems they could study. They found one in Tyler and then they found the person they were looking for: a consulting engineer in Denver named Tom Morrissey. An ex-Bell Labs employee, Morrissey understood coaxial cable and television transmission far better than they did. He was also willing to explain to them what he knew. He spent hours with the men, teaching them the basic principles of cable TV and how to put together a system that would work.

The Schneider brothers soon went up to Casper and began building the pioneering cable outlet in Wyoming. Richard became the head engineer, Gene ran the outfit, and Daniels continued in his role as the relentless promoter and fund-raiser for this newfangled enterprise. The brothers' mother, Gladys, loaned them some money for the venture and became the company's bookkeeper, a position she would hold for the rest of her life. They called their operation the Community Television Systems of Wyoming, Inc., because they felt that the term "community" would help their image locally, especially if they were ever sued. Now all Daniels had to do was go to AT&T and talk the gigantic telephone company into helping him transmit the signal, via microwave, from Denver's Channel 2 up to Casper, 250 miles away, a much farther distance than TV signals were relayed in the East. If AT&T said no, the investment was sunk because the telephone behemoth had a monopoly on all the existing microwave facilities.

This was the first time an attempt would be made to send television signals to obscure locations through the use of microwave transmission. AT&T thought over the offer and said they would be willing to try it, but needed a down payment of $125,000—a vast amount for a business that had no history whatsoever in the Rocky Mountain West. Bill Daniels had no customers, had no background in this field, and had thus far generated no income from this venture. He had no tangible evidence that he could actually bring all this off. Undaunted, he went to the partners and asked each of them to reach down further into his wallet because without more money, the deal was dead. The men listened and were persuaded enough to put up a $125,000 bond to kick-start the relationship with AT&T. It was a huge risk and everyone involved knew it. "Believe me," says Gene Schneider, "back then $125,000 was a lot of money."

Armed with Malarkey's business suggestions, AT&T's technological support, the engineering skills of the Schneider brothers, and his own determination, Daniels was ready to launch the system. Before that could officially happen, he went to the powers that be in Casper and obtained a permit to operate the system.

"I'm kind of sorry I did that," he once told an interviewer for The Cable Center in Denver, "because I don't think we needed them in those days, but I did it anyway. By going to the city of Casper, it started instant publicity in the newspaper.... I got some ink saying some guy...wants to bring television to Casper, and it was free publicity."

"We finally got the system built," recalls Gene Schneider, "in December of 1953 and turned it on. We had the opening in the National Guard Armory in Casper. There were no television sets in town. We did not want to be in the business of selling TV sets, so we had to convince appliance dealers to get some in so we had something to show the people what we were selling. These were black-and-white sets, about three to four feet across, with a twelve-inch screen in the middle. In the first two days at the armory, about twelve thousand people came through, a lot of them from all around the state, just to see a television picture. Casper only had about twenty to twenty-two thousand people back then.

"We signed up a lot of them, and it was probably the most successful system I was ever involved in. We charged $150 to hook up and $7.50 a month, which was a very high number for one black-and-white channel in today's dollars." Also, the system ran only eight hours a day.

"By the end of 1954," Schneider says, "we'd hooked up about four thousand homes and completely paid for everything in one year. Bill was just a super salesman. He could sell anything and was a great asset to the business in the early days."

The Casper venture was even more of a bonanza than Daniels had envisioned. His group of oilmen investors felt as if they'd just drilled scores of wells and none had come up dry. If things were this profitable in other places, cable would be an unstoppable industry. Every town in the West would immediately want to hook up a cable system. Everybody was anxious to get connected to TV. Flushed with this early success, the young entrepreneur was ready to take the system elsewhere.

One of the major issues Daniels and his partners had faced that first year in Casper was what fare to put on the one channel they were offering. Who made that decision? Every ninety days they sent their customers a poll and asked them to pick which program they preferred—*I Love Lucy* or the *Sid Caesar Show*. The majority ruled, at least that was the way they presented it to the public.

"We had to choose what to bring up on the channel over the microwave," says Schneider, "so we put out ballots to people to let them select. But then Bill and Richard and I would get together and decide what *we* wanted to see. Which, of course, were all the sports, all the fights. We never got any complaints about this. Nobody knew how we were operating this and many people didn't even vote. They probably wanted to watch sports, too."

While Daniels was launching his system in Casper, Jack Crosby was starting his own cable business out of his father's appliance store in Del Rio, Texas. For $10,000 he put up a TV tower right on the Mexican border. The reception was so bad, he once said, that "you could watch a football game, but you couldn't tell which team had the ball." During this time he received angry phone calls at home morning, noon, and night. He was finally able to build his own microwave system, which greatly improved reception and stopped the calls. He never imagined that he wasn't simply clearing up a TV picture but creating a system that would forever change the world of communications.

"I just wanted to be able to watch something on this wonderful new tube," he says. "We didn't have a big business attitude—it was simply let's see if we can get television. If you stop and think, one of the most remarkable things about cable is that it is a multibillion-dollar industry that started in the Del Rios, Texas, and Casper, Wyomings of the world and then moved to New York and Philadelphia and other big cities."

Throughout the years both Daniels and Crosby shared many responsibilities in the cable business, including the chairmanship of the National Cable Television Association (NCTA). One day Crosby got a call from one of his banking partners in Del Rio.

"He said there was a lady driving up to the bank in a Cadillac, from Mexico City, and she wants to cash an out-of-town check," Crosby said. "I said to him, 'You know, we don't do that without references.' So the person at the bank asked her who to call as a reference, and she said, 'Whoever owns the cable television system in town.' I asked the banker, 'Would she happen to be a very beautiful petite blond lady, going to Denver, by the name of Daniels?' The banker said, 'Yes, how would you know?' I said, 'Just a wild guess. Give her the bank!'"

Despite the good results from his first cable venture, Daniels was not in a position to quit his insurance job and go into the communications business full-time. While maintaining an office in Casper, he kept up his regular commutes to Denver and decided to open a cable office there in the Mile Hi Center building. He and his investors had soon started two more systems in Rawlins, Wyoming, and Farmington, New Mexico, two modest western towns much like the places Daniels had grown up in. He was comfortable visiting these locales and selling to these people; he had an instinctual feel for their backgrounds and understood that they were looking for the kind of entertainment

TV could provide. In some ways he was a modest man who was almost painfully aware of his lack of education. He'd been an average student in high school and had never gone to college. He was unpretentious in manner, in the western cut of his clothes, and in what he liked to eat and drink. One of his favorite meals, even many years later, after he'd hired a gifted French chef, was a peanut butter and jelly sandwich graced with pickles. Another favorite were the small White Castle hamburgers, which he ate by the handful.

His manner was rough-hewn and his language was salty. He liked risqué jokes and terms of endearment for women (such as "honey" and "darling"), and he would keep using these words long after they became politically incorrect. He liked to puff cigarettes constantly and would ignore many of the bans on smoking that pervaded America later in his life. He liked to drink, a habit he'd developed early and that intensified as he got older.

He was modest in all ways except one—and that was in his ambition to bring cable TV to the American West. From the moment Daniels first encountered this new medium, he looked upon it not just as a business but as a calling, a way to alter and expand the world around him, a way to keep himself amused and involved in the world for decades to come, a method to give back to others who had much less than he did. Cable TV was the doorway that allowed him to connect with people and change their lives, an opportunity to use not just his business acumen or financial resources but his spirit and heart and immense creativity. Cable TV was a labor of love that would take him places he could never have imagined—including Hollywood parties, dinner invitations to the White House, and friendships with several presidents.

All that was a very long way from his family's humble roots. He never forgot the underdog because he knew what it meant to be one. And he was the first person on either side of his lineage who looked at a job as not merely a way to survive, but as a means of self-expression. He hadn't lived just to go to work each morning and put in his time. He wanted to find some joy along the way—wanted not only to open a new office and help build a new industry, but to discover a new way of doing business.

Six

While searching for new cable markets in Wyoming, New Mexico, and other western states, Daniels drove throughout the Rocky Mountain West, stopping in dusty towns all along the way and looking for places that might be interested in getting wired for TV. He gave the locals his sales pitch about how cable was the coming thing and then moved on to the next community. He ran a very small-time operation, but at least he was getting out of the office and doing something he believed in. After returning to Casper, he called up those who were building the young cable industry around the country and made appointments. Then he traveled to meet them. He followed up his visits with notes and letters. He asked a thousand questions and then a thousand more. He learned which bankers were servicing the fledgling cable systems and which were reluctant to get involved in the business. Daniels was good with numbers and was developing a sense of the figures behind successful operations of different sizes. He was absorbing information from everywhere and everyone. If he was at a loss to explain the technical side of cable, he was at his best when bringing people together to talk about making new deals.

Without quite realizing it, he was starting to define his role in the industry. Nobody else was playing this role because it hadn't existed before Daniels came along. No one else saw the opportunity or took it. He was the man in the middle of everything—the guy who knew more about the business as a whole than anybody else. Within a few years after his first encounter with television, others around the country were beginning to take notice of this development. If you wanted information about cable anywhere in the United States, you phoned Bill Daniels. If you needed to get to know someone in Texas or California or up and down the East Coast, you dialed that man out in Denver, because he had all the phone numbers and had probably talked to that person himself. If you had to raise money for a deal, you phoned Daniels and he was ready with half a dozen suggestions; if the first five didn't work out, the sixth one just might. If you had a question about technology, he most likely couldn't answer it himself but could connect you with the right people. If you just wanted to talk about cable's possibilities, you phoned Daniels and heard the most optimistic response you could imagine about the future of the business.

If he was having trouble creating or holding together a family of his own, maybe the world of cable was becoming a much larger and ever-expanding family for him. And maybe that always shifting world of business was more suited to Daniels' personality and needs. Maybe it was change itself that he was most attracted to—change and growth and having new experiences and creating new opportunities for others—instead of doing the same thing over and over again. Maybe what cable needed more than anything else was someone with an unlimited view of the future, someone with a vision and the desire to talk about it.

Everywhere he went he would talk about cable providing television access to people in rural communities and providing better reception for viewers all over America, but that wasn't what he really wanted to tell people. His true interest lay in something that often sounded to others like a distant dream. He wasn't content with cable being merely a wire that hooked up distant towns to network broadcasts coming out of cities. He thought cable could do much more than that—generate its own programming and offer alternatives to network shows. He thought that once the nation was wired, once everyone had a TV set and was hooked up to cable, then cable itself could play an important role in the American culture. Why did millions upon millions of citizens have to depend on what the three networks—ABC, CBS, and NBC—were broadcasting from New York? Why couldn't people have more choices? Why couldn't there be programs for kids and programs for adults and programs for a whole variety of tastes? Why was the thinking so limited? This was what he really liked to talk about, but even many people inside the industry doubted that most of these things would ever happen. At the moment, they were just trying to keep their small businesses running.

Daniels wasn't getting paid for a lot of his activities on behalf of cable, but he was staying very busy and having a lot more fun than he had selling insurance. Then there were the side benefits. As a result of widespread networking, he was elected chairman of the National Cable Television Association for 1956–57. This was largely a symbolic position in those days, yet it greatly expanded his set of contacts and opportunities. At the same time, it limited his options for doing deals.

"I didn't feel that as president of the trade association, I should use that for my personal gain," he told The Cable Center. "That thought bothered me, but I advised people on how to build their systems, who to call, who to talk to.... I told them the same things that Marty [Malarkey] had told me, and helped them get on because we wanted the business to grow."

After leaving the NCTA office, he wanted to enter cable full-time, but many of his friends and advisers thought that would be a bad mistake. In the mid-fifties, television was still little more than a novelty, and cable TV was far less than that. Most Americans didn't even have a set. Fads like TV often came into vogue for a while before disappearing for good. Cort Dietler, an oilman in Denver, became acquainted with Daniels when they both worked at the Mile Hi Center. One day the two men engaged in a serious discussion about Daniels' future.

"I had an office on one corner, and Bill had an office on the other end," recalls Dietler. "He was still in the insurance business, very successfully. He'd gotten carried away with the television idea in Casper, and he kept telling me that this was great and we ought to do it everywhere. I said, 'That's fine, Bill, it would be a nice hobby.' He said, 'No, I mean, that's what I'm gonna do.' I said, 'Are you kidding? You have an outstanding business right now.' He said, 'Yeah, I'm going to get out of the insurance business.' That was the last bit of financial advice I ever gave him, and he never asked me again.

"Bill had the guts of an army mule. He became a very successful self-made man who didn't go to college, and I think he was always sensitive about that. He was a natural-born salesman because he knew how to project himself and he genuinely cared. He could be plenty tough when he needed to be. He wanted to win but not in a phony manner."

While Daniels' name was taking root throughout the industry, resistance to cable was growing. In 1952 the FCC had finally lifted its freeze on new TV stations, and many entrepreneurs rushed forward to get permits to build new ones. In the next two years, the number of stations tripled nationwide. Many of these new outlets were in smaller towns that had already been wired for cable. As broadcasters began to appear in communities where cable was present, conflict was inevitable. Local TV stations aggressively disliked competing with the signals that cable brought in from larger markets. They felt that they couldn't get either the local viewers or the national advertisers interested in their product, and that cable would eventually put them out of business. Politicians in these towns tended to line up behind the local broadcasters—at the expense of cable. In Asheville, North Carolina, the city council voted against building a cable system. In Fairmont, West Virginia, local broadcasters asked for the federal government to step in and limit cable systems. In Memphis, Tennessee, the homegrown TV outlet told the cable entrepreneurs that it wanted nothing to do with their services. In Reno, Nevada, the group that produced the very popular *Cisco Kid* series sued the local cable system

In 1952 Bill took on two commitments: cable television and his wife, Jeri, shown here on their wedding day along with her three children, parents, and sister.

because it was bringing in this program from a San Francisco station and directly competing with the Reno channel that aired the same show.

Cable was creating enemies everywhere, and its troubles were only beginning. As the industry quickly spread across the country, mostly through the efforts of local entrepreneurs, a host of technical problems had arisen with it. Many of the amplifiers and other equipment were homemade and only partly functional. They might work for a while, but bad weather was always a threat to these systems. When they inevitably broke down, frustrated customers erupted in anger. The pictures were often accompanied by "snow," the little bits and pieces of electronic fluff on the screen that make it almost impossible to see the action. Before long, consumers were getting together, approaching the local governments or utility companies, and asking them to regulate cable or force it to live up to certain standards.

Then the telephone companies, which had been allowing cable to use their poles for wiring, decided they wanted a bigger piece of the TV pie. For a few years they had been willing to collect a dollar or two per pole each year as a fee for their services, but as cable spread, they wanted to charge more or even start delivering TV programs themselves. Some of them dramatically raised their rates, while others stopped letting the cable outlets use their poles. Still others took the cable systems to court.

Cable was besieged on every side. With an increasing number of viewers, local broadcasters, telephone companies, and city councils lined up against the young industry, the film business then joined the pile. In 1954 a TV producer named Arche Mayers told the National TV Film Council that cable systems were trying to "cheat" the movie industry by paying no copyright fees on the material they brought into local markets. This conflict soon reached Daniels and his cable firm up in Casper. A local businessman, Burt Harris, wanted to build a TV station but reluctantly was going to give up his efforts, saying he couldn't make this work because Daniels was already bringing Denver stations into the Casper market. But Bill, who welcomed competition, encouraged Harris to enter the market with his local station.

Throughout the West, both TV and radio broadcasters were growing angrier with cable. They wanted help in their business struggles and were not getting it, so in 1956 they came together and filed a request with the FCC demanding that the feds step in and regulate cable. They asked the federal government to regard cable as it regarded the phone companies, which were known as "common carriers." These kinds of businesses were subject to having their rates and services controlled by lawmakers. The government began studying the problem and looking for solutions.

In addition to all these troubles, the early days of TV were filled with some unreliable operators and many technical challenges and difficulties. In the 1950s television ran on tubes, as transistors had not yet been invented, and tubes had a way of blowing out during the most crucial moments of sporting events or at critical points in TV dramas. Dark sets produced howls of rage and indignation aimed at local cable outlets. Wind knocked down cable lines, especially in states like Wyoming, where fifty-mile-an-hour gales are commonplace. Moisture became trapped inside of TV transmitting equipment, which generated pictures that resembled high-country blizzards. In cold weather, the copper core inside of the cable shrank and lost its connection to the amplifiers. A number of the original cable outlets were run by seat-of-the-pants entrepreneurs who would do whatever they could to cut costs, including splicing together pieces of worn-out cable. When conditions got tough, these pieces tended to snap in two, bringing cable a few more enemies.

Because of the powerful forces lined up against cable in the 1950s (and for many years to come), the industry needed true believers, even cheerleaders, as much as it needed anything else. It needed someone who was combat-tested and unafraid of a good fight, someone who was always ready to get up off the mat and come out swinging once more. It needed people who were impatient for change and never comfortable with the word no—people who were constantly looking for a new way to say yes. It needed someone who would never give up, somebody with the grit and the humor to see things through and keep enjoying himself even when things were bad. It needed someone who knew that business was not life and death but was above all a game to be played—yet played to win. And if you could win, the other guy could too.

In spite of cable's many problems, Daniels was eager to try something novel, which would only make the nation's film industry and broadcasters even more nervous about this upstart business. He wanted to deliver original programming, such as uncut movies or made-for-cable shows. In the fall of 1957, Daniels' new partner out of Wyoming, a man named Carl Williams, traveled around the huge Rocky Mountain region, from Great Falls, Montana, to Albuquerque, New Mexico, trying to get people interested in this offer. Daniels was not the only person ready to expand cable's services, as several other entrepreneurs were testing these ideas in markets elsewhere.

In Palm Springs, California, a branch of Paramount Pictures called International Telemeter built a cable system designed to bring pay-per-view films into that community. Local theater owners became so upset by this prospect that Paramount quickly shut down the service. In Bartlesville, Oklahoma, a business known as Video Independent Theatres (VIT) offered the same kind of programming to the 28,000 people of that community. VIT put on three first-run uncut movies a week on one channel, at a cost of $9.95 a month. The Bartlesville experiment failed miserably, even after the price was chopped in half. One reason was because the arrival of VIT had forced its main competition—the local TV stations—to improve their programming, so more people decided to stay home and watch television. A second reason was because the citizens of Bartlesville preferred to be able to choose the movies they wanted to see, instead of being given a very limited selection via cable. Third, they claimed that TV shows were more alive and spontaneous than what Hollywood was currently producing.

The pay-per-view experiments in California and Oklahoma bombed, but they left the major broadcasters more afraid of cable than ever. They banded together with the other anti-cable forces and demanded regulation of this new industry—which was putting forth the audacious notion that people should pay something to watch television. American TV was supposed to be free, wasn't it, just like American radio? Such luminaries as David Sarnoff, the esteemed chairman of NBC Television and RCA, announced that broadcasters needed protection from cable and then went further, saying that it was "a negation of... American broadcasting" to charge people to view TV. The conflict gathered momentum, and the issue soon reached the floor of the United States Senate, where the Commerce Committee hired a special counsel named Kenneth Cox to hold hearings about the broadcasters' complaints. After listening to much testimony, Cox came down on the side of the broadcasters, writing a report declaring that cable should be regulated by the FCC.

"It seems clear," Cox stated, "that the TV industry cannot thrive and grow, to the greatest ultimate public interest, if it continues to exist only half regulated."

In 1958 the FCC ruled on the widespread broadcasters' demand that cable be regarded as a common carrier and therefore subject to regulation. Despite the enormous opposition to unregulated cable, the federal government saw things differently, unanimously voting against viewing it as a common carrier. Cable was different from telephone and telegraph operators, the feds decided, because cable did not carry information indiscriminately but chose what signals to convey, based on the appetites of the consumer. In spite of this victory, the fight was only beginning.

Having failed to persuade the FCC to regulate cable, the broadcasters began heavily lobbying the U.S. Congress to achieve the same goal. Congressmen were soon introducing their own bills to limit cable's power and reach. In 1959 the Senate Commerce Committee held hearings in order to find ways to control the new business. This frontal assault on cable rankled many entrepreneurs but none more so than Bill Daniels, who'd been following the political battle from Denver, while traveling around the country promoting the industry.

"Having fought in World War Two and Korea," he told The Cable Center, "and having been in the cable business such a short time, and having the government tell me what I could or could not do, I deeply resented this. Because I thought, 'Now wait a minute, goddammit! I've been out there busting my ass and getting shot at, and all I wanted to do was make a living!'"

Like many combat veterans in the aftermath of World War II and Korea, Daniels felt that he had a right to return to America and earn money as he saw fit. When the U.S.A. had called on him to serve, he'd sacrificed his time and risked his life for his country, not just once but twice. He'd done this with courage and honor, and he now believed that his nation should not stand in his way when he was trying to build a business and kick-start an industry that could give consumers what they wanted, while providing many new jobs. He was angry that the powers that be, starting with the networks, local broadcasters, telephone companies, and parts of the U.S. Congress, were all threatened by the rise of cable and were committed to choking off its growth. This seemed to him not just bad business but unpatriotic, and Daniels was, as his career would demonstrate over the next several decades, first and last a very patriotic man.

He and Carl Williams eventually concluded that their efforts to sell pay-TV to the general public were premature. Not discouraged, Daniels began thinking of alternative ways to make money in cable. Where did he fit into the industry? What vacuum needed to be filled? He didn't have enough wealth to bankroll a lot of new systems himself. And he wasn't a manager of cable outlets, once they'd been built and were up and running. That kind of day-to-day work had always struck him as tedious and limited. He had a constant itch to move on, to close one deal and then look for the next opportunity, to meet new people and go new places. What could he do that wasn't being done anywhere else? How could he use his ever-growing body of knowledge about the business to his advantage?

"Bill reasoned that while there were many brokerages around the country specializing in television, radio, and newspapers," says Carl Williams, "no one was servicing the cable industry. At that time, the industry had only three hundred thousand subscribers and they were stretched out among a couple hundred systems. Some of the systems were very small, and the largest was a little shy of eleven thousand, in Cumberland, Maryland. Bill proposed that we start a [brokerage] partnership. With no articles of partnership, we opened a bank account. Bill put in $600 and I put in $400. A week later Bill sold a 10 percent interest in the company for $500 to his friend Winston Cox, who was on his board in Casper. So Bill owned 50 percent of Daniels & Associates, I owned 40 percent, Winston owned 10 percent, and away we went."

Daniels & Associates was the first office in the United States devoted exclusively to brokering cable deals. Now that it was in operation, it needed buyers and sellers and operating properties, so Daniels began doing what he did best. He got on the phone and started bringing people together and building the industry—spreading his vision of cable's future from coast to coast.

Seven

By the mid-fifties, Daniels had established cable connections throughout the United States. He was meeting men like John Rigas, a theater owner in Coudersport, Pennsylvania, who'd bought that town's cable system in 1953 for $100; Alan Gerry, a TV appliance dealer in Liberty, New York; and Bob Magness, a cottonseed buyer in the Lone Star State who'd stumbled into cable (much as Daniels himself had) while eating lunch in Paducah, Texas. These three men would eventually run, respectively, Adelphia Cable Company, Cablevision Industries, and Tele-Communications, Inc., the latter becoming the largest cable operating company in the world. In 1957 Daniels had just finished serving a term as president of the National Cable Television Association (NCTA) and after leaving office, he'd started Daniels & Associates in Denver. For the grand opening of his business, he mailed out a mimeographed sheet announcing his new venture to all of his contacts in the cable field. He soon received a call from Joe Sariks, whose cable system served 7,500 people in Bradford, Pennsylvania, and several surrounding towns.

Sariks wanted to sell his business and felt that it was worth $1 million. Daniels, who had no experience with accounting or pricing cable systems or dealing with figures of this magnitude, sat down and ran the numbers through his head. A million bucks sounded about right to him, and he added a $50,000 commission for himself if he could come up with a buyer. Before long he was speaking at a dinner in Rapid City, South Dakota, and in the audience was Charlie Sammons, a Dallas insurance executive who listened very closely to Daniels' enthusiastic talk about cable's prospects. Following the dinner, Sammons wrote Daniels a letter asking how he could get involved in the business. Daniels told him about the property in Bradford, and Sammons said he was interested but wanted to meet with Daniels and take a look at the company's balance sheet. He discovered that it was bringing in more than $50,000 a month in cash flow or $600,000 a year. Most successful businesses, Sammons knew, were put up for sale at the rate of five to ten times cash flow; this one appeared to be a huge bargain at less than two times cash flow. He had only one question for Daniels: Was he willing to take a check?

The answer was yes, and as the broker looked on in astonishment at how easy the sale had been, Sammons wrote out a check for $1,050,000. Word of this transaction quickly got around the cable community, and people began talking about how much Charlie Sammons had paid for the system in Bradford and how much Daniels had helped him in closing the deal. Daniels then sold a system in Bozeman, Montana, to Bob Magness and some other properties to Sammons. The Dallas executive didn't want to run such far-flung systems as the one in Pennsylvania, so as part of their working arrangement, he hired Daniels & Associates to manage the systems for him in return for a 20 percent equity position in each of the purchases. In many future transactions Daniels would make the same agreement with other buyers. They were happy to have someone so well connected and knowledgeable overseeing their assets and in return Daniels started getting a piece of the ownership in cable systems across the country.

Cable's first true believer had arrived on the scene. The industry presented him with many difficulties and challenges, but those were secondary to the chance it gave him to be who he was. The born salesman now had something to sell. His pent-up fervor for something more came into focus and his passion found a home. A young and uncertain business had melded with a man who supported it relentlessly. It was a perfect position for Daniels to be in. He had an effect on people that was much larger than he could have known.

"I got started in the cable industry in 1952," says John Rigas, "and hooked up our first customer in March 1953 in Coudersport, Pennsylvania. We promised our customer three clear pictures, and we ended up giving them two snowy ones. That was the best we could do in those days. We were getting signals from eighty or ninety miles away, and they were pretty inconsistent. As I look back on that period, the prevailing wisdom was that cable wasn't going to be a long-term situation because UHF (Ultra High Frequency) TV would come closer to the rural markets, but at least cable was a way to introduce TV signals. After a couple of years I started to realize that there was a real future in cable.

"I'm not sure of where I met Bill, but I certainly heard of him when he became active in the NCTA sometime around '56 or '57. He was the one that took a real interest in leadership in the NCTA. We were looking for leaders and for somebody who had a personality to motivate people and believe in them. Bill Daniels captured the imagination of us little guys right off the bat and right away communicated his leadership. Bill was a little guy himself. Well, physically he was a little guy, but he wasn't little in presence.

"We were all struggling to find our niche, and Bill was out West there with his cable systems. I remember so well when he brokered one of his first systems. He set a precedent because there wasn't a market for a system before. He brokered this deal and gave us hope. There were people out there willing to look at something, and Bill did it. I cannot stress to you how important it was to me personally because I'm sitting there with maybe three thousand subscribers, not an awful lot. But what is their value? I have a debt to Bill because he made that step forward. To me, it was one of the defining moments in my life and I think in the cable industry.

"I would say this about Bill and I know it's a cliché, but Bill, to me, was a man for all seasons. He truly was. Bill had an extraordinary sense of timing in his life. As I look back, he knew in the beginning that there was an important role for him to play as a leader. He saw something that was needed to bring a national recognition and a presence and a level of statesmanship to the cable industry. He was a father figure, a patriarch. As the years evolved, Bill sensed at different times, as generations moved on, that he had different roles to play. I believe that was one of his extraordinary talents. He was interested in all of us and never forgot any operator and enjoyed knowing about all of us. For many years I was just an operator out there in this little rural town of Coudersport, Pennsylvania, and yet somehow, some way, Bill always kept track of me. He was a mentor to anybody who was stepping out, and he was my security blanket. If I said that Bill had said something, I was believed and people had trust in me."

Rigas was part of Daniels' growing family, and as its members everywhere would learn over the coming decades, he kept track of a huge range of people—where they were living, what they were doing, their recent accomplishments or the hard times they were going through, either personally or professionally. When they reached a new level of achievement, he was the first to send them

Bill Daniels always knew a pretty girl could help promote any idea, even one as peculiar as this newfangled Cablevision service.

a note of congratulations, and when they were struggling, he offered advice, comfort, and sometimes money or a job. No matter the circumstances, there was always one person they could turn to when they needed an ear. Daniels was many things to many people but he was one thing to all: a great listener. People who met him casually were astonished that he would take the time to ask them in-depth questions about their background or family ties or career ambitions. They were even more astonished when they ran into him again a year or two later and he remembered their answers. He had a bottomless memory bank and a gift for setting aside his own personality so that he could explore someone else's. When he rested those deep blue eyes on people, they eagerly told him things they wouldn't share with others.

As part of his new role as broker to buyers and sellers, Daniels often traveled to New York to talk to the banking community about obtaining loans for these deals. When he tried to convince Manhattan executives to finance cable trans-actions, a number of them politely thanked him for coming and ended the meeting. Some weren't so gracious. In later years, Daniels would proudly claim that he'd been thrown out of more lending institutions than anyone in America. Bankers feared that cable was a passing fancy or that a new technological breakthrough would render the systems obsolete. They were reluctant to trust a young man from Denver who wore western-style clothes and had little business background and was trying to persuade them that something they knew nothing about and didn't trust—cable TV—was here to stay. They were not interested in making anything like five-to seven-year loans to fund the upstart companies. Most weren't even willing to agree to two-to three-year arrangements.

While the great majority of East Coast bankers Daniels encountered were not impressed with his sales pitch, a few took notice as he laid out cable's assets from a long-term financing perspective. First of all, it was a cash-flow business, which bankers understood and appreciated. Subscribers paid monthly fees, so money was always coming in. Second, because the technology was evolving so quickly, cable enjoyed more rapid depreciation schedules on its assets compared to many businesses. Whereas other corporate assets might take twenty years to depreciate, a cable operation could write them off in five to eight years. As a result, cable systems generated positive cash flow yet paid few taxes. The com-bination of rapid depreciation schedules and high cash flow made the young industry able to service its debt very efficiently, a key selling point to bankers. Once bankers had heard Daniels' presentation, cable started to look like a more reasonable long-range risk—at least to one group.

For years Charlie Sammons had used the Bank of New York for his financial services. He introduced Daniels to BONY, and among all the lending institu-tions in Manhattan, Daniels found the warmest reception there. He was soon taking investors to BONY and brokering deals through their offices. Other New York banks would eventually follow their lead.

When visiting New York, Daniels was not enamored of Broadway plays or the opera or art galleries but he did like to indulge his passion for athletic contests. "One night," recalls Joanne Ditmer, a longtime Daniels friend and reporter for the *Denver Post*, "Bill and I were going to Madison Square Garden to see a sporting event. We had tickets to both the press box and to the owners' box. He wanted to sit in the press box. This was in the early sixties and I said, 'Bill, they don't let women in the press box.' He said, 'But you're with the press. Don't you have a *Denver Post* press card?' And I said, 'Yes, but they don't let women in the press box.' Well, Bill Daniels never heard of things that didn't go his way, so he suggested that we see about that. We get up to the top of the stairs, and here's this little old gentleman in a uniform who greets us warmly and Bill presents the cards. The man said, 'Sir, you can go right in, but the young lady can't because we don't permit ladies in the press box.' Bill said, 'But she has a press card.' The gentleman said they didn't let women in the press box. Bill said, 'You've got to.'

"The gentleman said, 'No, but I'll tell you what. You can go in the press box and the young lady can sit right over there where you can see her.' Bill said, 'No, I don't think so.' So we then went down to the owners' box. At that time, the configuration of the owners' box was right against the playing floor and the balcony came out over it. The people who sat in the balcony over the box just had a splendid time all evening dropping popcorn in the laps of people sitting in the owners' box. Bill was not known for patience and he really got quite infuriated by that. I can't even remember the game because I spent most of the time trying to keep him from going up and wiping them out.

"Even in those days, it was evident that Bill had tenacity and I don't want to say ruthlessness, but you didn't cross Bill easily. If you were a friend, he was loyal to the end. But if you did anything that offended him or he felt was back-stabbing in any way, you were on the list. I think probably that rather steadfast outlook gave him such a fine reputation in the business world."

During his trips to New York, Daniels kept hearing about Irving Kahn. A five-foot-five-inch, two-hundred-fifty-pound New Jersey native, Kahn had been named for his famous music-composing uncle, Irving Berlin. After beginning his career in public relations in Manhattan, Kahn had gone to work at Twentieth Century Fox studios in Los Angeles. One day he noticed an actor trying to read his lines off a long roll of paper. Watching the young man struggle with this makeshift and very awkward cue card system, Kahn posed a question.

Why couldn't you build a machine that easily allowed actors and actresses to read their material from a screen as they performed? He soon quit the PR field, invented something called a TelePrompTer, and founded TelePrompTer Corporation. The TelePrompTer did exactly what Kahn had envisioned it would—helping thespians read their lines off a screen—and the device became very popular throughout Hollywood and beyond. In 1952 he assisted presidential candidates Harry Truman and Dwight Eisenhower in learning to use TelePrompTers at that year's political conventions.

Despite TelePrompTer's success, the company was struggling, so Kahn went searching for other opportunities. Large-screen TVs had been invented and Kahn wanted to use them to broadcast live, closed-circuit boxing events. He struck a deal with heavyweight champion Floyd Patterson and his manager, Cus D'Amato, which let Kahn show Patterson's fights in the closed-circuit medium. In the late fifties, as this venture was taking off, Bill Daniels called up Kahn seeking an appointment or Kahn phoned Daniels looking for advice (in later years, each man would claim that he'd made the initial contact with the other). In any case, Daniels first made the trek to Kahn's Manhattan office looking for the boss, but the boss was not in. Instead, the visitor met a young man named Monroe Rifkin, who'd quickly risen to the position of chief financial officer at TelePrompTer. Rifkin was an East Coast native who was very much at home in Manhattan. He enjoyed his job and felt good about his career path. He'd never really considered living anywhere other than New York. Like a lot of people who were first coming into contact with Bill Daniels, he didn't know that his life was about to change.

"It was 1959," he recalls, "and I was executive vice president of TelePrompTer, which was a small company. Irving Kahn had a big mouth, but it was a small company. It was lunchtime and, as usual, Irving was out to a two- or three-martini lunch somewhere having Greek or Afghanistan food. I was having the daily deli sandwich at my desk. This little guy came up to the reception desk and said, 'I'm Bill Daniels from Denver, Colorado, and I want to speak to whoever is in charge here.'

"Since Irving was out, I was in charge. Bill was ushered into my office and introduced himself. I put my sandwich down and I'll never forget his first words: 'Hi, nice to meet you. Let me tell you why I'm here. I've been reading about you folks in the newspapers, the sports pages, where you've been doing closed-circuit telecasts of fights. I want to tell you about another aspect of closed-circuit television.' I said, 'What's that, Bill?' He said, 'It's called community antenna television.'"

"He described the mountainous terrain out West and antennas on the mountaintops and how people couldn't otherwise get television. I said, 'Bill, that's very interesting, tell me more.' He said, 'Well, I'm one of the pioneers of building those systems, and I've just recently established myself as a broker. I've moved to Denver from Casper, Wyoming, and opened a brokerage office. You guys are big and I want to sell you some cable systems.' We had a nice conversation. He explained a bit about the business to me. What was intriguing to me were the prices you could buy systems for—$200 or $300 a subscriber. Three to five times cash flow. So we talked.

"Bill came back maybe a month later and presented to me some financials of properties so I could see the real numbers. It continued to look interesting. A few months went by and Bill would come into New York once a month. We would have a meal together and he would tell me more. He said, 'Look, the only way you're really going to get a feel for this is to come out West with me and I will show you some systems.' My devious mind started working. I had a vacation coming up, so I thought here's a great way to get my travel paid for and I'll go out West and see Bill, then have my wife join me and we'll vacation.

"So that summer of 1959, I flew to Denver on a Lockheed Constellation. It took about nine hours from New York with lightning hitting all around us. Never so scared in my life. We arrived in the evening and Bill was supposed to meet us. I'm looking for this dapper little guy, but I see a stunning, tall, slim young lady with two gigantic dogs. It was like a scene from some movie. She introduces herself as Eileen and said, 'Bill is in Casper. He's not here because he had his license revoked in Colorado for speeding too many times.'"

Eileen Kamm, as Rifkin now learned, was Daniels' third wife. She was bright, beautiful, headstrong, fiery, and as strong-willed as Daniels himself. She'd been the class valedictorian at Denver's East High School, a model, and a dancer. She had a son named Cliff, and she and Daniels were quickly embroiled in matrimonial conflict. If she wasn't exactly the right person for him to have married in 1958, when he'd rushed to the altar again, she was just the wrong person for him to divorce a few years later, in 1962. His other separations from his ex-wives had been fairly amicable and they'd remained friends. That wouldn't happen this time around.

On that summer evening in 1959, Daniels had stationed Eileen at the airport to make a grand impression on Rifkin, which was precisely what she did. Her job was to wow him and then to move him along quickly to his next destination.

"She put me on another plane to Casper," he says. "I get to Casper the next morning, and the dapper little guy meets me at the airport. He showed me around the Casper system, which is managed and partially owned by the Schneiders and Bill and some other people. There's not much to see, but it's an interesting little business. From there we drive to Rawlins, Wyoming, which has a cable system that Bill and some other people also owned. They scared me to death driving up this mountain.

"Casper was a metropolis compared to Rawlins. We continue this circle and get back to Denver and catch an airplane to Phoenix. In Phoenix we meet with Bruce Merrill, who was an equipment supplier with a couple of cable systems he built around Arizona. Bruce lives in a gorgeous home up on Camelback Mountain. He rolled out the red carpet. He had a cable system with about 800 subscribers in Silver City, New Mexico, which was an old copper mining town, and Bill was going to broker it for him. That is one of the systems Bill wants to sell to us. We go through that visit and hear about the cable industry through the eyes of an equipment supplier.

"Next stop on the trip, we fly to Farmington, New Mexico, which Bill owned a chunk of. This was another nice cable system. The thing that was remarkable about Rawlins and Farmington is that they had the same ownership group. All their offices were in little back alleys somewhere. When I inquired as to why, I was told that they didn't want to look pretentious, they didn't want to look prosperous. From Farmington back to Denver, I get on a plane to New York. Next morning, I go into the office and tell Irving, 'We've got to raise every nickel we can, sell everything we can sell: the TelePrompTer business, everything. There's a thing out West called cable television or community antenna television and it's undiscovered and it's a license to steal and we've got to do it.'

"I spent a few minutes giving Irving the whys and wherefores and the economics. He said, 'I like this idea, let's go for it.' I mean, we didn't even have a company. Everybody thought TelePrompTer was a big company, but we had no money. We were failing and were going to die. So I called Bill and told him we were serious about buying those properties. Bill said, 'Well, you really can't buy Casper because the Schneiders don't want to sell. But I'll talk to them. But you can buy Rawlins, Farmington, and Silver City.' And we did.

"When I made my second trip to Denver," Rifkin says, "I went to Bill's office in the old Mile Hi Center Building. I met Carl Williams, Bill's partner at that point. He started working on contracts and we went to contract with the three properties. We closed on the first one in December of '59—that was Silver City—and we closed on the second two in January of 1960. That was the beginning of my career in cable. At this point Irving Kahn had never seen a cable system. He lived vicariously through me. I took it under my wing. I liked it. It was building things, which I like to do. I mean, what can you buy that in three years is paid off?"

Even Miss America joined Bill Daniels' bandwagon promoting new advances in cable television. Here, Debra Brown joins Bill for the grand opening of Parson's Cablevision in 1966.

TeleprompTer paid $747,000 for the properties. In early 1960, the company made a public offering of stock to raise $2 million to buy ten more cable systems, plus a radio station. It was a great time for entrepreneurs in the budding communications business.

"I get a call and Bill had another deal for us," Rifkin said. "We pursued that deal. We bought Liberal, Kansas. We bought Elmira, New York, and TelePrompTer was off and running. We didn't do any further brokerage deals with Bill. For a period of time, he didn't show us any or there weren't any. But we were the only buyers and everybody in the world was coming to us. I think we amassed all of 25,000 to 30,000 subscribers, which was very big in those days. Then Bill called me in New York. 'Monty,' he said, 'you've got to come out to Denver and join me.' I said, 'You're crazy, Bill, I'm a New York boy.' Bill said, 'All right, but I'm going to persist in this.' And he did—for three years. He stayed after me to move and I was modestly interested."

In the summer of 1960, Kahn was the biggest star at the NCTA convention being held that year in Miami. Those attending the event watched the Floyd Patterson–Ingemar Johansson heavyweight championship fight via closed-circuit TV, thanks to Irving Kahn. He also showed the fight on his cable systems around the country. Kahn believed that this kind of pay-per-view television was where cable's future lay. He'd invented a device called Key TV, which allowed viewers to place their orders for films or other programs by pushing a button that relayed a signal from their television set to the utility poles outside on the street, the same poles that held the cable. These signals would be collected from the poles and would determine what the consumer wanted to watch. Based on this data, cable companies would then send out the programs on a pay-per-view basis. Kahn wanted to sell first-run movies in this manner—and take away business from film theaters. He also wanted to buy the rights to the World Series and sell it to the viewer at two dollars a set. He wanted to buy the rights to concerts at New York's Carnegie Hall and sell them to the culturally starved masses throughout the United States. When it came to cable TV, he thought as big as Bill Daniels.

Rifkin's job was to trek around the country, usually to backwaters, and look for the small cable systems to buy. He found a number of them and was having success, but he was also getting tired of all the travel and being away from his family. Meanwhile, Daniels kept calling him, telling him that Denver was the place to be, offering him a job in the Mile High City. Daniels had instant feelings about men and women—about their business acumen and potential to take advantage of the great ride that he was certain cable would be. He knew immediately whether he wanted to be associated with them or not, whether he wanted them on his payroll. His radar was excellent, and when it homed in on someone, he would not take no for an answer. He kept pursuing Rifkin and Rifkin kept resisting, but that did no good. When Daniels wanted either a new business connection or a new personal relationship, he simply dismissed the word no.

In the spring of 1963, he invited the Rifkins out to Denver for a weekend visit. Daniels had arranged for them to be feted at the Denver Country Club, where the couple was introduced to other people with young children. These couples told them what a wonderful city Denver was, especially for those raising families. They told them about the beauty of the Rocky Mountains and the countless recreational opportunities that lay just outside the city. The New York boy was starting to waffle and so was his wife. Denver, at least when you were sitting inside the country club, really didn't look that bad. Daniels made him an offer and Rifkin found himself in the position that many others either had or would find themselves in over the ensuing decades. Bill Daniels was very hard, if not impossible, to turn down. When he wanted you, he wanted you badly and he usually got you. Rifkin packed up and headed west.

He realized that he'd met the ultimate closer.

"Bill was charming," he says. "I saw him at the negotiating table bringing seller and buyer together and doing a good job of it. I saw him take the sellers out of the room when he had to. I don't know what he did—got them to give in on points or whatever—but we got those deals done. He was just a little razzle-dazzle charmer. After three years of his persuasion, I made the move to Denver. Bill once told me that his biggest dream at that point was to make enough money so he could take a year off and go to the Harvard Business School and get an executive MBA. I never heard of that dream again."

Rifkin took over as the head of the Daniels & Associates cable operating company. He'd dealt with a lot of powerhouse businessmen in New York, but now he was sent in the opposite direction to woo another mogul. Jack Kent Cooke was a Canadian who'd made riches working with a media tycoon north of the border named Roy Thomson. In time, Cooke decided to head south, take up residence in Los Angeles, and become a U.S. citizen. Like Daniels, he also had an insistent personality. When he learned that regular folks had to wait five years to earn American citizenship, he lobbied Congress to grant him this right instantly—and he won. After searching the U.S. landscape for business opportunities, he decided that he wanted to be involved in two things. The first was sports, so he went out and bought the Los Angeles Lakers basketball team and the Washington Redskins of the National Football League. As a passionate sports fan, he naturally watched a lot of athletic events on television and wanted to have the finest picture possible. He eventually noticed that the best images on TV screens came from systems that were hooked up to cable. At that point he decided that he wanted to get into the cable business too.

Daniels sent Rifkin to L.A. to sell Cooke properties and the young man did just that. Cooke bought four systems, two in California, one in Texas, and one in New Hampshire, for a total of $4.6 million. It was the largest deal Daniels & Associates had ever done and one of the biggest cable deals at the time. Cooke, now a player in the industry, called his company American Cablevision. Rifkin was starting to think that his relocation to the Denver had been a pretty smart move, after all. Because of Bill Daniels, the company Rifkin worked for was not only growing every month and extending its clout across the United States, but Denver was becoming the clearinghouse for the best information about the cable business, if not the home of the cable industry.

In 1968 Daniels & Associates, under Rifkin's direction, created the American Television & Communications Corporation (ATC), which included all properties being managed by Daniels along with properties owned by General Electric. ATC, reacting to the desire for cable companies to be publicly traded, did its IPO in 1968. While Bill Daniels was the largest individual share-holder, he selected Rifkin to become the president and CEO. Bill recognized that his greatest challenge was continuing to help build the industry.

Eight

In 1959 Senator John Pastore of Rhode Island held hearings on a range of proposals designed to support the findings of the earlier Cox Report, which had concluded that cable needed to be regulated in order to ensure the survival and good health of television stations across the country. Bill Daniels had already testified before Congress on the benefits of keeping cable free of regulation, but the fight was coming around again. He often told people that while the networks, local broadcasters, telephone companies, theater owners, public utility commissions, and a variety of government agencies were all lined up against cable, the young industry had two forces backing it: Main Street and Wall Street. Daniels had always believed that Main Street, the millions of viewers out there who were hungry for TV, was cable's ace in the hole—and the single most important element in the entire mix.

"Main Street is the public," he once explained to The Cable Center, "because the public wanted more television, or they wanted some television where there was no television. Or in markets where they had only one or two stations, they wanted more."

And Wall Street, he added, would always go along with Main Street: "The people who financed us, the bankers and so forth, were excited about us because they could see a new communications industry and we serviced our debt beautifully."

Whenever the federal government began threatening to regulate or curtail cable, Daniels and other businessmen told their subscribers to start writing letters to the FCC and to members of Congress. The people in small towns were the first to pick up their pens and start writing.

"Boy, they would write letters," Daniels told the The Cable Center. "Because, goddamnit, that was the only way they could get any television."

Daniels always contended that the people who held the real power in America were the consuming public, not the elected officials or the FCC. If congressional offices were flooded with mail supporting cable, the politicians had to listen.

By the late fifties, the politicians *were* paying attention—but to many different voices at once. Senator Pastore's hearings unleashed a fierce debate not just between those outside the cable business calling for regulation and those who opposed this, but also among those inside the cable industry itself. One group, led by the NCTA's board of directors and their head counsel, Stratford Smith, felt that regulation was inevitable and it was time to get behind the federal effort to do this, in order to limit the regulatory impact. The other group, led by Daniels and his allies, held fast for no exterior control at all. They were shoot-from-the-hip entrepreneurs who'd built their businesses from scratch and didn't see any need for the FCC to step in and tell them how to conduct their affairs.

As that war of words continued, the Commerce Committee put together a bill designed to accomplish four aims. The first was a provision requiring cable systems to obtain licenses from the FCC. The second gave the FCC authority to place limitations on cable systems in a given market as a way of protecting the interests of local broadcasters. The third made it mandatory for cable systems to carry all local broadcast signals and do nothing to degrade or otherwise interfere with them. The last prevented cable operators from bringing in programs that were already being aired by the community's broadcasters. Senator Pastore supported all four provisions and felt that the cable industry as a whole was essentially behind them. He was only half-right. The Daniels contingent decided to fight the provisions all the way to the Senate floor. The coming showdown would echo far into cable's future.

As Senator Pastore searched for compromises to get the bill passed, two cable powerhouses stepped forward and began pushing for the outright defeat of the legislation. Milton Shapp was the founder and president of Jerrold Electronics, which supplied the amplifiers and other electrical equipment that served cable systems; inside the industry, Jerrold had become the biggest name in electronics. Henry Griffing ran the VIT cable outlet in Bartlesville, Oklahoma, which had recently experimented with pay-per-view movies. Both men were highly respected within the cable field and both had apparently been willing to go along with some regulation of their business—until now.

With the Senate vote nearing, they aggressively began lobbying cable operators and politicians. The duo sent out telegrams to operators all across the nation, asking them to come to Washington and work against passage of the bill. A number of businessmen, including Daniels, took up the charge and threw themselves into the anti-regulation efforts. For two days, senators argued the merits of the bill in sessions that would long be remembered for their theatrics and rancor. Shouting matches erupted and bitterness was in the air. Down on the Senate floor, things quickly went from heated to hostile. Senator Robert Kerr of Oklahoma lambasted his fellow lawmakers for trying to rein in cable. At the crescendo of his speech, he stood before the United States Senate and began to cry. As tears rolled down his cheeks, he exhorted his fellow lawmakers to do the right thing and kill the bill.

Senator Pastore watched all this in shock. He too felt betrayed. He had seen himself as a friend of cable, who was trying to ease the way toward regulation while offering protection to both sides. Now his compromise solution was collapsing right in front of him. Publicly he sat and silently fumed, but privately he made remarks about lobbyists that were too purple to report in the historical record of the debate. As he listened in dismay, a vote was taken and those opposing the bill won by the narrowest of margins: 39–38. The fight was over and the cable forces had triumphed—for now—but the bad blood the victory had stirred within the Senate and the communications industry would not go away for decades.

Some of cable's key leaders had alienated major politicians and other potential allies. Men like Milton Shapp and Bill Daniels would continue to spread the word about cable and keep making deals and growing the industry, but new legislative battles would soon arise and they would be just as bitter. Those who felt that the cable industry had burned them back in 1959 had very long and angry memories. As the arguments flew back and forth, one thing remained constant: Main Street continued to demand more and more television as cable continued to spread. By the end of the 1950s, 640 cable systems nationwide were supplying TV to 650,000 American homes. If it was a controversial business, it was also—as Daniels had been preaching for years—the wave of the future.

Nine

In the mid-sixties, Daniels began wooing another young man for his company. John Saeman was living out in California and working for a wired pay-TV business called Subscription Television, which wanted to bring first-run movies, sports, and cultural events into people's homes. That plan had become clogged up in the courts after it was strongly opposed by the National Association of Theater Owners—NATO didn't want anyone else showing the American public new films. While the legal battle over pay-TV was unfolding in the courts, Saeman, a former marine, began calling cable operators and selling them on the first professionally organized sales and marketing service. He kept hearing about a man out in Denver named Bill Daniels and decided to fly to Colorado to meet him. They had a lot in common: both were ex-military, staunch Republicans, and always ready to close the next deal. Daniels was a number of years older than Saeman and quickly conveyed to the younger man the feeling that he was involved in a business that was taking off—not tomorrow or next week but right now.

"He had an amazingly upbeat setting in his office," Saeman recalls, "with the big copper fireplace, the huge desk, and controls that opened the drapes. I thought, 'God, this guy is really successful.'"

He went back to California and kept working for Subscription Television, but soon hooked up again with Daniels at a trade show in Arizona. As he was preparing to leave, Daniels called and asked him to have a drink. He declined because he was catching a plane to L.A. But Daniels, who always acted on gut instinct with people he liked, phoned the following morning and told Saeman that he wanted to hire him and make him a millionaire. Saeman laughed into the receiver. He was a farm boy from Wisconsin, with his feet planted squarely on the earth. He was intrigued with Daniels' offer, but it seemed unbelievable that he could ever approach being a millionaire.

He decided to check into Daniels & Associates more deeply before turning down the offer. He asked a contact at Dun & Bradstreet, one of the owners of Subscription Television, to review the financial status of Daniels' company. Twenty minutes later, the man told him that he'd better not go to work for Bill Daniels because the numbers were shaky.

Eventually, in May 1965, he flew back to Colorado and sat down with Daniels, who told him that he would make him a vice president in charge of marketing and sales. Saeman said he was willing to do this but that wasn't what really interested him. He wanted to get into the brokering end of the business—the buying and selling of systems, the money side. In order to take the job, he said, he needed a place to live in Denver. Daniels picked up the phone and passed this request along to a friend who quickly showed Saeman half a dozen houses. He bought one before leaving town. When he got back to California, his wife, Carol, asked him how the trip had gone. He told her that they were moving to Denver and he'd just purchased a home.

"That wouldn't work today," Saeman concedes.

When he began working at Daniels, he was immediately struck by the gap between the successful image the boss had portrayed and the reality of the company. Daniels talked as if both he and the cable business had already made it. Later in 1965, Daniels purchased a Learjet 24 for $10,000 a month plus operating expenses. This seemed like a grand extravagance in a small business that was surviving from month to month. The Daniels office had only six executives and three secretaries. Monty Rifkin was president and Dick Zell was the chief financial officer.

"I didn't have to worry about paying our bills," Saeman recalls, "but Dick Zell did. His fingernails were very short. They went back to about the beginning of his knuckles. The facade Bill put on, the image that he projected, the professionalism that he had, was such an integral part of who he was, and that was true his entire life. Bill was never poor. He was always rich.

"He bought that Lear jet, hired the pilots, and was in the air. He took great pride in the plane, saying that it helped him to get to business meetings first and that he could fly whenever he wanted to. A myth grew up around Bill having that jet, but a few years later he had to get rid of it. It never put any money in his pocket, but Bill liked it."

While Daniels worked to promote the company and the cable business, Saeman traveled throughout the country, usually to backwaters, taking care of the systems his boss owned. Whenever he doubted his future or the future of the industry he'd decided to join, he renewed his faith by returning to Denver

Bill Daniels and John Saeman each instinctively felt the chemistry was right for a solid and successful business relationship.

and spending time around the man who'd hired him. Daniels' eye was not just on next month or next year or even ten years down the road. It was on the spread of cable TV everywhere from coast to coast; and beyond that, it was on the *effect* this was going to have on the United States as a whole. He believed that the nation was going to experience a communications revolution unlike anything seen before. Anyone with courage to jump on this train now, anyone who could withstand the inevitable delays, sidetracks, derailings, and other temporary obstacles that were bound to happen in a revolution of these proportions was going to have a fun and prosperous ride.

"The most profound thing that Bill conveyed to those around him," says Saeman, "was his vision for the industry and his unwavering belief that we were going to be a wired nation for cable TV. It's not like he woke up every morning and called everybody in and said, 'Now don't forget, guys, this is going to be a wired nation and you gotta believe in that.' It was subtle but convincing. It's not something that I remember concentrating on or thinking about, but as we moved along the highway of the development of the cable business, it was always there.

"I was always mindful of the fact that this industry kept moving to the next level. When we got started and were operating cable systems that were only providing services that should be available—ABC, NBC, CBS, and a PBS station—in areas that didn't get those, that was the cable market. It went from that to one of us saying, 'If people will buy that, I wonder if we could bring in an independent station from Los Angeles or Chicago or Atlanta—would they buy that?' And the answer was yes, they would. Then that segment of the market had to be fulfilled. So it kept inching along. While there were ups and downs, the trend just continued to expand into the next market and the next market and on and on.

"We got into some markets where we struggled for a long time, but the belief Bill had that this was going to be a wired nation, cable was going to be the wire, and we were going to defeat all of our opponents and were going to originate our own programming—that all came true. He had the vision."

After working for Daniels for a few years, Saeman came up with a plan to get himself out of the office and back to where he wanted to live: California. He liked his job and his boss, but he wanted more freedom to do his own deals and run his own show. He asked Daniels if he could return to California and oversee their operations in that state, as well as in Oregon, Washington, and Nevada. He didn't merely want to manage cable systems—he wanted to act as a broker and sell them. Rifkin was cool on the idea, but Daniels saw its potential and decided to give the younger man a base on the West Coast. Saeman went to work in his new office, which was his garage in California. From there he widened and deepened the foundation of Daniels & Associates as a nationwide business and as the broker to corporations that were starting to pay attention to cable.

He sold a system to the Times Mirror company—the parent organization of the *Los Angeles Times*—for $3.6 million. The Daniels & Associates cut of this deal was $180,000. The office in Denver needed the money so badly that Dick Zell flew out to California for the closing, pocketed the check himself, and cashed it as soon as he landed in the Mile High City. Saeman sold other cable systems to King Broadcasting and to the *Seattle Times* in Seattle; to the *San Francisco Chronicle* Publishing and Broadcasting Company; and to the *Chicago Tribune.* Saeman was having as much success as both he and Daniels hoped he would. It was a near-perfect arrangement, but then one day in 1971, Daniels called and asked him to come back to Denver and, using the model from his West Coast operation, expand to a disciplined national brokerage and investment banking division. He wanted Saeman to make deals for the company from coast to coast, which was precisely what Saeman wanted to do, but he wanted to do it from California. After many discussions with his wife, they decided to return to Colorado.

From that vantage point, he watched Daniels in action on a daily basis. People who witnessed his management style never forgot it.

By the early 1970s, Daniels had established not only a growing reputation as the father of the burgeoning cable industry, but he was also building his own legend as a boss and a personality. One aspect of that legend was rooted in his favorite saying: "The best is good enough for me." He absolutely had to have things the way he wanted them.

"Bill was always very proud of his office buildings," says Ben Hooks, who worked for Daniels & Associates at their Palm Desert cable system and later managed their cable system in Tempe before going on to run Buford Media. "He wanted them to be very attractive in the communities we served. One time Bill came down and looked out the big front window with a view toward the highway. There was a billboard between our building and the traffic on the highway. Bill turned around and said, 'I don't like that billboard.' I said, 'Well, sir, I don't know what we can do about it.' He said, 'Well, buy it!' I don't remember what we paid, but it was dear. We ended up owning that billboard and getting it down so it wouldn't obstruct the view of the building from the highway."

One of Daniels' systems in California had a goldfish pond that was riddled with algae. To the employees the algae wasn't important—they were just trying to run a company — but they knew that the sight of this unkempt pool would push him over the edge. Once when Daniels was coming to visit the system and the pond had not been cleaned, Chris Scurto gave him the wrong directions so they could buy twenty more minutes to deal with the mess.

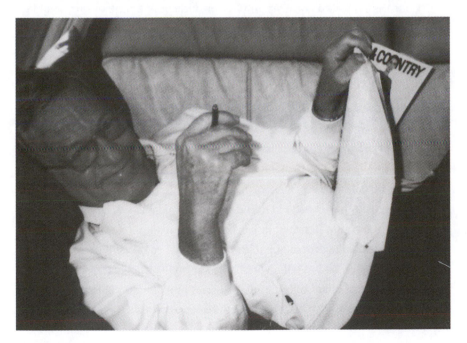

Bill Daniels, whose motto was "the best is good enough for me," relaxes in his Learjet during a flight to one of his cable television systems.

"We took that pool apart," he says. "We yanked it out, and all that was left was a cement podium. We took a plant from someone's office and slapped it on there. This left about thirty dead goldfish."

Around the office, Daniels demanded unconditional neatness. Every employee had to keep his or her desk as clean as possible—or endure a pointed lecture from Daniels on sloppiness. He smoked constantly but just as constantly emptied out his ashtrays (he couldn't go to sleep at night until all the trays were empty, all the dishes had been washed, all the floors had been picked up, all the newspapers folded, and everything else was put neatly in its place). If he was coming back to the Denver office from a flight or driving in from a distant location, he would usually call his employees to tell them how far away he was and when he would be arriving. They, in turn, would calculate exactly how long they had to straighten up the messes they'd created in his absence. Then they would start sweeping, rearranging, cramming stuff in drawers or shoveling it into wastebaskets with both hands.

"I once asked Bill to come up to Greeley and speak at one of our breakfast meetings," says Joe Tennyson, who ran the Daniels cable system in that Colorado town. "He gave one of his legendary speeches where he talked about the importance of opening the doors for women and all those corny kind of things that we all remember him for. I asked him while he was up here, would he mind just coming out to the office? He said he was planning on doing that. At the office the day of his visit, we were having a tech meeting and I look out the window and Bill is checking out the techs' trucks. Pretty soon he came in and I introduced him to everybody and he thanked them all for doing such a good job. But then he asked, 'Who drives truck number 5?' Poor old Rob Hastings—you could see it—his heart just went to his throat. He raised his hand, and Bill reaches into his shirt pocket and pulls out a hundred dollar bill and hands it to Rob. Bill said, 'I just want you to know I appreciate people who keep my equipment clean.' Needless to say, I never again had to tell anyone to clean up his truck. Here's a guy who's maybe making six dollars an hour and Bill gives him a hundred dollars."

On one occasion Daniels visited the Greeley offices and was upset because the employees were not wearing shirts with "Cablevision" emblazoned on them. He let his displeasure be known, and the Greeley crew decided this would not happen again.

"The next time we knew he was coming to visit," says Paulette Hastings, "we went to the store and bought white short-sleeve shirts. We had only forty minutes until he would arrive. I hurried and sewed 'Cablevision' patches on them. Then I rushed home to iron them. When Bill got there, all the guys had their 'Cablevision' shirts on!"

"I was free to buy or sell any property for Bill," says John Saeman, "but I would never have dreamed of changing the logo on our letterhead. That was his department."

His greatest weaknesses, Daniels often said, were his impatience and his perfectionism. The military had taught him punctuality, and if he'd scheduled an appointment with you at ten o'clock, you'd better walk into his office at ten sharp and not 10:01. Arriving at 10:02 would earn you a stern look and a lecture on tardiness. And if you were late for work in the morning, well... you'd better have an especially close relationship with the boss or somebody near you better have died the night before, and if neither of those things was true, you'd better be prepared for more lecturing. If people weren't at their desks on time, he would tour the office to see who was missing and then get on the intercom and start scolding in a huge, booming voice, sometimes referred to around the office as "the voice of God."

"You had to be at work by eight A.M.," says Gretchen Bunn, who went to work at Daniels in accounting in 1972 and eventually became the program director for thirty-five cable systems. "Bill wanted you there earlier than that. If you weren't there by eight, he would go down to the parking garage and look at the cars of everyone who was there—and everyone who wasn't. He never forgot those things.

"Alan Harmon was from Hobbs and Bill loved him and hired him, but Alan drove him nuts because he didn't have Bill's work ethic. He would show up at the office mid-morning just in time to check his messages and go to lunch for two hours, then return to the office to recheck his messages before calling it a day. Bill would always lecture him about getting to work earlier, so one day Alan arrived in the office promptly at eight A.M. He came in, looked around at everyone—they were just working. 'What's the big deal?' he said. 'Nothing unusual is happening here.' He left and never showed up that early again."

Daniels was, according to one of his secretaries, Linda Henshaw, "a high-maintenance boss." He would call her at 5 A.M. and ask her to take dictation. He would call her at 8 P.M. when he was out of town and ask her to feed his fish. She was required to hunt for his cat, Sydney, when she got lost—which was often.

"He had a favorite pen," she says, "but then they quit making them. I called every drugstore and every office supply store in the United States and was able to get the last hundred and fifty pens. I felt good about going through this process, knowing that I had done everything I possibly could. I had the final answer."

In the mid-seventies, Saeman hired a German immigrant named Erika Schafer, who failed her typing test, to be his secretary. In time she improved her typing and went to work for Bill.

"I learned very shortly," she says, "that in order to work for Bill, I had to always be a step ahead of him. I was so terrified that he would yell at me and scream because I blew something. That was my biggest challenge. He gave me all my chances and was a lot of things to me. Over the years he became my mentor, and he saw so many things in me that I would never have had the courage to see myself. Consequently, I achieved more than I ever dreamed possible."

After working for Daniels for nearly fifteen years, she wanted to open her own real estate investment company in Cherry Creek. Daniels invested $1 million in her upstart business, and she became a major developer in the area. And she, unlike many other people, not only paid him back but with interest.

When Daniels wanted to make a visual presentation in his office, he expected everything to run perfectly. If a tape machine was not cued up to the exact second, holy hell was raised. If you happened to be lucky enough to deliver a perfect presentation, with perhaps one small detail out of place, he would call you into his office to discuss that one small detail. If a secretary was unfortunate enough to send him a memo with one insignificant misspelled word, she would receive that same memo back, laminated. He not only wanted his own offices immaculate, but if he could have had his way, he would have tidied up the universe. He worried about where all the world's garbage went at the end of a day, and he took great pleasure in sharing his views on neatness. Once he made a surprise visit to a company he was about to acquire in

Houston. The offices were such a mess that he couldn't focus on the visit. As he was leaving, he curtly blasted the management and later said that the incident reminded him of dropping a bomb during World War II and watching smoke rise from the earth as he flew away.

Daniels himself was always on time and always prepared. Every morning he asked his secretary to type out a series of index cards, about thirty of them, and then he spread them out on his desk in long neat rows. He studied them diligently and shuffled them around until they were in the exact pattern he desired. They told him about potential buyers, potential sellers, bankers who desired stroking, and politicians who were on the fence concerning a cable issue and needed to be wined and dined. He felt that the only way to compete with the broadcasters for the politicians' attention was to treat them better than the competition was treating them. After studying the cards, he picked up

Bill Daniels and President Richard Nixon meet at a gathering of the nation's leading businessmen at the White House.

the phone and set the wining and the dining in motion. He couldn't comfortably leave the office for the day until he'd dealt with every single card. The following morning he would have another thirty ready to go.

The index cards spread out across his desk were more than a highly organized way to go about his work regimen. They were very much a symbol of his role in and his goals for the cable industry. As those who knew Daniels best always said, he never actually implemented anything either inside his own office or outside in the cable world. He was not a detail man in any sense of the word. He delegated the implementation of things to others and paid them very well for their efforts. His job was as an entrepreneurial thinker, a conceiver of new ideas and possibilities. He looked at the cable industry from above, precisely the way he looked at the cards on his desk and he constantly thought of ways to bring together this player and that institution, ways to get the regulators off cable's back, ways to bring Congress to where it needed to be, and ways to keep stretching the boundaries of the business. He didn't merely want to see cable succeed so that it could bring more viewers to television. He wanted cable to change the nature of television itself. By extension, because TV was becoming the most important media force in the world, if you changed this medium you would be altering the way people thought and felt and lived. It was a grandiose vision and he conceived of it while driving through the dusty towns of the Southwest in the mid-1950s when most people had never seen TV.

Beside his desk he always kept two or more briefcases packed and ready to travel, in case someone phoned and asked him to fly anywhere in America for a meeting on a new deal. When the phone rang, he grabbed the closest loaded briefcase and took off. During a flight, he carefully studied the background of the person he was going to see. He memorized the name of the man's wife and children. He prepared a list of questions to ask the individual, business questions and personal questions. He always had a backlog of questions so he could never run out. The relentless inquiries had two purposes. They built a rapport with a potential business ally, which might help close the next deal (Daniels understood, with the instinct of the true salesman, that most people loved talking about themselves and would do so continuously if you just gave them the chance). His questions also served another purpose: they kept the other person from asking him too much about himself and kept him from sharing his deeper thoughts or emotions.

Whatever was stirring in there—from his coming of age in the Depression, to fighting and killing the enemy in two wars, watching his father die early after suffering with diabetes and heart failure, jumping into and out of a couple of marriages, not having children of his own, his own uncertainties about the cable business—his real feelings belonged to him and nobody else. It was his job to keep the lid on them. It was his job to be strong and silent. Drinking helped him do that, so occasionally he drank a lot and partied late into the night with his friends or with a new girlfriend. But that was only infrequently. The alcohol was kept under control, and the ex-soldier remained in charge of himself.

When he wasn't having a party, he went to bed early and arose very early (in later years when he was living in California, his bedroom included some exotic decor such as a mink bedspread and mink pillows). He was often out of bed at four A.M. and already doing the things he most enjoyed: smoking cigarettes, drinking cup after cup of coffee, and devouring newspapers—provided they came on time. The man who was supposed to have the papers in front of Daniels before dawn each morning was Arthur Bell.

"Arthur liked to drink," says John Saeman, "and Bill was always putting him on a two-week suspension, but he always took him back. He exhibited unbelievable loyalty to Arthur. Bill believed in giving people a second chance but not a third or fourth or fifth one. Arthur was an exception to this. I think he was with Bill longer than anyone else."

When Bell was suspended from work, Bill hired Duke Saeman, John Saeman's son, to get up at four A.M. and drive from the distant suburb of Castle Rock all the way to the airport to get the national newspapers and bring them to Daniels' front door. By the time Saeman arrived there, his boss had read the local papers and was eager for the next batch. Not only had he read them but he'd most likely written some notes for his employees or others to review about the day's events. He expected them to be as current on the headlines as he was. Other than having a lifelong interest in sports, Daniels was never taken with the world of entertainment, but he loved absorbing the news. He read a handful of papers every day and constantly looked for TV programs that would give him the latest bulletins from around the world. (Back in the early 1960s, there were very few such programs on the air, especially at four A.M., but he imagined that one day that would change.) He also planned the coming day and the series of index cards he would tackle at the office. Sometimes, especially in the first decade of Daniels & Associates, his daily plans involved figuring how to make payroll or keep his creditors at bay.

"One of my earliest memories of Bill, but not the most notable, was when he was advertising in our magazine," says Stan Searle, who ran a trade magazine called *Communications Publishing* before founding Pioneer Cablevision. "This must have been around 1965. He had a $1,200 advertising bill with us, which was several months past due, and he didn't have the money to pay it. Instead, he mailed me a copy of his financial statement, suggesting that he could take it to a bank and borrow against it [to pay his bills]. He knew that no bank would do that, but it probably eased his embarrassment.

"I did study it out of curiosity and in the process got a valuable education. I saw that he had from five percent to twenty percent interest in several small cable properties, somewhere in western Oklahoma and possibly California. I got the idea from him of bootstrapping ourselves into the operating side of the cable business. We later had a twenty percent interest in systems in Duncan and Muskogee, Oklahoma, and interest in a Newkirk, Oklahoma, system and one-third interest in a Yakima, Washington, system, the first cable system there. We did all this mostly as junior partners to the people with capital. I got the inspiration for the important concept from studying Daniels' financial statement that he had sent me because he couldn't come up with the $1,200. Of course, later on he did pay that bill."

After driving to work, Daniels often buttonholed employees and asked them questions about world events. It didn't always occur to him that these people had probably not been up since four o'clock reading newspapers, and even if they did arise early, they might have been raising families or negotiating with spouses or doing things other than preparing for a news-event quiz. They had lives apart from their connection to the cable business. With every woman Daniels married, he was given the opportunity to father his own children and raise a family, but each time he declined, before moving on to the next round of romance or matrimony.

He didn't seem to want to be the husband of just one woman or the father of any particular child. Rather, he was starting to define his role as the patriarch of the growing clan that both Daniels & Associates and the cable industry as a whole were becoming, as the business spread from coast to coast.

"He was like a father, not only to me, but to many, many people," says Jerry Presley, who worked at Daniels & Associates for many years. "When he would talk to you at a party or in a group, he would give you a hundred percent of his attention. He never had wandering eyes. Therefore, I think that he touched people one-on-one.

"He demanded loyalty, but you were absolutely assured that he was going to give it back to you. You never wanted to cross him, lie to him, or take anything that was his, but you knew he would treat you with the same respect. I always remember when Ross Perot sent in private troops to rescue his employees from some backwater country. Bill Daniels would have done exactly the same thing."

Ten

Another unmistakable Daniels trait, as Monty Rifkin and John Saeman had found out during the process of relocating to Denver, was his tireless pursuit of talented people—even after they'd repeatedly resisted him or the cable business. When Glenn Jones was a young man in the coal mining area of Pennsylvania, he won a scholarship to Yale but passed it up for the chance to put on boots and workgloves and take a job in a local steel mill. His father was a coal miner and became so upset with his son's refusal to further his education that he himself enrolled the teenager in Findlay College in Ohio, an institution associated with the Church of God. When the brass at Findlay learned that young Jones was playing piano in a vaudeville act while attending their classes in order to earn a few bucks to help support himself, they wondered if he might be better off taking a degree elsewhere. He transferred to Allegheny College back in Pennsylvania and earned a degree in economics.

During the Korean War, he served in the navy's underwater demolition unit and took apart sea bombs. Following his discharge, he found a job in Denver with the Martin Corporation, a defense contractor, testing the explosive components of the Titan 1 ICBM systems. He also went to night school and earned a law degree from the University of Colorado. He began his legal career in very modest circumstances. He was eager to go back to Pennsylvania and practice there, but he didn't have the money to move across the country. His car could barely make it to Boulder and back, a round trip of about fifty miles. He had a wife and children and was struggling to cover his bills. One evening in the early sixties, he found himself in his apartment building hanging out laundry and talking to another resident. The man was very interested in Jones' legal background and began asking him about changing jobs.

"I basically met this guy over the clothesline," Jones recalls. "It was Carl Williams, who was Bill Daniels' partner at the time, and we became good friends. I had decided to start my own law firm. I was practicing out of a doughnut shop on Florida Street and Holly, but it got embarrassing after a few months. My clients would meet me there, and I didn't drink that much coffee or eat that many doughnuts. Carl just kept hitting on me, asking me to move into their building at 2930 East 3rd Avenue. He wanted me to do legal work for them in exchange for rent. I put it off for a while but finally I moved in and switched out rent for legal services. This must've been 1961. I sort of became the deal lawyer for Daniels & Associates. I would close the deal for Daniels, representing a buyer or the seller, and then when either the buyer or the seller did their next cable deal, they would call me. I was soon representing cable companies all across the country."

In 1964 Jones ran for Congress but lost, perhaps because he didn't have enough time to devote to his campaign.

"I practiced law so intently in those days," he says, "staying up until the sun came up the next morning, putting deals together. I remember having papers strewn all over the stairs up to Bill's office. After midnight, the stairs were just layered with documents. By the time everybody came to work in the morning, they were completed documents. But I did burn myself out doing deals. Bill and I had a great relationship. He would just write his signature on the bottom right-hand corner of a whole bunch of seven by eleven pieces of paper and I'd go out and put deals together on top of his signature. I always knew where he was, hiding out down in Phoenix or Scottsdale. I could always find Bill when others sometimes couldn't."

After a few years of working for Daniels, Jones tried to quit the legal field, but that was more difficult than he'd imagined. He moved up into the mountains and lived out of his Volkswagen, anxious to get away from those demanding his professional expertise in the cable business. People would hunt him down and demand his services. They'd heard about the easy money to be made in cable and wanted his advice and help. To get rid of them, he would tell them that he was out of cable now, but they persisted. Then he would quote them a huge rate for his time—$350 an hour—certain that this would put them off. No problem, they said, as they pulled out their checkbooks and began writing out the numbers. Finally, he decided to buy and operate a cable system himself in the mountain village of Georgetown, about an hour's drive west of

Denver. The property had under a hundred subscribers, and many of them had been refusing to pay their bills, because their service was so bad. The seller had wanted $400 down, but Jones hadn't been able to raise this payment, until he'd borrowed it against his Volkswagen. He got the loan and entered the business. Another future cable magnate, who'd been introduced to the industry through the Daniels' office, was making his debut in the field of modern communications.

While pursuing the Georgetown deal, Jones continued working for Daniels and learning the cable business. The education he was receiving was unparalleled, but there were drawbacks.

"Bill was kind of slow paying in those days," he says. "When he got into me real deep, I would go to his people and say, 'We all have to eat.' They would laugh and ask how much I needed. I'd say I needed five thousand dollars out of fifteen thousand or whatever and they would write me a check."

Part of Daniels' cash-flow problems had stemmed from the fluctuating nature of free enterprise; another part was caused by the opposite sex.

"Every few years," Jones says, "Bill would have to liquidate some holdings to pay for his bills—his lifestyle, basically. And of course, he got divorced a couple of times. I handled one of the key witnesses in one of his divorce cases, the one with Eileen. She was a gorgeous blonde and she would have been devastating in court. It would have been bad to have her on the witness stand. I ended up having to take her to Hawaii and convinced the judge that we could use her written testimony. The opposing attorney just went crazy over this.

"Bill had a great joie de vivre—he was just bigger than life. He was one of the world's best salesmen. I've seen him do amazing things on the telephone— turn people around. From a business standpoint, I admired his aggression. Bill took no prisoners. I remember he used to drive Cadillac convertibles and he'd have a bottle of Jack Daniels between the seats in the front and people would steal his car once in a while or he'd leave the key in it. He'd come out of the office and it would be gone.

"We were going up to Greeley one time and we got stopped—for good reason because we were really moving. The scotch bottle was hidden but it was interesting to watch him handle that policeman. And he didn't get a ticket either! He was very confident with the cop, got his name and address and Bill told him he was going to write his supervisor and tell him how professionally he handled himself."

Jones' first act as a cable operator in Georgetown was to go up and down the streets of the small town and collect back pay from the disgruntled subscribers. Many customers nagged him about their poor reception, but he fixed this by hooking up a TV monitor to the system and instantly improving the picture. He soon expanded his operation, which he had dubbed "Cowpoke Cable," to include the nearby mountain town of Idaho Springs. He renamed his business Silver King Cable after a local mining outfit but then finally settled on a much simpler handle: Jones Cable. He began flying back and forth across America looking for other small systems to purchase, and when he found one, he borrowed every nickel the banks would give him to make the buy. He was becoming a cable player, but a few more years would pass before he turned into a force. His rise was helped along by creative funding.

The oil industry, in order to finance the high cost of energy exploration, had recently begun using a strategy called the limited partnership. Well-heeled investors, often doctors or lawyers in search of tax shelters, put up the money for drilling, while independent oil companies oversaw these operations for a fee. The partnerships usually lost money for a while, which helped the investors taxwise, but when they eventually went into the black or wells were sold for a profit, the operator took 25 percent and the investors 75 percent. The system was designed to help those who needed tax breaks during their prime earning years and retirement income later on. Jones applied the same concept to cable, and then went looking for backers.

In 1972 Jones and his brother, Neil, raised $150,000 for their initial fund. Four years later they turned a $300,000 profit for their investors. Confident that the partnerships had a future, the brothers worked full-time to find new sources of money, and soon they were making presentations on Wall Street to the biggest names in finance, from Dean Witter to Prudential Bache. They eventually raised more than a billion dollars for their cable investments, and by the 1990s Glenn Jones was running the world's eighth largest cable operation. His Denver-based business had 1.5 million customers and was worth between \$2 to \$3 billion. Another seat-of-the-pants entrepreneur had made the Mile High City the home of the cable industry.

Because Denver was the address of the industry's leading broker and several successful cable enterprises, Daniels believed that it should also be the center of the trade publishing business. In the seventies, he began a campaign to make this happen. At that time Stan Searle ran the trade magazine company Communications Publishing out of Oklahoma.

"Bill told me," Searle says, "that if the trade magazines would move to Denver, then it would truly become the cable capital. He was influential in getting other people to move here too. I've always wondered how many people he gave that speech to. In any case, he had Alan Harmon call me and ask if I was really serious about moving to Colorado and I assured him I was. Alan asked me if he got me an appointment with the governor, would I come up and see him? I told him I would. And the following Tuesday, Bill had arranged for me to meet with Governor John Love, who in turn put us together with bankers who facilitated our move and also the construction financing of our new building in Englewood. Alan Harmon, who became a friend of mine, graciously handled the introduction at the governor's office and confided to me just a few years ago that he himself had never met Governor Love until that day. He carried the introduction off in a manner that made me think they were old buddies.

"Bill was always focused on business. After a flight he would immediately jump out of the plane and head for a phone booth with his fat little notebook in hand. He would spend every minute on the ground pursuing whatever deal he was working on. I remember an anecdote that I heard about Bill getting out of a cab in Seattle. He was engrossed in conversation with whomever he was riding with and pulled a twenty dollar bill out of his money clip. He walked into the hotel and noticed the twenty dollar bill in his hand. He'd given the money clip to the cabdriver, who had long since disappeared."

When he wasn't inadvertently giving away his money clip to cabbies, he was constantly dropping huge tips on waitresses, barbers, bellhops, shoeshine men, repairmen, and maître d's at tony restaurants. On one occasion he sent a Daniels employee ahead of him into a fashionable eatery in Washington, D.C., to make certain that their party got a good table. The employee was clutching a hundred dollar bill which he slipped to the maître d' while asking for the best seat in the house. The grand gesture was unnecessary. When Daniels arrived at the restaurant, his group was the only one there.

The first time Daniels visited John Rigas' cable system in Coudersport, Pennsylvania, he wanted Bill to visit a dive called the Texas Hot. Daniels had a soft spot for dives and waitresses who worked there, and he preferred sitting at the counter. At the Texas Hot he ordered a hot dog with everything on it and a cup of coffee, asking the waitress if he could take a menu home with him. Several weeks later Daniels sent Rigas the menu laminated on a plaque. He didn't tell Rigas that he'd also sent the waitress a note complimenting her on her work and giving her a $100 tip. Decades later, shortly before he died, he sent her another $100. Throughout his life, whenever he would see Rigas, he'd cup his hands and holler, "Hey, John, how 'bout one Texas Hot with everything on it?"

Bill Daniels devoted long hours in the 1960s to brokering cable television systems and gaining equity interests in various cable properties.

Eleven

In the early 1960s, the TV networks began embracing the old maxim that if you can't beat 'em, then you might as well join 'em. Having lost the fight in Congress to regulate cable, the networks decided to start buying into the industry. In November 1963, CBS, the so-called Tiffany network because of its prestige and clout, stepped forward and purchased a cable system in Vancouver, British Columbia. The following year the Westinghouse Broadcasting Company bought four cable systems in Georgia. Allen Gilliland, a broadcaster in San Jose, California, commenced bidding on cable properties in the Golden State, while Newhouse Broadcasting purchased a small system in Rome, New York, and applied for a cable franchise in its home city of Syracuse. Lucille Buford, the owner of a TV station in Tyler, Texas, bought half the interest in a cable outlet in Lufkin, Texas. General Electric Broadcasting established a cable unit with the idea of opening franchises throughout New York State and beyond. And broadcaster Burt Harris formed Harriscope, which purchased cable systems in Flagstaff, Arizona, and Palm Springs, California.

Daniels & Associates was the broker in 80 percent of these deals and in several cable acquisitions made by the powerhouse Cox Broadcasting Company. One day in 1965, Daniels received a call from Sol Taishoff, the publisher of *Broadcasting* magazine, who asked the broker to meet a friend of his. Daniels had coffee with Leonard Reinsch, who ran Cox, a communications empire that owned radio, TV, and print media. Daniels was impressed with Reinsch because the latter saw cable not as a rival that was going to harm broadcasters but as another communications medium with a golden future. One of Daniels' key insights into the communications media was that each branch of it—TV, radio, magazines, cable, newspapers, etc.—fed every other branch.

This idea directly challenged conventional wisdom, which held that new media would eventually replace old media, as the printing press had once replaced hand-printed manuscripts. But things were operating differently. The advent of radio hadn't put newspapers or magazines out of business. When television came along, it didn't cause the demise of radio, as many predicted it would. TV didn't wipe out movies, either. Television only made the public more and more interested in reading about or watching people in the film business when they appeared on TV to promote their new motion pictures. And now cable, instead of threatening to ruin network TV or the film industry, was serving to bring more entertainment to mass audiences. The American public, Daniels believed, had a bottomless hunger for both entertainment and information, and that hunger had only begun to be tapped. All forms of media were simultaneously pushing forward the endless appetite for stimulation. His unswerving faith in this perception would eventually be worth millions to Daniels and billions to the cable industry.

Reinsch was used to buying TV stations at six to seven times cash flow. When Daniels told him that he could pick up cable outlets for three times cash flow, Reinsch asked where one was available. Daniels located a property in Aberdeen, Washington, with 9,500 subscribers, and Reinsch purchased it for $1.5 million. Cox didn't have anybody to manage the operation, so the Daniels office took over that role. Daniels & Associates collected one fee for brokering the deal and another for running the system.

Reinsch then invited Daniels to a luncheon in Dayton, Ohio, where he introduced the Denver broker to Jim Cox, who headed the empire. After meeting with Daniels, Cox decided to invest heavily in cable and was soon purchasing more properties through Daniels' office. When his fellow broadcasters saw what Cox was doing, they wanted in the game as well. All of the tub-thumping for cable that Daniels had been doing throughout the past decade or so was starting to pay off. He was perfectly positioned to help those with real money invest in cable when they were ready to make a move. And why not make those moves with the numbers that cable was generating?

In 1964 the Federal Communications Commission released the first ever officially sanctioned study of cable's profitability. It reported that the average operating profit margin per cable system was 57 percent, a huge figure that nearly doubled the margin for broadcasting outlets. When these figures quickly spread through the communications business, cable systems began emerging everywhere. Soon a hundred or more new operations were being launched across the United States every six months. A backlog of a thousand new permits stacked up for entrepreneurs anxious to leap into cable. Daniels & Associates could barely keep up with all the deals that were swirling around the office.

The more sales that Daniels brokered, the more he was able to spread his essential message: Cable wasn't an adversary to anyone or anything in the broadcasting field. It was simply the newest branch of the communications industry—and would add to the whole pie without eliminating any part of it. Cable would one day bring more sports, more entertainment, more political news, and more specialized programming of every kind to the American public. It was only a matter of time before people began using this untapped potential. The future of TV was in appealing to the specific interests of more segments of the population than the three networks could reach or satisfy. In a word—think bigger, much bigger, because that was the direction everything was moving toward.

In the late 1960s, Bill Daniels' fleet of cable service vehicles spread throughout the West. Bill is pictured with his Colorado Springs Cablevision sales-and-service team.

By the mid-sixties, Daniels was taking this message to some of the most powerful businessmen in the communications field. In New York, he delivered it to ABC-TV executive Fred Lieberman as he was pitching the network on buying cable systems. He delivered it to the brass at CBS and to David Sarnoff, the head of NBC. After listening to Daniels present his vision of cable's brilliant future, Sarnoff added a note of skepticism that would prove to be prophetic. Despite cable's growing success, it still had many enemies who did not embrace the new medium and had not forgotten the bitter defeat of the cable regulation bill on the floor of the United States Senate back in 1959. These forces were gathering momentum for their next assault on cable's freedom in the marketplace.

"Young man," Sarnoff declared, "if you can solve your political problems, I think this is very exciting."

Daniels was not one to worry about a future fight because he always believed that he would ultimately win. While political heavyweights were building up anti-cable sentiment, he was enjoying the 1960s—the go-go years in his business and in his own life as well. He began driving faster cars and living more luxuriantly. He generated more cash and spent it more aggressively (he liked to tell people that certain things in life were difficult but the easiest thing in the world was making money). He went through more homes, more clothes, more marriages, and more relationships. He lived as hard as he had when he was a young man buzzing the treetops of Hobbs with a small aircraft. In his forties, he was not much different from the fellow who'd slipped out of the New Mexico Military Institute in the middle of the night to have a rendezvous with the lieutenant governor's daughter.

One person who spent time around Daniels in the 1960s was Matt Tinley, Jr., his great-nephew from New Mexico. He experienced the Daniels lifestyle firsthand.

"Bill had two sisters, Dottie and my grandmother Bobette," says Tinley. "Bobette's son was my father. My relationship with Bill started the day I was born because my dad, as he was wont to do, was in Las Vegas gambling when I was born. Bill brought me home from the hospital. He was a surrogate father in many ways. He and my dad had a very close relationship but a very rocky relationship. I think because they were both a lot alike in many ways. Their strengths were their frailties. As Bill used to say, 'I was flying first class when I couldn't afford coach.' Or, as they say in Ireland, 'I'm living next week now.'

"Bill was the kind of guy who always had the free cash, the girlfriends, the Cadillacs, the T-Birds, the fancy clothes, and he threw the best parties. My dad left Texas and came to work for Bill and started living that life. They had an apartment or a house together and a swimming pool in Cherry Creek [an upscale Denver neighborhood and shopping district]. On the weekends they would hire models from the Playboy club here in Denver, and they hired a bartender and had parties by the pool. No one in Denver did that sort of thing, but Bill had a lot of Hugh Hefner in him. He loved women, but he loved them in a way that men loved women back then. If you could make a good drink, had a nice body and a pretty face, if you wore perfume and had nice nails and laughed at their jokes—then, hey, you were great. There was a spot for you.

"So my dad had all of this thrown at him early when he and Bill began living together. The problem was that Bill was a little more advanced and more sophisticated than my dad. He had the know-how to live on the edge. And he was twenty years older. My dad started living this very fast life before he was ready and he started the drinking and the gambling and moving to Vegas and all this kind of stuff. I think it all just overwhelmed him really.

"In my early years, Bill was always just very, very kind to me. My dad died in a car wreck when I was seven, so I stayed with Bill for a really extended length of time. I went to the funeral with Bill in his jet. It was pretty amazing back then. I thought he was the richest guy on earth. He couldn't make payroll, but he'd still have a jet! I mean, you'd think he was like a nut. That was so Bill.

"The funeral was like the lowest moment of my life. You know when your dad dies and you're seven, it's like your whole world has evaporated. This shattered my world, but Bill was so kind to me. After the funeral, we went to a 7-Eleven store and I was a huge baseball fan and he bought all the baseball cards in the place. He made the poor clerk go in the back and get all the cards from the inventory, and we went out to his Cadillac carrying loads of Tops baseball cards.

"The most valuable things Bill did for me were not what he would think they were. It wouldn't be financing a business. It was teaching me to have guts and not to be afraid of anything. To take risks and maybe fail, but sometimes you have to get out there and just do things. More important, his life taught me that being an entrepreneur is really lonely. He told me once his biggest regrets were not the things he'd done and failed at, but the things he hadn't done. That is what I feel most strongly about.

"He paid my way through Harvard, financed things, and those things were very kind, but his biggest contribution to me was to let me sit beside him. I miss him. He's an irreplaceable person. Relationships are a lot better when there is tension in them. You learn so much more about a person. My best relationships go up and down because there is true love and true emotions. If your relationships are always on an even keel, there's no passion and no heart to them."

Twelve

In the late fifties, the cable industry had barely won the congressional vote that had kept it from being regulated, but the fight was only beginning. In the sixties, microwave technology arrived, which meant that cable systems could use it to import programming from much farther away. These imports often interfered with local broadcast stations that were showing the same programs. Microwaves only heightened the longstanding conflict between broadcasting and cable. If cable had the power to bring entertainment from New York or Chicago into homes in small towns across the country, how could the local stations compete? The broadcasters intensified their efforts to curtail or stop the spread of cable and lobbied hard at the FCC, which in 1962 ruled that it would deny any new microwave licenses that economically damaged a local station.

The TV networks were of two minds about the growth of cable. On the one hand, they were using Bill Daniels as their primary broker to buy up cable properties around the nation. They could see that the systems were profitable and had a place in the ever-expanding communications field. But they were also worried about how much clout cable might accumulate. At the same time, many congressmen still felt betrayed over the cable industry's change of mind at the last moment and its refusal to back any portion of the 1959 regulation bill. All of this was brewing when the stakes and the temperature of the debate were suddenly raised.

An enterprising man named Charles Dolan applied for a license to bring cable not to a village in Pennsylvania or Kentucky, where a system might improve the reception or provide a few more channels, but to the communications capital of the world: New York City. Like Daniels, Dolan felt that just because the residents of Manhattan already had a wide number of programs to choose from, they would always be interested in having more (in the late

Always the innovator, Bill Daniels launched in 1979 Showcase I and II as pay movie channels to enhance the profitability of the numerous cable television systems he owned or managed.

fifties, Daniels had tried to convince the city fathers in Denver that the Mile High City should be wired for cable, but his plan had gone nowhere; decades would pass before he would see his ideas come to fruition in the so-called capital of the cable industry). If viewers had a dozen channels now, Dolan reasoned, why wouldn't they want two dozen or three or even four? Now that color TV was becoming more and more popular, with millions of Americans rushing out to buy the latest innovation in the medium, wouldn't cable be even more important because of its ability to deliver a clearer, cleaner image? If TV screen ghosts were bad in black-and-white, they were intolerable in color. The post–World War II hunger for entertainment that had fed the rise of television wasn't nearly sated yet, was it? Dolan knew only one way to answer these questions.

His application for a license hardly went unnoticed. Another enterprising New Yorker, the irrepressible Irving Kahn, was determined not to be outdone in his own backyard and soon asked for permission to sell his own cable system in the city. TelePrompTer wanted a piece of the action, and so did the media conglomerate RKO General. A bidding war was under way. As news of these developments spread outside New York, operators rushed forward to wire other major cities. Los Angeles and Philadelphia quickly faced battles over cable, while the Cox Broadcasting Company laid plans to bring new systems to Cleveland, Toledo, and Pittsburgh. Cable TV, which had its roots in rural America, was coming to the urban centers.

If broadcasters had been alarmed about the triumph of cable in the hinterlands, now they were really worried. The networks, and ABC in particular, loudly protested the movement of cable into the cities. Daniels had recently tried to get ABC to stop fighting the spread of cable and to buy into the industry, but the network had rejected his advances. Some of ABC's own advisers had tried similar tactics, but they too were brushed aside. As soon as the ABC brass learned that New York was in the process of being wired, they launched a blitz at the FCC, the first time a network had ever lobbied the federal agency so directly in an attempt to get cable regulated once and for all. ABC wanted the feds to draw boundaries around cable's activities. The network brought up the same cry that had been heard from broadcasters ever since cable had first appeared: if the government did not step in and take control of the situation, the American public would soon lose what it had come to take for granted—free television. The only way to preserve free TV was to restrict cable.

ABC found allies throughout the broadcasting world. The network had one major weapon that cable simply could not compete with: it could offer politicians airtime, while cable did not yet have enough clout or reach to have this capacity. The 1960 presidential election, in which John Kennedy had narrowly defeated Richard Nixon, in part because of Kennedy's superior performances during televised debates, had convinced politicians everywhere across the United States that success on TV was now the most significant avenue toward winning at the polls. They had no choice but to pay attention to those who held power in the TV industry, which meant the broadcasters.

The National Association of Broadcasters published a study of the negative impact of cable on their businesses, claiming that when cable operators brought signals into markets where local stations already existed, the locals consistently lost money. Cable leaders tried to fight back against this position, but the momentum was building against them. When it became clear that something had to be done to placate the broadcasters, the FCC took action. In the spring of 1965, the agency issued a new set of regulations for all cable systems. They stipulated:

> *Cable could not duplicate a program shown in a market by a local broadcaster for fifteen days before or after the local outlet had aired the same program. Cable systems had to carry all the local stations in each market. There would be a freeze placed on the granting of all new microwave licenses on systems designed to serve major urban populations.*

The new rulings appeared to have given the broadcasters a huge victory in their fight against the spread of cable. Five years after losing on the floor of Congress, they'd seemingly gained the upper hand. Broadcasters and their allies—telephone companies and theater owners—had finally put cable in its place. Or had they?

Despite the FCC's decisions, Charles Dolan and Irving Kahn were determined to go ahead with their plans to wire the island of Manhattan. While the feds

Bill Daniels was a magnet for beautiful women. He is pictured here with three women at a Denver fund-raising gala.

were attempting to limit cable's influence, the duo had brought together a group of potent New York political figures and convinced them that cable was good for the city. After much wrangling, Dolan and Kahn (along with a lesser third competitor, CATV Enterprises) won the right to build a cable system in Manhattan. Essentially, Kahn got everything north of Eighty-Sixth Street and Dolan got everything to the south. After dividing up the island and getting ready to go to work, there were more disputes and delays. New York Telephone tried to stop the construction of the new system, as did CBS-TV and Universal Pictures, but in the end the push by Dolan and Kahn, as well as the consumers' desire for cable, was simply too strong.

The city government cautiously gave in to them and allowed the plans to go forward, but only if the price was kept reasonable. The system could not sell pay-per-view programming and as a goodwill gesture it offered free services to local hospitals and the police department. With these conditions in place, the wire that would bring more TV to New York began being strung up and down the length of the island. Cable, which had its humble beginnings in the small towns across America, now made its debut in Manhattan. Roughly fifteen years after it had arrived in places like Tuckerman, Arkansas, and Astoria, Oregon, cable had now gained a foothold in the largest city in America.

A paradox lay at the heart of the young industry. It was growing each day by hundreds of subscribers, but the struggle against it was also gathering force. Every time cable won a victory, the anti-cable powers vowed to renew the battle. The backers of regulation had political strength and money on their side, but they lacked the one thing they most needed to triumph in the long run: the underlying desire of the population. Or Main Street, as Bill Daniels always put it. From New York City to Casper, Wyoming, to Southern California, the American public wanted access to as much information and entertainment as possible. The politicians weren't leading this fight—they were merely following the demands of viewers for more TV.

It would take many more years and many more battle scars before these dynamics would fully play out, but once cable had begun, it could not be stopped. In the end, it was the vision of Daniels and others like him that prevailed. Time was on their side because their intuition about what Americans really wanted ran deeper and truer than the opposition's. Senators and congressmen would inevitably embrace the movement because it led to more votes.

Thirteen

Daniels had launched many cable deals through funds provided by New York financiers, and those connections were growing stronger. Initially, he'd only been able to secure three-to five-year loans that had been personally guaranteed by the principals of the cable companies; under these circumstances, the bank itself assumed very little risk. When this arrangement proved successful, the banks signed off on the same loans without demanding a personal guarantee. Then the loans grew from five years to seven years and later from seven to ten, with the bank holding the first mortgage on the property. Once Daniels became the most reputable cable representative inside the banking community, he turned his attention to insurance companies, handing them a list of cable's investment virtues. It was, first and foremost, a cash-flow business, so it serviced its debt very efficiently; it had far fewer defaults than was the norm in many other industries; it paid very low taxes or none because of its enormous write-offs; it had been around long enough that loan officers could see that it was not going to be replaced by the next technological innovation.

He soon put together financing from the Travelers Insurance Company, Allstate, John Hancock, Equitable, and Teachers. While Charles Dolan and Irving Kahn were wiring Manhattan, Daniels was solidifying cable's relationship with America's major financial houses. The investment community's belief in cable opened the way for what would become known as MSOs, or Multiple System Operators, the giant conglomerates that eventually jumped into cable. They could do so because the infrastructure for the financing for these deals was already in place. The MSOs, comprised mostly of the larger companies who bought cable systems (often newspaper publishers), and the broadcasters were becoming the industry's major players. From the beginning, Bill Daniels was the glue that bound the financial network together and got the money flowing. Without him, the bankers and insurance companies would have stayed safely on the sidelines—at least for a while—and missed an unprecedented opportunity to earn untold millions of dollars. Daniels was the economic and the spiritual leader of cable because he did one thing better than anyone else: he made business fun.

"Bill and Irving Kahn hit it off quite well and had a great deal of respect for each other," says Les Reed, who worked at TelePrompTer in the sixties. "I would end up having incredible dinners with them at the finest restaurants. Bill was always the guy who would come across a crowded convention floor and see you and ask, 'How are you? You okay?' I would always smile at him and say, 'You know something I don't? Am I on short notice somewhere?' He always had time to say hello, and we had a wonderful long-distance relationship. He led the way in everything cable did. When he started his system in Colorado Springs, he brought in buses full of people for the promotion and had tractors there and had all the sales forces dressed in uniforms. It just looked so snazzy. Marketing was the key back then. That really got people's attention.

"Bill became the 'music man' with the garbage can—banging on it and saying, 'Let's get some attention going here and make this thing happen.' When you think of who was marching around the countryside, it was Bill who was always telling the cable story. He formed the cable associations, he was involved with the regional state groups, getting them moving in the right direction. He was big on the programming side too. He saw a lot of the excitement in what was coming there. He got involved in the sports side because of his love for sports. He put his money where his excitement was. Here was an individual who had such a good time he brought everybody else along with him. He never did this stuff alone. I always remember knowing that if you were ever in Denver, his home was always open. Events were always going on around him." Like countless others inside the cable field and beyond it, Reed was amazed by Daniels' energy and style.

"Bill had such a charming way of staying in touch. He never just went to one cable show but showed up all over the country. When he came into a convention, he would always make it exciting just as he thought the business was exciting. I remember the shows where Bill would have a suite—the suite to end all suites. He would have one of the greatest floating card games that you could ever imagine. Whoever was feeling heavy in the pocket would participate. It was always too rich for my blood. I used to sit and get such a kick out of it. I can remember walking out four-thirty in the morning and they were still going. And Bill always had the best-looking woman on his arm. It never failed."

In the mid-sixties, after Daniels had watched the broadcasters use their clout with politicians to fight against cable, he formed a plan to beat the regulation forces at their own game. Long before there was a C-SPAN network that covered national politics, he conceived of just such an idea. He kicked off his strategy by contacting a young man named Tony Acone, who'd been working at Leisure World in California. Leisure World had built a cable system that produced a variety of programs for its customers. Acone was on the air every day doing a sports show and political interviewing. Two cable operators in San Clemente, Vern Gill and Bob Hilliard, had asked Acone to put his programs on their system. The men introduced Acone to the National Cable Television Association and told him that he had to meet the most important figure in the entire cable community, a Denver man named Bill Daniels.

"Several weeks or months later," Acone says, "Vern called me when I was on the air and asked me to come to his office. He told me that he and Bob decided to sell their cable system. The guy handling the deal was named John Saeman, a broker for Daniels. I meet John at this luncheon and he is very gracious.

"Fast-forward to June 1968 and it's the NCTA show in Boston at the brand-new Sheraton Hotel. Hotter than a bugger in Boston. It's probably a hundred degrees and the humidity is ninety percent. Brand-new hotel and the air-conditioning isn't working. So I coordinate and meet with John to meet with Bill. We go to the top floor of the hotel to Bill's suite and we walk in, and it is wall to wall with people. Hotter than hell, people drinking, smoking, the noise is unbelievable. Here's Bill in a light blue short-sleeve silk shirt. He says to me, 'Hi, how are you, come over here and sit down.' Bill wants to know all about my family—my brothers, my sisters, and my aunts—everything about me.

"I'm going to say we sat there for half hour, forty-five minutes. But the amazing thing is that during the first few minutes of our conversation, the room went silent. His was the only voice I could hear. We communicated like there was nobody else in the room. I knew when I got up from that meeting that I had met somebody who was really meaningful in my life. When I left, Bill says he will see me somewhere down the road.

"Later that summer, a guy named John Druckenbroad, who was a PR director for the NCTA, calls and asks for my help on a PR campaign to educate the Congress and the Senate on cable television. He said they were going to put together a slide show and invite the legislators over to the Capitol Hill Hotel and take them through this slide show. I said, 'I will help you, but that is maybe as bad of an idea as I've heard in a long time.' I told him that nobody would come, and those that did would be put asleep by this slide show. I told him that he was trying to educate them about cable television, not still photography—it's television, for gosh sakes.

"I suggested to him that they put these guys on television. Why don't they show a congressman and a senator what cable television can do for them? I told him I was interviewing these guys left and right, and I would send him some tapes. Get the administrative assistant of the congressman to be the associate producer of the show so they have content control. This is a chance for a congressman or a senator to talk about something he wants to talk about rather than a reporter sticking a microphone in his mouth. Produce the show, ask and answer questions, stick a mailbag in there the last ten minutes of the show. They will get immediate evidence of what cable television is doing for them because their constituents will be right there asking questions. So he calls me back and says the chairman of the PR committee wants to fly me to Washington to sit down and discuss this. I ask who the chairman is, and he says, 'Well, it's a guy named Bill Daniels.' So I've just told the father of cable television that his idea stinks and I've got a better one.

"I fly to Washington, walk into the NCTA offices, and Bill is sitting there with a little smile on his face and says, 'I told you I'd see you down the road somewhere.' And then he said, 'I understand you don't think much of my idea.' It turns out Bill got the idea for the slide presentation from Tom Johnson, who worked for Bill. Tom invented this briefcase which held a slide machine, and you push this button on the briefcase whereupon the slide show would come on. So in Bill's mind, this was a neat thing. Once I learned this, I understood why the presentation was focused in that direction.

"I laid out this whole idea for Bill, and he says he wants me to go around and talk to as many congressmen and senators as I can about this idea. Write up a report and get it to him. Bill asked if I could do this, and I said, 'Well, yeah, but you know I only came here for a couple of days. I only have a change of underwear and a fresh shirt.' Whereupon Bill reaches in his pockets, rips off I don't know how much money, and tells me to go and get a couple of suits, sports jackets, whatever I need. I do all that—I get through maybe a hundred and sixty congressmen and almost half the Senate, including Everett Dirksen, who was wonderful, and the whole thing was very positive.

"Bill wants to build a studio on Capitol Hill, and limousines would pick up the congressman or senator and bring him to the studio. The format of the show was already done. The guy's interviewed, the show is done, you move him into an edit room and they look at the show, maybe make a few changes, and the limo takes him back to wherever. Next case. Bill is just beaming; he loves this thing. John Saeman and I put together this rather exhaustive business plan. We were going around visiting RCA, Ampex, all these companies who make equipment, because we have to build the equivalent of NBC Burbank—virtually a master studio on Capitol Hill. I found a big, beautiful house, and the plan was to build the studio there.

"We were way ahead of our time. But we had to get permission from the Capitol Hill Restoration Society. I hire an artist who does a rendering, and we pass with flying colors. Get this entire thing going. By the time John and I finished putting it together, the numbers didn't work. The cost to do all of this against the payback just made it a bad investment at the time. There weren't enough systems at the time capable of playing back programs. Local origination was practically nonexistent then. So now I have to go to Denver and tell Bill it's a great idea but it can't be done. We had to unwind all of this. Bill said he understood and appreciated our candor. He asked me what I was going to do next and I said I would go back to Leisure World and make home movies. He said, 'All right, I'll be talking to you.'"

As usual, Daniels kept his word. Undaunted by the temporary defeat of his latest plan, he kept generating new uses for cable. He had so many ideas for spreading the medium that he was soon back in contact with Acone.

"Maybe two to three weeks later," Acone says, "I'm sitting in a barbershop in Santa Barbara getting a haircut. The phone rings and the barber says, 'Yeah, he's here,' and hands me the phone. It was Mary Jo Klingberg, who says to hold on for Bill. Bill says he is on his way to Dallas for the Texas Cable Conference and says, 'I want you in Denver Sunday night and be in my office six-thirty A.M. Monday morning.' He says, 'I got an idea—can you be there?' I said, 'Yes, sir.' I stay at the hotel that Bill helped build somewhere on Colorado Boulevard. The phone rings in my room at five A.M. and Bill tells me that his brother came into town and he's running a little late. So we meet at some restaurant at five-thirty A.M. and I meet Jack and have a bite to eat and we end up back at the Daniels office.

"He says, 'All right, here's my idea—I want to build the first color television studio on cable in the country. Can you do it?' I said, 'Yeah, I'll try it.' He says, 'I want to do it in Palm Desert, California, not far from you. You'll love it.' I say, 'Oh, yeah?' He says, 'That's an order!' So he picks up the phone and calls Keith Burcham and tells him he'd just hired me and that I was going to work for Keith. I was going to come in and build this studio. I went out there and goddamn—we did it! Keith was absolutely great. He would give me all the time and direction I needed."

Burcham grew up in Hobbs, New Mexico, and knew the Daniels family well. After Bill returned from World War II and then from Korea, Burcham, who was ten years younger than the ex-soldier, regarded him as a swashbuckling hero. Burcham himself spent six years in the Air Force flying F-100 jet fighters. While he was trying to decide on a career, Alan Harmon, a Hobbs friend of his who worked at Daniels & Associates, invited him to the office.

"It was a wonderful, futuristic type of place," Burcham says, "and Bill was there and they showed me around. They took me to the Brown Palace Hotel for lunch and Bill signs a $100 chit and here I am, making $660 a month. That really looked good! Alan said that when my time was up with the Air Force, Bill and he would like me to work for them."

Burcham resigned from the Air Force to take the job—despite the advice of some people in Hobbs.

"Bill Daniels," he recalls, "was the world's best salesman—bar none—and promoter. He promoted the cable industry, he promoted Daniels & Associates, and he promoted Bill Daniels. I don't say that in a negative way because when he was promoting Bill Daniels, he was also promoting Daniels & Associates. Some people didn't particularly care for his aggressive promotion of what Bill did, but the majority did. I had some people in Hobbs who said, 'Well, why are you going to work for him?' I said that this man has been up front and honest with me. He cares about my family, he knows my family, so I am ready to go. And they said, 'Well, you know he does that with everyone.' I said, 'The key factor is that he does it. For whatever reason.' I worked for him for over twenty years and that never faltered. Even after I no longer worked for him, that same thing was there all the time."

Burcham went to work for Daniels in Olean, New York, where his first day on the job it was thirty-two degrees below zero. After nine months he was transferred to Barstow, California, where it was one hundred and twenty degrees when he arrived. Nine months later, Daniels called and said that he'd just brokered a cable system in Palm Desert, California, and he wanted Burcham to run it. For almost a decade he managed the systems in Palm Desert, Cathedral City, Rancho Mirage, Indian Wells, LaQuinta, Indio, and Coachella.

"I got to escort a lot of people through our property and show them what cable systems were and how we operated," Burcham says. "I would get calls from Bill saying that the governor of Colorado is landing in two hours and I want you to meet him and I want you to say that you welcome him to the desert area on behalf of Bill Daniels and if there is anything I can do, let me know. Or I would get a call from Bill and he'd say, 'There's a lady in the hospital in Palm Springs. I want you to go over and check on her and find out if there is anything that I can do for her and whatever it is, do it.' She was the wife of the guy who shined his shoes at the Brown Palace."

When Daniels became interested in cable TV creating its own programming, his company purchased the first color cameras and built a TV studio in Palm Desert. Then he hired Tony Acone to produce local shows, while Burcham oversaw the operation. But Daniels oversaw Burcham—often without any warning.

"When Bill would come to town," Burcham says, "he would come unannounced. He would check with the Henny-Penny Chicken place owner, who

Despite his penchant for long hours and relentless travel, Bill Daniels always found time to mug for the camera. For Bill, life was more than work. It meant having fun, too.

he knew was on the chamber of commerce. He was checking up on me because I was also on the chamber of commerce. He would talk to every one of those chamber's members checking on me. And I would get these reports back. Or a little Volkswagen Beetle would arrive unannounced and a very attractive young girl would get out one side and the driver would get out of the other side. As I looked through the window, I saw it was Bill Daniels. He and an airline stewardess had driven from Los Angeles, where she was stationed. They'd come to the desert to spend several days.

"There were times when I would get a phone call from Bill and he'd say, 'I don't want girlfriend number one or girlfriend number two to know I'm seeing girlfriend number three. So if girlfriend number two calls, I spent the day with you in the desert. And I just left and you don't know where I'm going.' So the phone would ring an hour later and here's girlfriend number two trying to find Bill!"

Daniels taught Burcham one of the secrets of his success: when you wanted to do business with someone over a long period of time, begin the relationship by making a grand gesture toward that person—offer him a lavish, unexpected gift or send him and his wife on a trip somewhere exotic or do something else that was big and memorable.

"Bill told me," recalls Burcham, "that the majority of the time, the individual will turn it down, but they'll always remember that you made the grand gesture. Then he said that if you have to make good on the gesture, work it out the best you can!"

Daniels used this philosophy with Burcham himself. Whenever he and his wife, Audra, moved into a new house, within a week the Daniels Learjet would arrive in town and the boss himself would step out, anxious to see where they were living and that they were well taken care of. One time Daniels took them to dinner and asked Audra about her aspirations and dreams. She said, "Well, what I've always wanted to do, I haven't done. I've always wanted to take banjo lessons and learn how to play the banjo." The next day a man came to their front door and presented her with a banjo. But in return for his largesse, Daniels demanded loyalty and performance.

"The key value that Bill Daniels had," says Burcham, "was that he hired you, he gave you the responsibility, and he let you do your job. And he didn't second-guess you. He didn't interfere with you. By the same token, he would go to my systems people, usually on a Sunday, of all things, and he would get the system manager out of bed and the office manager, and meet them at the office and quiz them. And then Monday morning I would get the questions, 'Why did he do that on a Sunday morning?'

"You never knew what you were getting into with Bill because, again, the phone would ring and he'd say, 'There's a cable operator having a problem with a city council member in Northern California, and I want you to go up there.' It wasn't our system, but at the time I was president of the California Cable Association and he wanted to help out his friend in the cable business. So I made a trip up there and met the lady who was the council member who was giving them so much trouble and I researched the situation. My worst mistake was that I prepared a written report for Daniels, which was very candid, as if he and I were chatting. He immediately fired off the report to the city council lady. So the next time I saw her, she was a little huffy. For which I don't blame her. But I learned anytime you write a memo to Bill, write the memo as if the person you were talking about was going to read the memo. Because he was just going to send those memos around!"

Fourteen

Tony Acone, like many other people over the years, enjoyed working for Daniels because of the essential simplicity at the heart of this entrepreneur. He liked action and he liked honesty. It was better to hear the unpleasant truth than an oily lie.

"I'll always remember the day Bill hired me," recalls Acone, "and what he said: 'There is one thing I will ask of you and that is, don't ever tell me yes if you think you should tell me no.' Then he gave me that look over the glasses—you know that look? I still have the power of attorney he wrote in my name for the Capitol Hill thing. It basically says I could do anything I want. Which was Bill's way of saying, 'I trust you.' He did not invite you to challenge his orders, but he was always open to hear if I disagreed. Once a decision was reached, you better be the good soldier and follow orders. But at least you had your shot at disagreeing with him."

The over-the-glasses look that Daniels gave Acone on this occasion had become legendary within the Daniels office and throughout the cable industry. The expression was constantly mentioned—"Did he give you *that* look?"—and was never forgotten. Once you'd seen it, you didn't want to see it again. Daniels often wore his spectacles balanced on the end of his nose so he could look down and read through them when necessary or look up and over them when talking to someone. If you happened to be the someone he was looking at, he made certain that you would not turn away from his piercing blue eyes or stop listening to his words. It was too simple to call this expression a glare or even a withering stare. A glare carried hostility and "withering" usually implied a put-down. This look was a far more complicated and multilayered affair. It revealed the essence of the man.

First of all, his eyes told you that he'd seen things and done things that you hadn't seen and were never going to do. They told you that he'd once been able to beat up and knock down just about anyone he got into a fight with, and he still had these abilities if he wanted to use them. They also told you that he'd been in two wars and had not only survived them but emerged from combat as a hero who'd been willing to go into battle and defeat the enemy, no matter the circumstances. He'd never allowed himself to be controlled by fear, and he had a hard time understanding why anyone would choose to live that way. All of life's great adventures, those blue eyes were implying, began with going inside and confronting your own fear, looking it right in the eye and moving toward it rather than running away from it. The best way to overcome the dread that everyone felt from time to time was to acknowledge and embrace it rather than turning it into your worst enemy. If you were willing to do that— just this one thing—your own life could be more thrilling and filled with more possibilities than you'd ever imagined. It might even start to be as rich and unpredictable and fun as his was.

The expression said other things as well, although Daniels often delivered it in complete silence. It said that even if you doubted yourself and your potential for creativity and success, and even if that was acceptable to you, it was not acceptable to him. He would never have hired you and put his trust in you if he'd felt that way about you. Regardless of how limited your faith in yourself was, his faith in you was unlimited. He saw things in you (with those wide-open, penetrating blue eyes) that you did not see, and he saw your fears as well, and for your own sake more than anyone else's he wanted you to get beyond their clutches. He wanted you to improve yourself and have joy and success perhaps even more than you did. In that sense, the over-the-glasses look could rightly be compared to a godlike expression. It saw more than you did because through experience he'd removed some of the filters of fear and of human limitation.

Daniels was always more comfortable soliciting information from others than divulging it about himself, and he rarely told anyone about his philosophy. He'd acted on it as a young man when his country needed him to fight against fascism, and he'd done it throughout his cable career, when he'd discovered that the best thing about starting an industry was that there were no hardened rules or "right" ways of doing things, so you could invent the business from the seat of your pants. Nothing was more educational or exciting than that. His philosophy was about being willing to enter into the unknown and having the

In 1974 Bill Daniels campaigned for governor of Colorado but was defeated by incumbent John Vanderhoof in the Republican primary. Despite the odds against him, Bill's patriotism led him to be an outspoken businessman's candidate.

courage to create from there, instead of doing the same things over and over again and getting a rote result. Whenever he was willing to take these risks, the right people and the right opportunities kept showing up, and he kept matching or exceeding his expectations of success. Some might call this luck or magic. Some might call it good timing. Others might refer to it as being tapped into some deeper rhythms and processes in life—processes that caused the world to respond to confidence and action and energy because it wanted to create more, too.

After receiving this bespectacled look from Daniels, a few of his employees slithered off and decided they didn't want to play the free enterprise game at this level of seriousness or intensity (there were, after all, less demanding bosses to work for and smaller mountains to scale). For Daniels himself, making money was just the obvious part of this game; the deeper contest was seeing how far you could stretch yourself and your self-imposed boundaries. Most people did not slink away but were ultimately reassured by his expression, because if someone like Bill Daniels saw all this untapped potential within them, then it must be there. They could do more than they'd thought they could and would now set out to prove that to him. Sometimes, leadership involved more than a lot of fiery speeches and other forms of haranguing. Sometimes just one look at exactly the right moment would do.

"The very first production from that [color TV] operation in Palm Desert was in 1971," says Tony Acone. "It was the groundbreaking ceremony for the Eisenhower Medical Center. And that was with Bob Hope and a number of dignitaries. It occurred the day after Thanksgiving and we were the live cable television outlet that carried the event. We were licensed [to do this] by the White House. Keith Burcham thought I was nuts because I wanted to call the White House and get permission for this. The next thing you know, Rosalee Rojas came running into my office and said, 'Tony, the White House is on the phone!' I said, 'Tell 'em to hold on.' Of course, she looks at me like I'm nuts. It was the director of White House communications, and then I got a call from the president."

Not only did Acone get permission to televise the event live via color cable TV, but the dignitaries that were present for the groundbreaking included President Richard Nixon, Vice President Spiro Agnew, Jerry Ford, Bob Hope, and Frank Sinatra.

"We had a dais full of really top-heavy people," Acone says. "We weren't put together like a big NBC operation but had a little truck, and I had to be within fifty feet at most of that truck because my cable lengths were short. White House operations didn't like us being so close, but we worked it out. They decked out our truck in red, white, and blue bunting, and we were all decked out in red, white and blue.

"As it turned out, we weren't broadcast, but John Conti, the actor, happened to own the TV station in Palm Springs—the NBC affiliate. So I called him and told him I needed a favor and had a deal he couldn't refuse. I told him I had the right to produce this show, but I needed a quadraplex tape copy of the program and would feed it to him live and he could carry it live on his TV station. That turned out to be the first time ever that cable was the originating production for a broadcast program. So our stuff ended up the next day on *The Today Show*."

One of the millions of people who watched *The Today Show* that morning was the man who'd hired Acone to make innovative things happen with cable.

"Oh, Bill was beaming," Tony says. "He just loved it, and it went out to all the trades."

As Daniels went about his daily work, making his countless phone calls and moving the index cards around on his desk, a communications revolution was taking place all around him, and it was bigger than the visionaries who were driving it forward. As often happened with truly creative spirits, the effect they were having on the world and on those around them would not be fully seen for years to come.

Fifteen

Daniels' first two marriages had known their share of tumult, but his first two divorces had been relatively peaceful. He'd escaped some of the more painful legal and economic consequences that can follow the breakup of a household. He'd also managed to stay close to the children of his second wife, Jeri. He would not be so fortunate with his third divorce. In the early 1960s, after his latest marriage unraveled, he and Eileen Kamm engaged in a rancorous settlement for alimony. She had a son named Cliff, from a previous marriage, and she was known for being strong-willed and stubborn. Those traits surfaced when she hired a lawyer named Fred Epstein to represent her in divorce proceedings.

"Fred was a very aggressive attorney and very good at what he did," says Arlan Preblud, a fellow attorney who worked with Epstein in the mid-sixties before going on to become an attorney for the American Basketball Association. "At the time of their divorce, Fred was just beginning to make a name himself in the area of family law."

Daniels, sensing what was coming from the legal team pitted against him, decided not to attend an initial hearing on the financial settlement of the divorce. He had unlimited courage when it came to aerial combat or charging into banks in New York and asking for cable loans, but this had the possibility of getting downright unpleasant. He sent his lawyer and his accountants to the hearing instead. This went against protocol, and it greatly offended the presiding judge, Mitch Johns. It also gave extra leverage to Epstein.

"The judge came out of his chambers," Preblud says, "and took the bench. He called the case of *Daniels* v. *Daniels*. Mr. Epstein stood up and said, 'Your Honor, Mrs. Daniels is present and we're ready to proceed.' Bill's lawyer stood up and said, 'Your Honor, I represent Mr. Daniels. and Mr. Daniels could not be here today because he had some important business to take care of, but we have his accountants here who are prepared to testify.' The judge was taken aback by that because no one was going to question the dignity of his court. For a party to a case not to show up was reprehensible. He said, 'Well, that's just fine, but this court considers this an important matter, and the fact that Mr. Daniels isn't here does not persuade me at all. The fact that his accountants are here doesn't impress me at all either. I want Mr. Daniels here.'"

Bill's lawyer, representing his client the best he could, stood and repeated what he'd just said. The judge turned red, looked at Eileen's attorney, and asked him what his client was asking for in the settlement. Epstein gave Judge Johns a laundry list of her demands and desires.

"I don't recall the specifics," Preblud says, "but she wanted everything and then some. She wanted possession of the home, she wanted him to pay all the bills and, basically, she wanted everything and she wanted Bill to pay for it."

After listening to Epstein's litany, Judge Johns pointed at him and said, "Prepare the order."

When the attorney asked him how he should prepare it, the judge impatiently told him to prepare it exactly the way he'd just outlined it before the court. Judge Johns was granting the woman essentially all that she'd requested.

When Daniels' lawyer raised an objection to this ruling, the judge told him that he could object all day long, but because his client had failed to appear in court today and refused to speak for himself, the divorce settlement was going forward under these terms. Epstein prepared the order, which the Daniels team later tried to fight, but the judge would not be dissuaded. The final terms of the arrangement were all in Eileen's favor.

"Several years after the divorce," recalls Preblud, "I reminded Bill of this story. In a way that only he could do, he kind of laughed at it, a laugh of 'I wish I'd been there that day'—a laugh that didn't take any joy in what had happened."

Daniels' third marriage and third divorce would almost make him swear off matrimony for good—almost, but not quite. A few years later, after many girlfriends, he encountered someone whom he thought might snap his pattern of temporary infatuations that ended either with sudden breakups or sessions in court. If he'd been an aggressive suitor in previous situations, he now brought out all the artillery with his fourth and last wife, Devra Fox. He would go after her with the tenacity that had made him a driving force in the cable TV industry. He was incomplete without admiring and giving attention to a female—and receiving these things in return. This would not change until the day, more than three decades later, of his death.

If his final marriage had worked out differently, if he'd stayed with Devra, his life might not have evolved the way it did. He may have devoted more time to family and less to building his cable empire, not becoming the extremely wealthy figure and great philanthropist that he later turned into. The renowned Irish poet W. B. Yeats, writing in the early part of the twentieth century, said that we all wither into the truth at forty. This may have been true for an older generation, but when Daniels reached his forties, he was still discovering who he was and defining his role as a man. He was still creating his identity in the business community and in his personal life. If he believed that making a living was supposed to be fun, he also believed that the only way to find out if something would work was to experience it no matter what barriers were standing in your way.

Life was a challenge to be wrestled with—until something changed.

"I first met Bill at a party when I was pregnant with my son, Mitchell," says Devra, "but he didn't remember that meeting. Then we saw each other when Mitchell was three, my daughter Cindy was five, and I was getting divorced. We started seeing each other. This must have been 1963 or '64. Naturally, nothing was easy. I was dating someone else very seriously, and Bill kept calling me and I wouldn't speak to him. He went to Europe with his best friend, Bob Clark, and he kept calling and writing me letters from Europe. I wouldn't read his letters and I wouldn't take his calls. He hated Europe and he hated being there. When he came home, he called me and was very apologetic. He was writing letters about why I wouldn't speak to him. I just thought it wasn't going to go anywhere, and I was very happy dating other people.

"But Bill began following me, driving by my house, calling and hanging up—teenage things! Fifteen years older than me and doing teenage things in his powder blue Cadillac. I was getting annoyed! I was dating somebody who lived just a few blocks away and Bill would go by his house too."

Daniels' antics were also being noticed by Devra's young son, Mitchell, and his sister, Cindy.

"My first memories of Bill," Mitchell says, "are little snippets of when I was very small in the early sixties. One story I remember involves Bill coming to our house with, I believe, a case of Visine eyedrops. You know, he always did things in a big way, so rather than bring just a bottle, he brought a case. It was apparently a guise to see my mother, and he posed that he couldn't put drops in his own eyes. So he would come over and have my mother put these drops in his eyes. My mother loved taking care of strays, so she'd do it.

"This whole time there was another guy competing for my mother's attention. This other guy, Bob Ellis, had a Labrador with a litter of puppies. He kind of hung out at Denver Country Club and played cards and had these girls. He had a trampoline in his backyard. So Bill had very tough competition. He didn't have a trampoline and he didn't have any pets to speak of. But of course there was something in Bill that even a seven-year-old kid could pick up on. He was special—he was so much fun to be around and so exciting. So we were pulling for him."

"Bill," says Cindy, "would take my brother and me to his home and make us those greasy hamburgers or maybe fried chicken or pork chops. I remember going to the Brown Palace with him, and we would sit in the Palace Arms, in the first booth. We would dress up and he would take us out for dinner.

"I adored Bill but was so shocked when Devra said they were going to get married, because she had been dating Bob Ellis for two years and I don't even remember Bill being in the picture for that period of time. Then, all of a sudden I was at Bill's house and she called up and said that she was getting married. I said, 'When are you and Bob getting married?' She said, 'No, I am not marrying Bob, I am marrying Bill Daniels.' I was in shock and was like, 'Who? What?' It seemed so out of the blue."

The wedding plans had come up rather fast.

"One night," Devra says, "Bill called me about twelve-thirty A.M. and he said, 'I need to speak to you. Put some coffee on, mix me a drink, you're going to need it!' And he came over about fifteen minutes later and asked if I would marry him! I was dating somebody else seriously! I never answered him—I never said yes. He said, 'We have to go down to your mother's apartment.' Her building was where Bill lived, and we went down there about one-thirty or two in the morning. He called my mother and told her the same thing—to get up and make some coffee, which he was doing all the time anyway because they lived in the same building. She lived on the fourth floor and he was on the fifth floor.

"My mother answered the door and asked what Bill wanted, and he said, 'I want to marry your daughter. May I have her hand in marriage?' She said, 'Sure.' She just wanted to go back to sleep. I still hadn't said yes to Bill, and he wanted to get married in Tahoe but for some reason we couldn't get to Tahoe in his airplane. But I still hadn't said yes! He had given me gifts the past few years, which I had never used. He had given me blank checks, which he had signed, but I'd never cashed them. I would never accept anything from him. So he would give things to the children and I couldn't say no to those. That would be ongoing.

"When I wasn't seeing him, he would call my house at three or four in the afternoon and say, 'Get the kids ready. I'm picking them up and we're going to dinner, shopping, and they're spending the night.' And I'd say, 'Okay.' I'd hang up and think, Now wait a minute, he's not their father, he doesn't have any visitation rights. But he loved hanging out with the whole family. So I'd have them ready at five and he'd come pick them up. He would take them out and buy them clothes. They'd go to the grocery store and pick up goodies and they would spend the night with him. Mitchell would sleep in the bed with Bill, and Cindy would sleep in the other room. They'd come home with their new clothes, which I could certainly afford but I didn't splurge with them."

After Daniels had gotten Devra's mother to sign off on the marriage in the middle of the night, he took Devra over to his office.

"It was Labor Day weekend and it was now Monday," she says. "He called a friend and told him we were going to get married, but I still had not said yes! It's about seven in the morning and we had not slept! Then another friend called us and said, 'We're going to Lake Tahoe for your wedding.' I said, 'Well, I don't really know.' Bill said, 'We're leaving and I want to call your boyfriend and tell him we're getting married.' I said, 'Well, we've been looking at houses in Devonshire.' And Bill said, 'Well, that's just too bad.'

"Then he took me over to the house he had bought, at 4190 Shangri-La. We're looking through the house and I'm saying, 'How is everybody going to fit in this house?' I was a package deal—two kids and cats and dogs. He said,

'Well, the house next door is for sale too.' He called a real estate agent and said he wanted to buy the house next door and the property next to that because I liked gardens. So then we had two houses and a piece of property and I still hadn't said yes. He wanted to call my boyfriend and say, 'Ha ha, we're getting married, you're not.' I said, 'Bill, I need to do this alone.' So I called the boyfriend and he came over. I had made Bill leave the house. I told my boyfriend, 'Something's come up, I think I may be getting married.' He said, 'To who?' I told him, and he kind of stormed out—wasn't really thrilled.

"Bill called his mother, Adele, whom I was extremely close to way before we even got married. He also called Jack, his brother, before the wedding to tell him we were going to go to Vegas. Jack said to his mother that he thought they should go. Adele said, 'Now, Jack, if we went out of town every time Bill got married, we'd all be broke.'"

Although she still hadn't officially said yes, Devra began packing her bags.

"Bill," she says, "had given me a set of luggage, red leather with needlepoint from Neiman Marcus, which was in my storage room, in the original plastic. I

Bill is pictured with his mother. She would always be the woman in his life.

wouldn't use it and it had sat there for about four years. So I started packing using this luggage. I thought I might as well give up. He's going to drive me crazy. I did love him, but he scared me to death. So I packed and the next thing I know is we are on the plane, flying to Las Vegas. There was something wrong with getting into Tahoe—storms or something. I didn't really want to get married in Las Vegas. So we're on the plane with four friends: Chuck and Jeannie Reiff and Alan and Sidney Harmon. I wore a blue dress with a matching coat—a Jerry Silverman I had bought at Montaldo's.

"We get to Las Vegas and my aunt and uncle were there. Bill walks up and says, 'Hi, Aunt Norma, hi, Uncle Lenny.' Of course, he's older than all of them! Bill takes me to this ballroom where chairs are set up in the living room and candles are everywhere. There's really going to be a wedding! I asked my aunt to be the flower girl and she's twelve years older than I am. I washed my hair and curled it and put on the dress and the coat. My aunt goes down the aisle with rose petals and she's throwing rose petals in an emerald green dress and jacket. So we got married. I can't remember who was Bill's best man, Chuck or Alan."

Now that Devra was legally his wife, Daniels insisted that she have a new wardrobe.

"I had to buy all new clothes," she says, "because he didn't want me wearing anything I had worn with anybody else. Bill had good taste and helped me pick out clothes. He liked hats, so I had tons of hats. It was hysterical."

Chuck Reiff remembers the wedding and the events leading up to it somewhat more fully.

"Bill had recently started dating Devra and going on trips with us," he recalls. "He was very smitten with her, but he was also dating Devra's sister-in-law! He dated her for a while and I guess it all blew up. She ended up moving to Santa Fe. Then I got a phone call from Bill saying, 'I'm getting married.' He said I had to be at the airport—we're flying to Vegas and I had to be there. We had been at the Broadmoor in Colorado Springs and went back to Denver, got more clothes, and flew to Vegas with Alan Harmon and his wife.

"When we landed, Bill said, 'Chuck, you take care of everything.' So I went to the front desk and told Harry Williams, the vice president there, that we needed a justice of the peace and a ballroom for tomorrow night. Harry Williams was in shock! I then went around and spoke to a couple of the hookers there about being bridesmaids. They just couldn't believe they were being invited to a wedding. I told them that probably, if necessary, Bill would pay for the dresses.

"Harry Williams was there and the owner of the hotel. I told him Bill would take care of the bill and he said, 'There's no bill.' That's how close we were to all these people. I think Bill lost about two thousand dollars playing baccarat, and we all flew home and were depressed because we lost money."

As Reiff points out, Daniels was well known in Las Vegas because of his many business and recreational trips to that city.

"The one and only time I challenged Bill," Reiff says, "was when he found this girl in Las Vegas and I knew her. I told him, 'Bill, she's going to take you like Grant took Richmond. I know her from years back.' He said, 'Stop thinking for me. I can do this myself.' And sure enough, two days later, he said, 'Oh, Chuck, you were so right.' She took him for a lot of money. Bill never was sophisticated that way; he never realized that those women were out to hook him. I actually think he was pretty naïve in certain ways—for all his worldliness. A lot of people took him for money, but he knew he wouldn't get paid back. He just figured that he wouldn't get paid back and would be so surprised if they did pay him back."

Chuck Reiff had met most of Daniels' paramours, but he'd also met the woman behind all the women in Daniels' life—his mother—and she'd made a great impression him, as she had on so many others. The person she'd made the greatest and most lasting impression on was her oldest son. When Daniels met a new woman in Denver or elsewhere and the two of them were having fun late at night, he would usually stop the action so he could go to the phone and call Adele, who was asleep down in Hobbs. He did this regardless of whether it was ten P.M. or midnight or one in the morning. And he kept doing it after his mother had reached her eighties. He did it because he wanted the person he'd just met to meet his mother and talk to her, get to know her a little before anything more transpired.

This habit cost Adele so much sleep and put her in such an awkward position that she eventually went to her other son and asked Jack to tell Bill to stop doing this. Jack knew it was never going to happen and tried to explain to her: Bill had a profound need to feel close to her because she was the most important woman—and person—in his life. She was everything he kept looking for in a woman (and everything he kept looking for in himself). He kept hiring one executive after another at Daniels & Associates who had the traits that did not take after him as much as they did his mother. He wanted family men in his office, men who could make commitments and keep them, just as his mother could. Adele had held the family together through bad times, through drinking and tragedy and death. She'd watched her oldest go off to two wars, watched her husband die too young, and she was still taking care of her mentally disabled daughter, Dorothy, who'd never been able to function alone in the world. She could keep life going and make love work, and when someone needed her, even at one in the morning, she was always there. Bill kept phoning her and Adele endured these calls, much as she'd endured

Bill Daniels is shown with his mother, Adele, sister Dorothy, and younger brother, Jack. Bill had an unwavering devotion to his family, which included sister Bobette (not pictured).

many other things in her life. Even at eighty and beyond—even when she looked frail and life was fading away from her—she was far more resourceful and resilient than she appeared to be. She still liked to sing and play the piano and have a good time.

One night Chuck Reiff was visiting West Texas when he decided to drive over to New Mexico and take Adele to dinner. It was a memorable excursion.

"I got on the highway," he says, "and about an hour down the road, an accident had happened right in front of me. A car hit a truck and the driver was stuck in the car and we couldn't get him out. So I actually showed up in Hobbs all dirty, after trying to get this guy out. I found Adele's place and she was all excited and took me to about three bars in Hobbs! She'd walk in and say, 'Jim, I'll have my regular.' She's trying to impress me that everybody knows her.

"She knew me because every time Bill and I would get a little loaded in Vegas, he would call his mother and put me on the phone. She was a tough woman. She was like the women who must've made the West—I swear to God. Tough as nails. She gave up her whole life for Bill's sister, who was retarded."

Sixteen

As the sixties began to fade, so did the go-go years of cable. The first rush of expansion was passing, and regulatory forces were gaining momentum. After the FCC delivered its comprehensive new set of rules in 1965, the Southwestern Cable Company, which carried television signals from Los Angeles stations to customers in San Diego, decided to fight the FCC rulings in court. Southwestern Cable won in the appeals court, but the matter climbed up the legal ladder all the way to the top. In June 1968, the case reached the U.S. Supreme Court, where the justices voted unanimously, 7–0, to throw out the lower court's decision and gave the FCC nearly unlimited power to regulate all communications carried by wire or transmitted through the air. It was a smashing victory for those favoring regulation.

More bad news was coming for cable. Back in 1960, United Artists Television, Inc., which distributed movies and produced TV programs, had brought a lawsuit against two West Virginia cable systems owned by the Fortnightly Corporation. United Artists took the broadcasters' longstanding position that Fortnightly was breaking copyright laws by picking up the signals of shows that UA had created and charging cable subscribers to watch them. By now cable systems were employing microwave technology to bring in signals from afar, and this made the TV producers only more determined to stop this practice. Without its permission or some form of agreement, UA felt that Fortnightly had no right to air this programming. When the issue went to court, the anti-cable forces won again, in the District Court and then the U.S. Court of Appeals. When Fortnightly (which had recently been bought by Jack Kent Cooke) took the fight to the U.S. Supreme Court, it went up against Louis Nizer, one of the most formidable attorneys of his day. A showdown was approaching and it would be both dramatic and unpredictable.

Nizer had long been known for his condescending manner and courtroom arrogance, and in this case he reached new realms of smugness. Twenty years of anger at what broadcasters had always regarded as their illegitimate cousin—cable TV—were concentrated in Nizer's presentation to the nation's highest court. He was not simply working for the broadcasters; he also was reflecting their core attitude, which many of them weren't eager to express in public. Nizer acted as if it were obvious that his side was right and the other side was little more than an annoyance, a way to postpone the inevitable court decision that would deal cable yet another setback. To his surprise, a few of the justices began to poke holes in his reasoning. They weren't the pushovers he'd been anticipating. They had their own ideas about the law and who owned what. Nizer had made a bad miscalculation.

In a decision that shocked the broadcasting industry, the high court ruled 5–1 that it was Congress' responsibility—and not the justices—to clarify broadcast copyright law. The court found against United Artists and Louis Nizer. Cable had won but again this was hardly the end of the conflict.

The broadcasters then challenged the Supreme Court ruling, taking the battle back to the Federal Communications Commission and to Congress, where they lobbied hard for more regulation. The FCC quickly issued a new round of cable restrictions, ruling that cable could import *no* signals into the nation's one hundred largest TV markets and putting limitations on what it could do in the smaller ones. These decisions were unfolding during the presidency of Democrat Lyndon Johnson, who was the broadcasters' natural ally because he himself owned TV properties. President Johnson and many congressional members felt that keeping television free and available to everyone was a solid democratic principle that needed to be defended. Cable was cast in the role of the heavy, bent on taking away this right and making people pay for their news or entertainment. All of these factors combined to drive the industry into its worst period in more than a decade. Business casualties were everywhere.

The cable system owned by Cox Broadcasting and the *Cleveland Plain Dealer* shut down entirely, no longer able to sustain $20,000-a-month losses. Another system in Akron, Ohio, run by TeleVision Communications Co., sold out in the early seventies. Many other systems simply quit operating. In 1968 there were 250 cable start-ups; the following year there were only 90. As a

By 1978 Bill Daniels was legendary as the nation's leading cable broker and a person who had played a major role in bringing large corporations into the business.

result, cable manufacturing firms began laying off workers. In addition, the economy as a whole began to sag. Cable operators were used to having access to cheap loans, but that was about to change dramatically.

As cable began moving from installing systems in small towns to wiring America's major cities, the operators needed more and more funding. At the 1972 NCTA convention, Amos Hostetter, a vice president at Continental Cablevision, announced that cable was about to become the first industry ever, besides telephone and utility companies, to attempt to borrow more than a billion dollars in one year. Cable would have to raise the same amount annually throughout the next decade if it were to succeed in cities. Under any circumstances, this would have been a daunting prospect, but given the recent history of borrowing and other economic factors, the challenge was even more difficult.

Between 1965 and 1969, the prime lending rate that banks charged their best customers roughly doubled from 4.5 to 8.5 percent. The price of copper, which was becoming scarce because of its massive use in the cable industry, rose by nearly 50 percent. Cable's programming capacity was about to jump from twelve channels to nearly twice that number, which caused more and more franchise operators to leap into the business of providing these services to local communities. The operators were coming under greater and greater scrutiny. When cable companies wanted to raise their rates to keep up with rocketing costs, city councils could easily find another cable system that was offering a better deal. Competition among operators was fiercer than ever, as was competition for bank loans. On the one hand, cable was being more heavily restricted by the federal government, and on the other, it was being squeezed by the dynamics of free enterprise. Many operators would not survive the inevitable shakeout of the late sixties and early seventies.

Cable historians would one day refer to these years as the start of the industry's "dark ages."

"We all had the idea," says John Malone, chairman of the cable conglomerate TCI before moving on to head Liberty Media, "that cable could be pretty big and pretty interesting if you could ever get ahead of the debt and ahead of the politics, the regulatory issues. Mostly, I'd say, we didn't spend a lot of time thinking about it because we were just worn out fighting the daily fights with the politicians, with the regulators, with the banks, with the technology and just getting the job done. We were having enough trouble getting quality service on a simple product, let alone these increasingly complex products. So the promise was always there, but I'm not sure to what degree any of us believed we'd see it in our lifetime.

"Bill was always the guy who put on the suit of armor and went out to do battle with the industries that were our adversaries, whether it was the broadcasters or the telephone companies or whoever. Bill was always upbeat. Always positive and always throwing a little money at the game to have a study done about how important cable is to the economy of the communities it's in. He was always thinking that way whether he was a broker or a major investor."

Times were tough enough for cable in the early seventies, when the industry received another body blow to its image. Irving Kahn and his company, TelePrompTer, were cable's largest systems operator. Like Daniels, Kahn had

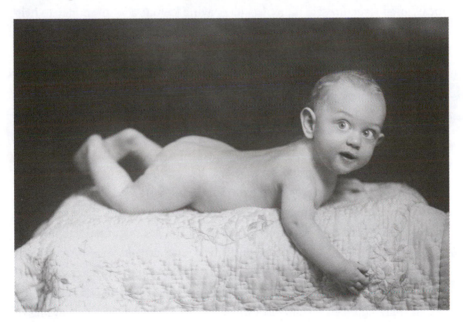

Because Robert William Daniels III was born on the first day of the month, when all the family bills had to be paid, they decided to call him "Bill."

always done things in a big way, but unlike Daniels, he'd been known to push the legal envelope in order to help his business. There were reports that when he began selling televised reruns of professional fights, he occasionally contacted boxers before their bouts and encouraged them to carry an opponent a few extra rounds because longer fights were easier to sell than shorter ones. And perhaps Kahn inflated the number of cable subscribers he'd wired on his Manhattan system in an effort to boost his company, yet these were minor infractions compared to what happened in Johnstown, Pennsylvania.

For years TelePrompTer had owned and operated the system in Johnstown before the state legislature made it law that cities had to formalize this arrangement with one business. Nearly all towns in Pennsylvania had given the official franchise to the current operator but not Johnstown. Its mayor decided to open up bidding. To Irving Kahn, who was busy wiring New York City, winning the Johnstown franchise was a minor affair. At the same time, he didn't want to lose this contract. Kahn didn't feel like making a lot of trips between Manhattan and Johnstown or going through innumerable steps to impress the local power structure. He didn't feel like paying lawyers a lot of money to help him make his case. When somebody suggested that he would get the franchise by contributing $5,000 to the campaigns of the mayor and two city councilmen, he reached for his checkbook, not even bothering to pay for these favors in cash.

Kahn was dragged before a grand jury and forced to testify under oath. He'd always been prone to exaggeration, and solemnly swearing to tell the truth before God did not change his habits. He swaggered into the courtroom and swaggered out. The grand jury indicted him, and he was faced with various counts of perjury. Kahn was tried, convicted, and sentenced to three five-year terms in a federal penitentiary. While the case made headlines throughout the nation, giving cable a bad name, Kahn himself was undaunted. He went to prison and signed up for a correspondence course at Penn State University in cable technology. During his twenty months behind bars, he studied hard and earned credits as a certified cable technician. Even before he was set free, he began applying for new franchises in New Jersey and oversaw the building of microwave systems to service them. Nothing as confining as prison could stop Irving Kahn from growing the cable industry.

After leaving the pen, he was not warmly received back into the business community. He had "cast a pall over the entire cable industry," according to *Business Week*, and some bankers and other cable players treated him as if he were a pariah—at least for a while. A year after his release, he was asked to speak to the Texas Cable Television Association convention, but decided not to accept the invitation. He was embarrassed by serving time in jail and felt that it was best to keep a low profile. Not everyone agreed with him. When Daniels learned that Kahn had refused the Texas engagement, he called him up and told him to come out of hiding and make the speech. It was the only way to put the past behind him—just face people head-on, keep your chin high, keep working, and say what you believe. Life offers no hiding places, and sooner or later you have to confront reality. After listening to Daniels, Kahn changed his mind and went to the Lone Star State.

As he rose to speak that evening, nobody in the audience knew what to expect, and everybody was concerned about the impression he would make. Gazing out at the audience in the tension-filled room, he cleared his throat and began with "Now, as I was saying before I was interrupted..."

People roared, and Kahn was welcomed back into the cable community with humor and relief. He would never again be quite the force he was in the past, but he was still a major player.

His criminal behavior made it more necessary than ever that someone with integrity and a clean reputation, someone with unflagging energy and optimism, be at the forefront of the embattled cable industry. As had been the case for the past two decades, more than anyone else that person was Bill Daniels. In good times and bad, his role was the same.

"Bill took it on himself to be the emissary of cable television to the world," says Doug Dittrick, an industry friend of Daniels in the 1960s and the founder of Douglas Communications. "Bill was always selling the cable story. He would go wherever he had to go to tell it. He did things on a grand scale, and it was interesting to watch this. He would say that the cable industry was going to provide fifty thousand jobs, and this was back in the sixties when we didn't have fifty thousand anything. Yet he was there writing the president of the United States and saying you have to treat this industry with respect and recognize it because it's going to do this and that. When you were around Bill, you had a dangerous feeling of being part of a legend whether you wanted to be or not, because of the way he did things. He did things on a legendary scale. He made the rest of us, quite frankly, think, Why the hell not? Why can't I?"

Everyone from his barber to his banker to his team of cable executives consistently noticed one thing about Daniels—a trait that came with being a leader.

"He always knew when somebody needed to be pumped up a little," says Dittrick. "He would look you right in the eye and focus only on you. When you're able to do that, the person comes away feeling you care about them and that they're somebody."

Because he'd been involved in cable for almost two decades and had built long-term relationships with most of the major players in the field, and because few deals were done anywhere without his knowledge or participation, Daniels was not as adversely affected by the dark ages as many others were. His roots and connections in the industry ran deeper than anyone's. He'd convinced Bob Magness to leave Texas and resettle in the Rocky Mountains, and Magness was well on his way to building the massively successful cable outfit Telecommunications, Inc., or TCI. (And when Bob and Sharon Magness decided to get married, Bill insisted on "interviewing" Sharon to make sure she was the right woman for his good friend. She passed muster, and Bill was always fond of saying how happy she'd made Bob and what good care she took of him later in life.)

Daniels had brought together a group of small cable companies and introduced them to the Narragansett Capital Company, which provided critical financing. Royal Little ran the company and relied on Daniels and Monty Rifkin to tell him which cable systems he should back.

"Royal Little," says John Saeman, "had three pots of money, and he filled all of them with cable investments. Narragansett Capital was a venture capital company. Memorial Drive Trust was the employee pension fund of the A.D. Little Company. Then 60 Trust was the employee pension fund of Textron. Royal Little put the maximum allowable dollars of exposure that he could out of each of the pots of money that he controlled into the cable systems through Bill and Monty. It was an unbelievable thing to watch."

With Little's support behind them, Daniels' employees found cable systems all over the country that were for sale, wrote up presentations about them, and gave them to Daniels or Rifkin. The two men then passed the information on to Little, with a recommendation to make the acquisition.

"To my knowledge," remembers Saeman, "Little always said yes, which was a real tribute to Bill Daniels and the relationship he had built there."

These newly acquired properties laid the foundation for what would become American Television and Communications Corporation, another highly successful cable operation. United Cable, another major player, grew out of Daniels' early connections to Gene and Richard Schneider and the first system the trio had built in the early fifties in Casper, Wyoming. Daniels helped George Storer with his initial cable acquisitions, and Storer eventually evolved into a large operator. Daniels had continued working with Charlie Sammons, Irving Kahn, and Cox Broadcasting in their collective efforts to buy and manage cable properties. The legwork Daniels had done back in the fifties, when he was serving as the president of the NCTA and later, when he was

In 1995 Bill Daniels and close friend U.S. Astronaut Pete Conrad landed Bill's private Learjet at Denver International Airport. It was the first private aircraft to land at the newly constructed international airport.

building a reputation as the most important broker in the field, was now pay-ing off in exponential ways. It was not quite true that all significant cable deals had to go through his Denver office, but most of them did. And yet he wasn't the man who handled the details of these deals, but the one who was always looking for which partner ought to be dancing with someone new.

"People say Bill was a deal maker, and there was never any question about that," says Saeman, "but he wasn't a huge deal maker in the sense that people typically thought. People thought that he put this person with that person. Bill's deals were more at the macro level of introducing people to the cable industry and giving them a level of comfort about what this business is all about. His greatest skills were his constant pounding of what this industry was going to be, the circles he ran in, and where he spent his time. He made it a point to meet the important people in the telecommunications industry—the principals from Cox, ABC, and others. Bill tried to sell at those levels. He was-n't selling deals per se. He sold the industry and the vision of what this indus-try ought to be.

"He knew which people ought to have their foot inside the box so they could play in the industry. He had an ability to identify characteristics that were impor-tant to a deal—why somebody should want to buy, why this person should want to sell, why this industry should be able to project itself well into the future—and he brought all of this into a very focused environment where he could excite people to get going. That, to me, was Bill Daniels, the deal maker."

Daniels had another trait that was rare in any industry, and he used it to great advantage to build his business: he genuinely wanted to see others succeed, even when they were competitors. Success for anyone in cable, he believed, ultimately meant more success for all.

One response of cable operators to the tightening economic conditions of the late sixties and early seventies was to take their companies public. In 1968 Cypress Communications was the first to do this and in the next two years ten more cable outfits followed suit. One of the most prominent of them was run by someone Daniels had lured to Denver and taught the art of brokering cable deals: Monty Rifkin. While working at Daniels & Associates, Rifkin had traveled throughout the country and put together numerous cable packages. In time, he wanted to step away from Daniels and develop his own niche. As would be the case throughout Daniels' career, he did not discourage the talented people he'd hired from going out on their own. Instead, he became their major supporter.

In 1969 Rifkin combined sixteen cable systems in fourteen states owned by Bill and his investors and created a public company known as American Television & Communications Corporation. He hired Doug Dittrick as the head of finance. Public cable companies had an edge on privately held ones, especially in a tight lending market, because they could raise money through the issuing of stock. Daniels himself would become the single largest shareholder at ATC, but he would sell his stock occasionally when he needed funds for his own business or for personal reasons. ATC was quite successful. Income grew steadily from its operating systems, while it poured most of its resources back into expansion and acquisitions.

In future years, one executive after another would leave Daniels & Associates to start their own businesses and make their own mark in cable. The boss would miss them but not try to stop them. His children were leaving the nest, as they were supposed to, because the father of the business had taught them how to create for themselves. The next generation of cable magnates was moving out into the world.

This did not mean that Daniels was taking a backseat in the industry. After Rifkin's departure, his office was left with only two properties to manage, one in Palm Desert, California, and the other in Naples, Florida. It was always looking for new investment opportunities and at Daniels' urging, the venture capital arm of Travelers Insurance, known as the Prospect Company, decided to put nearly $8 million into a new entity called Daniels Properties, Inc. Beginning in 1971, DPI commenced buying cable systems in five locations in Texas, plus others in Wyoming, California, and Louisiana.

Cable's dark ages were about to come to an end. The next decade would see unimagined advances. The vision Bill Daniels had been promoting for years would start to take shape right before everyone's eyes.

In a sense, he'd done his work for the industry, or at least the first phase of it, and was ready for new worlds to explore.

Seventeen

Like many successful men in their fifties, Daniels wanted to try different things and take on new challenges—such as politics. He'd had considerable experience dealing with congressmen, promoting cable interests at regulatory forums, serving on the GOP's national committee, and meeting with the current president of the United States, Richard Nixon. So lately Daniels had begun wondering if he could be elected to office himself. A bedrock Republican, he felt that too often business, and particularly the communications business, was hamstrung by city or state legislatures or federal agencies. With all the rulings that had recently gone against cable, he believed that his industry needed stronger political representation than ever before.

If he was going to run for office, he would not start at a low level, as that had never been his style. Daniels liked making a big splash no matter what he did, so he began putting together a plan to become the next governor of Colorado. Some people thought he was too forceful and uncompromising to be a good politician. During his campaign, for example, he was asked at a public forum about water rights in western Colorado—a very serious topic in the region.

"Bill said, 'Water? I never drink water,'" recalls Dan Forey, one of his campaign managers. "He said he never drank water because fish live in it and so do other things. I fell over laughing."

Other people, however, felt that Daniels would have made a very good politician.

In the 1960s, Brian Lamb was a public affairs officer in the navy who served in the Pentagon. Following his military release, he went to work for Colorado Senator Peter Dominick, and in the early seventies he became the assistant to the director for the Office of Telecommunications Policy under President Nixon. By then Lamb had considerable experience in Washington, D.C., and what stuck in his craw the most about the nation's capital was that the public

"My feeling has always been 'go for it.' I don't know that I could live with a five-year business plan." —*Bill Daniels*

knew very little about what took place in Congress or how the government actually functioned. He was fascinated with the TV medium and its potential for educating American citizens, but no news stations covered the government in any depth. The closer he came to the core of power in Washington, the more he felt that the people of the United States needed to be better informed about what their elected officials did. At the Office of Telecommunications Policy, the quiet and unassuming-looking young man was nearer to that core than he'd ever been before.

The office, which had about sixty employees, was located a block from the White House. Lamb's boss was Clay Whitehead, whose job was to develop broadcast policy for the chief executive. If there was an issue concerning cable TV or public television or satellite communications, the office determined Nixon's stance on the matter. Whenever a lobbyist came through the front door, the first person he met was Brian Lamb. In 1971 someone new walked in.

"I remember Bill sitting on the couch in my office," Lamb recalls. "I wasn't very important, but I worked for somebody who was, so Bill was there to tell me what he thought about telecommunications. The first impression I got was that he was short and well-dressed and a fast talker. Bill had polished finger-nails. I don't know why I remember that, but it was clear to me that this man worked hard at his appearance and his life. After that first meeting I came away with the impression, right or wrong, that he was a close friend of Richard Nixon, that he had visited with the president either in person or on the phone in the recent couple of weeks, and that the president said that Clay Whitehead and I were doing a great job. It was very important that I listen to what he had to say about the future of cable television.

"There was no doubt in my mind that when Bill Daniels left my office, he was somebody I was going to see again. He was not a shrinking violet and was willing to tell me exactly what was on his mind. He was always very good about complimenting you, which was part of his style. He would tell you how important he was. A lot of people walked in that office over the years and you never remember them and they never left a trail, but Bill Daniels was clearly the father of cable television. He cut a wide swath. From that day forward, I would take his phone calls and deal with him. I didn't make him happy all the time, but he was a player.

"I think Bill would've made a good politician. It's not all complimenting the roses at the White House. Politicians have to absorb a lot of people coming at them wanting things, and Bill knew how to deal with people. He had strong views. But he also was the kind of person that wanted to win—politicians like to win, so they compromise. What was Bill's business over the years but compromising? Working two sides, convincing one side and then the other of the merits of a compromise. He was a great one for always trying to make people feel good about themselves and feel good about whatever they did for him in the way of business. That's what politicians do. Bill did it for money directly. Politicians do it for money indirectly. Bill was always able to bring all the enormous egos in this business together."

With John Love as governor and facing his last two years in office, the party machine endorsed Daniels to run for governor. But, subsequently, Love was called to Washington to become the country's first energy czar, and the lieutenant governor was named governor. In effect, Bill was now the challenger in the primary against the incumbent.

When his older brother decided to run for governor of Colorado, Jack Daniels, a bedrock Democrat, took a dim view of Bill's chances. The two men argued vigorously about politics, and neither gave an inch. In their heated discussions, Bill talked just like a conservative Republican and Jack just like a free-spending Democrat. Yet it always befuddled Jack, who had a reputation as someone who liked to stretch a dollar, to learn that his sibling was constantly making substantial anonymous donations to the poor or giving money away to charitable causes or trying to get someone out of prison and help him land a job or just handing out large sums of money to people in a jam. It seemed to him that Bill was a sucker for almost every hard-luck story he heard—a notoriously soft touch. To his younger brother, Bill handled money in ways that would make pork-barrel liberals blush.

"The first time I went with him to the Brown Palace Hotel in Denver," Jack recalls, "he was handing out fifty-dollar bills to the bellhops in the lobby. He gave everybody one. Every time he turned around, those guys did handsprings for him."

Bill, as his brother knew, was a mover and a shaker, someone driven to get things done and get them done now. He generated ideas, he delegated the

Bill Daniels was a staunch advocate for cable television's growth and often fought battles with banks, bureaucrats, and broadcasters who tried to block cable's expansion.

responsibility for carrying them out to others, and he expected them to start performing immediately. He had virtually no comprehension of the word no. His way of making a deal—even a multimillion-dollar deal—was going to a restaurant with business associates and laying out the terms of the agreement on a dinner napkin. He liked broad strokes much more than fine points. Once the general terms were in place, he'd call in his legal and financial team to negotiate the rest. The team usually approached these missions with curiosity—and some trepidation.

Daniels shot from the hip, and results were his passion.

"He would never have made a good governor," his brother says, "because the bureaucracies would have driven him crazy. With all the things he wanted to do in office, he would have needed half a dozen lawyers to keep him out of jail."

Former Colorado governor Dick Lamm agrees: "The best way to put it is that Bill was a no-bullshit politician—he was not even a politician at all. He was just a no-bullshit type of guy. He was someone that I could always rely on to talk over problems with and get advice from. Being governor is tough, and I certainly don't mean this to be disrespectful, but while it's easy to say that Bill could do anything well, I don't think that his forte was dealing with stupidity."

In the Republican primary in 1974, he took on incumbent governor John Vanderhoof and ran on a platform that included creating a constitutional amendment to end school busing, a return of the death penalty, and a ban to be lifted on the killing of coyotes. He spent $425,000 of his own money on his campaign, a Colorado record at the time, and pursued the governor's office in somewhat the same way he'd once entered the ring at the New Mexico Military Institute. He came out swinging. Governor Vanderhoof was not used to such a bruising approach, especially in a primary, and took exception to Daniels' tactics. He once said that his opponent "is not only cutting me up, but he is attempting to cut up the entire party."

"Bill was a warrior," says Daniels' friend and the former U.S. senator from Colorado Bill Armstrong. "There was, of course, a gentle side to him, but he would've been right at home with General Patton. I think he relished the combat. To be a boxer, I think you've got to like to hit people and not mind getting hit yourself. He was a person for whom the battle had its own value, aside from the victory, whether it was in business or politics.

"If his political career had taken a little different turn, he might have had a significant impact on the political situation in Colorado. When he ran in the primary for governor, it sort of positioned him outside the establishment. He basically took on an unwinnable race and having done that, there wasn't a natural fallback position for him. With him, you didn't have the sense that you have with so many political figures, that they'll just tell you anything. He was very honest and outspoken. If he had been willing to take a little different step or be a little more patient or had laid the groundwork a little differently, he would have succeeded."

Before deciding to pursue the governor's office, Daniels had called John Saeman into his office and told him that Saeman was going to run the company from now on. If Daniels was elected, Saeman would carry on as the head of the business. If Daniels lost . . . that topic was not discussed.

Daniels was soundly defeated in the primary, and the loss was devastating for him. During his bid for governor, his secretary Fran Harding had acted as his schedule coordinator throughout the campaign. She watched from close range what her boss was experiencing, and she knew that the "warrior" was also a man with scars and vulnerabilities.

"I don't think people realized the depth of Bill's depression and grief over losing the campaign for governor," Harding says. "At that time, the cable business was not doing well either. It was a real struggle to pay the bills. Our accountant Dick Zell used to pull his hair out and say, 'How am I going to pay these bills? Hold this check—don't pay that.' Back then it was totally different from how it was later in Bill's life. One time after the election, he was in a motel room in Colorado Springs, really depressed. John Saeman and I were so worried about him, we drove down to get him."

"After Fran and I drove down to Colorado Springs," Saeman recalls, "Bill told us he was leaving and didn't know when we'd hear from him again. His bags were packed and he had some wine on ice for his trip. He was drunk and I told him I didn't think he should go. He said, 'How the hell are you going to

When Bill Daniels campaigned for governor of Colorado in 1974, he was popular as a law-and-order candidate. He is pictured here visiting the Denver city jail.

stop me?' I said, 'In your condition, that wouldn't be hard.' He asked me what I wanted him to do, and I told him to go back to Denver and he did. I asked him to stay in our house, but he wouldn't do that, so he checked into the local Marriott and we got together each day.

"We'd just purchased a large group of cable systems in Nebraska for about $8 million and had financed this through a $10.5 million financing with a group of insurance companies. We momentarily had $2.5 million of excess cash which was earmarked for capital expenditures. This made Bill happy because when he looked at the numbers, he thought this was his money and he could do whatever he wanted to with it. He had a girlfriend in Holyoke, Colorado. Her father owned a small country bank that was struggling, and he wanted to have us send a $500,000 deposit to his bank. I said, 'Bill, I can't do that.' He said, 'You'd rather get fired than do this?' I said, 'I guess so, because to do it would violate our loan agreements.' We didn't move the money. After a week he said he was ready to leave the Marriott, and off he went. What happened back then—this was 1976—was not what I would call an intervention in his life. In those days I didn't regard him as an alcoholic. Denial was just a daily part of life."

A full-blown intervention would not come for another decade when no one could deny the problem any longer.

Despite his political defeat in 1974, good things emerged from his venture into politics. He met Gerald Ford, who was about to become the thirty-eighth president of the United States, following Richard Nixon's resignation over the Watergate scandal in August 1974. Daniels and Ford shared a lot of common ground. They had the same political philosophy, similar military backgrounds, and a passionate interest in sports. Ford had served in the navy, spending two years on the combat carrier *Monterey*. He'd been a very good football player, playing center and becoming the most valuable player on the 1933 University of Michigan team, which won the national collegiate championship. He'd gone on to coach boxing at Yale and much later became an avid skier who regularly vacationed with his family in Vail, Colorado. When he met Daniels, President Ford was impressed with his boxing stories, his service as a naval pilot during the war, and his unflagging drive and desire to take risks and start new projects. Daniels was a man of action, a doer, just the sort of person whom the president believed would make an excellent leader in Colorado. Ford supported him during his campaign, and they stayed friends once the primary was over.

"Bill was multifaceted," says the former president. "Very few people could challenge his success in the business community. He started from the ground up and went to the top in a relatively few years. He was also a dedicated, patriotic citizen, whether you look at his record in the military as a navy pilot or if you look at his contributions as a participant in the political arena. They were all A+. I can just see Bill in a fighter plane. I wouldn't want to be the Japanese he was after."

Despite the two men's friendship, it wasn't President Ford who would have the most impact on Daniels' life in upcoming years, but the chief executive's wife. Betty Ford would play a much larger role after she stepped forward and publicly acknowledged a substance-abuse problem. Following her admission, she started the Betty Ford Center in California, which offered help to many famous (and not so famous) people who were trying to recover from alcohol or drug addiction and remake their lives. In time, Daniels would find his way to her door.

In the 1970s, his drinking continued and sometimes it deepened to a level that was impossible to ignore. He drank when his business produced so much stress that he needed instant relief from the tension. He drank when the voters of Colorado rejected him for someone else. He drank because of the pressures from the bankruptcy of the Utah Stars and the financial burdens that imposed on his company. He drank because his fourth marriage to Devra, like the other three marriages before it, was not going to last. He drank when a new love affair quickly assumed the old pattern of not bringing him long-term happiness. It only left him restless, anxious for something else, something more. He drank because he was full of questions and none of them had easy or simple answers. He drank because he didn't seem able to make and keep commitments the way some people did, and it didn't appear that this was ever going to change. He drank because he was getting older and certain things were only growing more painful. He drank because money could not keep away pain or loneliness or longing for things that were hard to name. Daniels was a perfectionist, but he knew he was imperfect himself, just a man with human frailties. Colorado's Governor Lamm once compared Daniels to F. Scott Fitzgerald's fictional character Jay Gatsby, the title figure of the renowned novel *The Great Gatsby*, because the cable tycoon seemed to have everything that money could buy except genuine companionship.

Often during the winter holidays, he went to poor neighborhoods in Denver and secretly left cash on people's doorsteps or had others do so for him. He worked in soup kitchens and handed out food to the indigent so he could be reminded of all that he had and how little some other people got by on. He encouraged everyone who worked for him to be charitable toward the needy. He demanded that those around him treat everybody they met with the same level of respect. He advised both men and women who were starting love affairs that they could judge the future of their relationships by how their lover interacted with those working in restaurants, hotels, and other services businesses; if anyone treated these people badly, Daniels said, watch out, because that was the way you were eventually going to be treated.

"Somebody once said, 'Observe the turtle, he progresses only with his neck out.'
I think the same holds true for us two-legged creatures." —Bill Daniels

Sometimes Daniels, the bedrock Republican, was tormented over why he was able to generate wealth and so many others weren't. Because of this, he felt the need to share with others who were less fortunate—even when they took advantage of him. He wore a tough mask in many situations, but Daniels was sensitive in ways that he virtually never talked about and was perplexed by things that were difficult for him to express. Men of his generation had been taught to remain silent in the face of their own pain and confusion. This tendency had been reinforced a thousandfold by going to war as late adolescents and being told to kill as many of the enemy as they possibly could. His inner life was rich and complicated, yet he kept almost everyone he met at arm's length when it came to getting a real look within.

"Even after working with him for a while," says Bob Russo, the corporate communications officer at Daniels & Associates for many years before becoming executive vice president of marketing and administration, "it was hard to get to know him. Most of the time Bill maintained the bravado of a commander—strictly business. He was quick to challenge you, grill you, or point out your mistakes. However, over the years I got a better sense of his deeper feelings and values. He really wanted people close to him to be honest. And he wanted to please people, even if that meant compromise. He also had a very soft side in terms of his ability to get in touch with other people's emotional feelings. After a while, you believed he loved you."

As Daniels grew older, he confronted some of his interior issues with his personal physician, Dr. Abe Kauvar, and with his spiritual adviser, Methodist pastor Ed Beck. He opened up to Reverend Beck more than anyone else, and revealed himself not just as a businessman who'd helped create an up-and-coming American industry, but as a spiritual seeker who deeply wanted to understand more about life's mysteries—and about himself.

"What gratified me more than anything else," says Bob Russo, "was hearing that Reverend Beck had had some deep and meaningful conversations with Bill, where Bill bared his soul to Ed about what life and death was all about."

"Bill," says Reverend Beck, "was certain about his standards in the business world. He was less certain about his personal life. When I would say to him, 'God accepts even the unacceptable in you,' that was very difficult for him to believe. He felt God's expectations were very high for him. He called me one day and said that somebody had sent him something that said, 'Where much has been given, much will be required.' He asked what that meant.

"I told him that if he wanted to 'do' or 'give' out of gratitude or thanksgiving, fine, but you are not doing it to earn brownie points or merit badges or Golden Gloves trophies. I told him that God already loved him, that he was God's child and God loved him dearly and deeply. Bill was a person of faith who found, at times, his faith wanting."

Not all of his conversations with Reverend Beck were serious. After Daniels' fourth marriage ended in divorce, he began joking that he was going to create a bumper sticker and distribute it around Denver. It would read "Honk if you've been married to Bill Daniels."

He talked about his divorces with Reverend Beck and asked him a question that humankind had been pondering for millennia.

"One time," the pastor says, "he called and said, 'Ed, what do you believe about reincarnation?' And I said, 'Well, how long do you have to talk? You have thirty minutes or so?' He said, 'Yes, I'm very interested.' We talked about different belief systems, and I quoted him a couple of them. I said, 'Bill, I'm just curious, do you believe in reincarnation?' He said, 'Well, I don't know. Sometimes I do and sometimes I don't.' And I asked him what he wanted to come back as. There was a pause, and he said, 'One of Bill Daniels' ex-wives.'

"I must've laughed for five minutes. When I caught my breath, I asked him why. He said, 'Because they're taken care of better than anyone else.'"

"If you've never taken a chance on yourself, at least think about it. Unless you do, you may never know what you're missing out on. And neither will the rest of the world."
—*Bill Daniels*

Eighteen

Daniels would not try politics again but turn in a different direction, one that had intrigued him since childhood. He jumped into the world of athletics and, more particularly, into the very expensive realm of professional sports ownership. Before long, he would begin referring to these investments as "charities."

In the early seventies, he converted his lifelong fascination with speed into an involvement with car racing. Daniels had met astronaut Pete Conrad, of the Apollo 12 moon mission, and through Conrad he'd gotten to know race-car driver Jim Rathman. The latter called him one day and said that another driver, Lloyd Ruby, was looking for a sponsor for the Indianapolis 500. What, Daniels immediately asked, could he do to help? Rathman told him that if he backed Ruby with a quarter of a million dollars, Ruby would put Daniels' name on his vehicle. The proposition had everything Daniels liked: speed, risk, competition, daredevil driving, free advertising, and an adventure into the unknown. He said yes and Rathman told him to mail out a check for $250,000 to Gene White, the owner of Ruby's car.

Daniels began learning more about the race-car circuit, absorbing knowledge and stories by hanging out with Rathman, Ruby, and some other drivers, including the famous Unser brothers, Al and Bobby. Daniels soon found out that there were people who liked cutting up behind the wheel of a car as much as he did—maybe more than he did. One night, several of the men were returning home from dinner when they decided to have some fun at the expense of one of the passengers.

"Al was driving," Rathman recalls, "and he said to Bobby, 'Give me the test.' We were running about seventy, eighty miles an hour down the interstate and Bobby reached out and put his hands over Al's eyes. Bill was sitting in the back with me watching all this and he went crazy! So then they faked it a little bit— going in the dirt and scaring Bill some more."

Backed with Daniels' cash, Ruby drove an 800-horsepower Laycock Mongoose at the Indianapolis 500 that Memorial Day. He lost the race and the venture cost Daniels somewhere between $250,000 and $300,000, but he'd had a great time with the racing crowd and would hang around with them for years to come. Neil Jones, a friend and political colleague of Daniels, was part of that crowd and relished the memories.

"We would drive right up to the Speedway Motel," Jones says. "It was the place that the drivers stayed, and anybody that was anybody had a room at this motel, right on the speedway grounds. We would find a parking spot, get out, and sure enough, someone would stick their head out of one of the motor homes or a room and yell, 'Get your ass up here.' That would be Jim Rathman, who won the Indy 500 back in the 1960s. Or Lloyd Ruby—'The Rube.' Bill and whoever this was would treat me like one of them. Sit around, listen to them tell lies to each other, smoke cigars, drink a beer, and just clown around."

Daniels, the spiritual seeker who was pondering ancient metaphysical questions with doctors and pastors in Denver, was equally at home sniffing the fumes at Indy's famed Gasoline Alley. And he was always ready to play one of his favorite roles: that of matchmaker for his friends. During his racing escapades he introduced Pete Conrad to his future wife.

"One day," says Nancy Conrad, the wife of the late astronaut, "Bill asked me what I was doing June 20, which was not an uncommon question. And I said, 'Bill, whatever you tell me I'm going to do!' Bill said, 'Well, honey, I think you're going to fall in love.' I said, 'That would be great, I've never been in love.' Bill said, 'I've got somebody for you. He's as smart as you are, he's as funny as you are, and he's as short as you are.'"

When the time came for Nancy to meet Conrad in Del Mar, California, she and a friend of hers named Karen decided to surprise both Conrad and Daniels. They dressed up in full geisha costumes; they put on wigs, white faces, kimonos, and other Japanese regalia. They hired a white limo to take them to the meeting and wrote a poem for the occasion. They arrived and began striking poses in the garden.

"The two men approached us," Nancy says, "and you could tell what was going through Bill's mind: 'What in the Sam Hill is this?' And Pete is grinning from ear to ear. According to Pete, he was immediately smitten. He really couldn't see me; I had all this white makeup on. All he could see, so he said, were great big eyes and dimples. He was hooked. Afterwards we took off all that makeup and had a really great dinner and evening. It lasted twelve years. And we never stopped talking. Bill gave me my whole life when he introduced me to Pete.

"If I could sum Bill up, I would say that his legacy is a tremendous awareness of how to truly share. He had thrown the Apollo 12 party for Pete. When Pete got back from the moon, he gave Bill a picture of himself standing next to the *Surveyor* on the landing site known as the Ocean of Storms. The inscription said, 'Sorry I couldn't be at the party, I was out of town on business.' Bill had it in his office for years and years."

Some of Daniels' racing buddies were interested in searching for hidden treasure on sunken ships in the Havana harbor, but Fidel Castro was opposed to this. When the men went to Daniels for his help with the challenge, he told them he would make some calls and see what he could do. He phoned a friend down in Atlanta named Ted Turner, who owned a small TV station that was struggling to survive. Atlanta's Channel 17—or WTCG (Turner said this stood for "Watch This Channel Grow")—wasn't growing at all and was barely staying on the air. It ranked fourth in a four-station market. Turner had been closely following the developments of cable TV and satellite technology in particular, and he believed they might provide a path that would rescue his station.

When Daniels called him, Turner was broadcasting baseball games in Havana, so Daniels asked him to contact Castro and get his permission for the divers to explore the ships. Turner, who was a successful sailor and open to almost any adventure, wanted to help, but obstacles were everywhere. Finally, the mission proved too difficult to accomplish. Still, Daniels maintained his friendship both with the divers and with Turner. He greatly enjoyed being around athletes, and despite his losses in race-car driving, he was not discouraged about investing in other sporting endeavors.

In the early seventies, he became aware of a heavyweight fighter named Ron Lyle, who was doing time in a prison in Cañon City, Colorado, on a manslaughter charge. Daniels had tried to help other ex-cons or junkies once

they left prison because he held the (quite liberal) conviction that inmate reha-
bilitation was not something our prisons do very well. He had always believed
in giving people a second chance. And because of his own background in the
ring, Daniels had a special affection for boxers. He could identify with the
fighter's mentality in ways that went beyond hitting an opponent on the chin.
He'd recently had to get up off the mat after several divorces, losing his bid for
governor, and countless swings in the cable business, his company once or
twice flirting with bankruptcy before making a recovery.

When he heard that Lyle was doing a stretch for his involvement in a
complicated domestic shooting, Daniels was quick to offer assistance. He met
Lyle and helped him win parole by promising to give him steady employment
upon his release. The parole board agreed to these conditions, and Daniels
took over the management of Lyle's career as a serious fighter. While assisting
him, Daniels also started a boxing club in Denver with the help of Lou Lopez.

Bill had become a dominant force in cable television, and had tested the political
waters. Now, his relentless drive brought him to professional sports. Here he is
flanked by pro driver Lloyd Ruby and members of the Indy 500 team.

The two men put together the Denver Rocks, which offered fighters of every weight class a chance to step into the ring and test their skills. They were trained by the well-known boxing veteran Bobby Lewis, and they fought at the Denver Coliseum in front of enthusiastic crowds.

"The Denver Rocks offered good amateur boxing," says John Saeman, "and the club was important because the support Bill gave to boxing in Denver became the footing for the local Police Athletic League and its involvement in sports. This helped many disadvantaged kids."

While the Rocks remained amateurs, Ron Lyle had much bigger things in mind. He trained hard and was very ambitious; so was his manager. Daniels was determined not just to find him work in the ring but to bring him up through the ranks and get him a shot at the heavyweight championship of the world—against Muhammad Ali.

"Most of the Republicans I know," Jack Daniels said, "would never have gone down to Cañon City and taken a guy out of the penitentiary and tried to make something of him. That's what Bill did with Ron Lyle. I'm a Democrat and I wouldn't have done that."

After leaving prison, Lyle began fighting and beating a lot of mediocre opponents. He was getting back in shape and polishing his skills. Daniels had been supporting him to the tune of several hundred thousand dollars, but Lyle was giving a good return on this investment with his steady string of victories. In 1971–72 he was undefeated in nineteen fights, and most of the time he knocked out his opponents in the early rounds. Gradually, he was becoming a legitimate contender. In 1973 he lost to a decent fighter named Jerry Quarry but then rebounded and won seven more times in a row. The following year he beat two name boxers—Oscar Bonavena and Jimmy Ellis—and in May 1975 he finally got his title shot in Las Vegas against Muhammad Ali.

This was a great moment for Daniels, who'd been a Golden Gloves winner himself. He was thrilled to be at ringside for what many regard as the biggest prize in sports: the heavyweight championship of the world. He was even more thrilled that one of the fighters was his friend and business associate. He was extremely proud of Ron Lyle; the man's efforts since leaving prison affirmed everything Daniels believed about the value of giving people another chance and working hard to improve your circumstances in life. With Daniels' money and Lyle's sweat and grit in the ring, the two of them made an excellent team. Tonight would show just how far they had come together.

Lyle came out strong and in the early rounds gave Ali all he wanted. For a while it looked as though he might upset the champ, but other fighters had been in the same place before with Muhammad Ali, who often saved his best effort for the later rounds. As the bout wore on, Ali took over and put Lyle away in the eleventh. It had been a good fight and Lyle had distinguished himself as a worthy contender. This night in Las Vegas was the height of his boxing career and his relationship with Bill Daniels. Following the match with Ali, Lyle decided to break his contract with Daniels and eventually he did. The end of their connection was both mysterious and painful—for both men.

"I came from rock bottom, from Cañon City," Lyle once told the *Denver Post*. "Bill Daniels introduced me to something and opened the door for me to compete as a boxer. He's a good man, an honest man, a sincere man. I hold him in high regard and appreciate what he did for me, but there are times in a man's life when he has to take his own steps. He has to move on. I was at that point after the Ali fight. I wanted to make something of myself. I wanted to have what Bill Daniels has and that was difficult. I don't hold anything against him, and I hope that a man of his stature doesn't hold anything against me."

"What the hell?" Daniels told the *Post* in response to Lyle's remarks. "I got Ron Lyle out of prison, got him a job as a fighter, paid his salary, told him I would get him a shot at the heavyweight championship of the world against Muhammad Ali. I fulfilled that obligation. We were partners, with a fifty-fifty deal. I never owned Ron Lyle. Nobody owns any man. I set up a trust for him and gave him some ATC [American Television Corporation] stock. After he lost the Ali fight, he wanted to break the trust and our partnership. I was crushed. It was probably the biggest disappointment I've ever had in a fellow human being, and I've known a lot of people. I will never figure out why he wanted to break up our arrangement. It was like being sued by your brother."

Walter Gerash, a famed Denver defense attorney, filed suit against Daniels to get Lyle out of his contract. In 1986 *Denver Magazine* published a cover story on Gerash and the article described various high-profile cases of his, including the Lyle case. Shortly after the article appeared, Gerash received a plaque that contained an embossed cover of this issue of *Denver Magazine*. He was surprised that anyone would take the trouble to get the cover embossed and put on a plaque. He was much more surprised to learn that the plaque—and the accompanying letter—came from his old adversary in court, Bill Daniels.

"The date of the letter," says Gerash, "is March 7, 1986, and I believe that article came out in February, the month before. The letter reads, 'Dear Walter, although to this day, I think you gave Ron Lyle some very bad financial advice as to his trust I set up for him and although at the time I personally resented your hostile attitude towards me, I do admire you as a defense attorney. I wanted this permanently preserved for you and your heirs. I hope it brings you some moments of reflection. A hell of an article. Respectfully, Bill Daniels.'"

Gerash kept the plaque on his wall to remind him of Daniels.

One person who became angry at the falling-out between Lyle and Daniels was Jo Farrell, the founder of JF Images, the leading modeling agency in the West. She had met Bill only in passing at a cocktail party but she had been professionally involved with Lyle and he'd treated her the same way he'd treated Daniels. When she read in the paper about their falling-out, she picked up the phone.

Bill with Joe Louis, one of his lifetime heroes.

"You know, I'm very Irish," she says. "My hair turned flaming red because I was so angry at Ron for what he'd done to Bill. When Bill came on the line, I told him, 'I want you to know there is somebody in this city that is so angry with Ron on your behalf. I know what you have done for him and I want you to know somebody out there really, really understands.'"

This was the start of a friendship that spanned almost a quarter century. When Farrell once needed help to keep her business going, Daniels loaned her $100,000.

Daniels was very lenient about many things because he understood that other people had just as many weaknesses as he did. But that tolerance did not extend to those either within his company or outside it who he believed had been disloyal.

"Bill's whole understanding of loyalty," says Reverend Ed Beck, "was almost an obsession. 'A good obsession,' I would tell him, 'that God accepts you and expects loyalty from you. You accept other people knowing that they have some glaring weaknesses.' He just couldn't see the reason why someone would deliberately set out to rip somebody off, whether it was himself or somebody he cared about.

"He didn't set out to get them, but he certainly wouldn't turn a thumb to help them. He just isolated himself from them. In some cases, I think those persons felt he had misunderstood or misinterpreted. He lived in a very black-and-white world when it came to loyalty and commitment. He felt there were very few variables. He felt that if someone was competent in the business world, then they should be that in their personal value system."

Despite having once again been burned in connection to a sporting venture—this time emotionally instead of financially—Daniels was hardly finished with professional athletics. Every now and then he would get bored with cable and dive back into the realm of romance and fantasy that the sports world represented to him. He poured lots of money into these pursuits, and, almost predictably, he lost lots of money, causing great consternation in the offices of Daniels & Associates. His executives knew how to broker cable deals and make the company profitable, but they didn't always know how to keep the boss from throwing cash at these very high-risk propositions.

"Sports," says Zelbie Trogden, a banker with Security Pacific Bank in Los

Angeles who worked with Daniels & Associates, "were a disaster for Bill. Not sports programming on television, but sports teams. Whether it was his boxing club or his racing deal or the Grand Prix of Denver or the United States Football League, he had the Midas touch. Everything he touched turned to mufflers."

While Daniels was campaigning for the governor's office in Colorado, he purchased the Los Angeles Stars professional basketball team in the American Basketball Association and then moved them to Salt Lake City. The ABA was an upstart league that was attempting to compete with the much more established National Basketball Association. The NBA, founded in 1946, was rooted in major cities like New York, Chicago, and Los Angeles, while the ABA was trying to make a go of it in places like Denver, New Jersey, and Salt Lake City. The concept of a group of teams from smaller locales creating their own identity and providing quality sports entertainment held great appeal to Daniels. It was another example of his natural tendency to want to help the underdog.

Bill Daniels made sure his interest in sports enhanced the development of the cable television industry.

When Daniels bought the California franchise, recalls attorney Bob Nagle, "it was near the end of the season. I remember there were about eight games left that year. The team was way behind in the standings. They were dispirited and had been traveling around in a bus, practically not getting paid. The day we closed the deal, they played not too far away from their home base, and Bill brought in his own jet and another jet and flew them to the game. By God, they started winning and won, I think, maybe not every game to the end of the season but enough to get them in the playoffs."

Under Coach Bill Sharman, the Stars won the ABA championship that year but the coach failed to show up for the championship dinner. Two days later Daniels confronted Sharman in the office about his absence. Sharman, who was still under contract in Utah, told him that he had just signed a deal to coach the Los Angeles Lakers. Daniels was shocked—and hurt. He valued loyalty and honesty and fulfilling your commitments above all else.

"Bill was the type of person," says Tony Acone, "that if Sharman had gone to him and said that he'd been offered a position to coach the Lakers, Bill would have said, 'My jet is fueled up. Why don't you take it to L.A., find out if it is something that you want to do, and if so, great. If not, we'll see you next year.' Instead, this guy didn't say a word, and he didn't respect his players enough to show up for the dinner."

Daniels never forgot a broken promise. Years later he bought a 5 percent interest in the Lakers, and Bill Sharman was still the coach. In Daniels' mind, this meant that he was paying 5 percent of the salary to someone who had stiffed him.

"Bill told me that because of this he was not sleeping very well," says Acone. "He said to me, 'I want you to get together with Jerry Buss [the Lakers' majority owner] and get Sharman out of there.' We had just signed the papers for partnership in the last forty-eight hours, and I get marching orders to go to Jerry and tell him to get rid of Sharman. I explained to Jerry that Bill was having trouble sleeping, and I will never forget the look on Jerry's face. 'Bill is having trouble sleeping?' I told him the story, and Jerry said Bill was right but if we do a termination without just cause, we would all get sued."

After Daniels had moved the Stars to Salt Lake City, he hired former pro basketball player and Olympic gold medalist Vince Boryla to be their general manager. Boryla thought that Daniels was a great boss, but his soft spot for athletes caused problems.

"Bill loved to come into town," Boryla says, "and get his arm around the ballplayers and talk to them about this and that. It really is kind of a sensitive area because it is a business and the players' perception of what he has in mind and what he's doing was not necessarily the same as the owner's. Bill was such a likable guy and I'd be doing things one way and he'd be talking to people around town another way. The bottom line was that I watched Bill's nickel ten times better than I would have watched my own. Bill spent more money accidentally than I spent on purpose, trying to be everybody's friend."

In spite of the Stars' run of success, Daniels and the team were faced with large challenges in Salt Lake City. Basketball did not have much history or tradition in Utah. Utah was largely Mormon and overwhelmingly white. By the 1970s, pro hoops had become the ultimate urban black game. Nowhere in America was there a larger gap between the audience and the stars of the sport.

"It was very interesting," says American Basketball Association lawyer Arlan Preblud, "to sit in the arena and look around and see all of these blond, blue-eyed white people watching predominately black ballplayers play. And cheering them. It really was a dichotomy to watch. My understanding of the Mormon church at that time was that I don't think they even allowed black people into the church. But they certainly grabbed hold of the Utah Stars and treated them incredibly well."

The locals may have liked the Stars, but the franchise, as well as the entire ABA, was strapped with severe economic problems. There simply weren't enough entertainment dollars to support every new sports team that was emerging across the country. It was a constant struggle to pay the bills, and before long the Stars were moving straight toward bankruptcy. In 1971–72, Daniels took over as the president of the ABA and heightened his efforts to help his own franchise and the league as a whole, but this was different from promoting cable TV. In the cable field, one's adversaries were fairly well defined: the networks, film industry, theater owners, telephone companies, and certain members of Congress. In pro basketball, nothing was as clear-cut and many sports fans simply felt that the most legitimate pro basketball was found in the NBA. Daniels, as usual, was undaunted. He dug further into his

A somber Bill Daniels in 1975 announces the demise of his ABA basketball team, the Utah Stars.

own pockets and persisted, determined that the Stars were going to survive and be a first-class operation.

"The team was in trouble," Fran Harding says, "and I think Bill dealt with his political loss by throwing himself into working very hard to get the Stars going. He moved to Salt Lake and lived there for at least six months, maybe nine months, in hotels. It was his way of escaping from people in Denver all the time and talking about the loss. You know, in the old Salt Palace [where the Stars played] there were a couple of private boxes and you couldn't really see them very well from the floor. He would be up there many times by himself. He just needed the space to try and get over things and move on. There were some hard times and he took it really hard."

Eventually the bad times carried the Stars into bankruptcy—and the Daniels' management group to the brink of despair. Daniels always made his own decisions and then left the legal details up to his team of attorneys, led by Bob Nagle and Ken Farabee.

In Daniels' absence, John Saeman was overseeing Daniels & Associates and Daniels Properties, Inc., when he became aware of what his boss was doing in order to keep the basketball team afloat. As the fortunes of the Stars turned more and more sour, Daniels began using the DPI stock as collateral to get loans for the sports operation. With cable itself enduring a shaky time, the banks that held the company's loans regarded their stock in DPI as their security.

"We found ourselves dealing with bankers," says Saeman, "who wanted to foreclose on our cable company. The lead lender at first wanted to take us over and liquidate our cable systems. I'm the new president of Daniels, in office only a short time when this happens. We worked closely with our bankers and our partners and bought time. As a result, we avoided bankruptcy."

This venture into pro basketball cost Daniels personally an estimated $5 million, but he was not the only one who lost money. When the team folded in mid-season of 1975, the season ticket holders felt severely let down, since they were deprived of watching their team play the last thirty-three games on the schedule. Salt Lake was filled with grumbling about the Stars' management, and Daniels took as much heat as anyone. When the final game was over, he made a commitment to himself (and a silent one to the fans) that in the future when he had the resources, he would return to the city and pay off every single ticket holder and other creditors the balance of what he or she was due because of the shortened season. This was not something he was legally obligated to do, and most local people never expected to see a penny of what they'd lost. For years many fans remained angry at Daniels because of what had happened to the Stars.

"I remember when Bill had his problems in Utah," recalls John Malone. "We used to tease him about this and say, 'You better take a detour around Utah because if your plane has to go down in Salt Lake, we may never see you again!'"

Humor aside, the combination of everything that was unfolding around Daniels—the loss in the gubernatorial primary, the unraveling of his fourth marriage, the bankruptcy of the Stars—all drove him toward seclusion. He began spending most of his time on the West Coast and left Saeman to run the office back in Denver.

"Bill did a Howard Hughes on us," Saeman says. "He just disappeared and went into hiding for a long time."

Through his attorney Bob Nagle, Daniels had given Saeman an unlimited power of attorney to do whatever the younger man felt was best for the company. Then he retreated to California to deal with his perceived failures in the only way he knew: through alcohol and Valium.

"He just drank himself through it," Saeman says. "He basically shut people out of his life because of the embarrassment. There was nothing going on in Bill's life that Bill could be proud of and take credit for at that time. If Bill had not been drinking heavily, you would have seen him come in and roll up his sleeves and say, 'Here's what we're going to do.' But because he was drinking heavily, he was impacted and went into himself until such time he could come back with pride."

What started to bring Daniels back was a deal initiated by Saeman in 1976. That year DPI bought a cable system in Nebraska that served a total of thirteen communities, the largest of which was Lincoln, for $7.7 million. This acquisition helped stabilize Daniels' finances in the wake of the Utah Stars fiasco. With new assets in hand, Saeman was able to begin paying the banks that had been waiting a long time. Then in 1980 he decided to sell DPI to the renowned Newhouse family, which had been a major force in the publishing industry for decades before moving into cable. After the sale of DPI, Daniels had significant cash flow for the first time in several years, and Bill Daniels knew exactly what he wanted to do with some of the money. He went back to Utah and made good on his word. He paid off all the creditors and ticket holders—giving the local fans the value of their remaining 1975 season tickets, plus eight percent interest per year. This cost him nearly a million dollars, but he didn't stop there. He also paid off the people who'd sold concessions at the games of the failed team. When he was finished with the payback, he could finally stop thinking about the Stars' bankruptcy.

Daniels had often said that when he left the earth he never wanted to owe anyone anything. For the past few years he'd felt in debt to the people of Utah, and that had been a constant source of torment. With this burden removed, he was a changed person. Paying off his creditors, says Saeman, "was for Bill like a shot of adrenaline. It really ignited him. The press picked this story up around the country, and this gave Bill the energy surge that caused him to put all that other stuff behind him."

The tough times that had persisted throughout the 1970s were starting to come to an end for Daniels & Associates.

"We had management revenues coming in," says Saeman, "and we were covering our overhead. Not to say we were General Motors and didn't have any worries, but compared to what we'd had, it was a walk in the park. The greatest concerns we had were in the 1976–1980 time frame when Bill was over in Salt Lake. [Daniels executive] Steve Halstedt jokingly talks about the time Bob Nagle said that Bill would jump off the tenth floor of a hotel, but we really thought that was a serious issue. We called Bill on a regular basis to talk to him. It turns out there was every reason to believe he was suicidal, because he was drinking like crazy and he was on Valium and those two are dangerous bed partners."

The Stars' backers weren't the only ones Daniels rewarded for staying with him through the bad times. Daniels had always insisted that his employees own a piece of his company (so they would work harder and take more pride in the business). And beyond that, he was known for giving out big bonuses, when he could afford it and sometimes when that was questionable. During a holiday season in the late 1970s, Daniels gave Saeman an envelope and told him to open it with his family on Christmas Eve. Saeman did as requested and found a check inside for $10,000.

"At that time," Saeman says, "this was a huge amount of money. I think I was making like $40,000 a year, and I was intimately involved in the finances of our company. I was thinking how in the world could he do this—it just didn't make any sense. Bill would never surprise you with anything short of magnificent. If you got a gift from Bill, it was truly outstanding, always more than you could have expected. As a result of that, he instilled in people an enthusiasm where the person says, 'Hey, I've got to do as much as I can for this guy.'

"So it was a great psychological ploy. His bonuses weren't based on anything other than motivating the hell out of people to cause them to do better. The mere fact that he would share ownership with his employees was a real tribute. In hindsight, which is very easy now, everybody ought to do it because look at how successful it was for Bill. Not only did the associates make a lot of money but he made a lot of money."

The Utah Stars' bankruptcy payback generated a lot of publicity for Daniels and became part of his legend. Many people who worked for him and then went on to run companies of their own later said that they were far more giving to charitable causes and more concerned with ethics and fairness as a whole because of the atmosphere that dominated the Daniels & Associates office.

"What distinguished Bill more than any other single thing," says Paul Maxwell, a cable industry journalist and publisher, "was his integrity. I've never met anyone who would keep his word like that, even if it hurt him. Of course, it never hurt him in the long run other than a minor glitch or something. The example he set made cable unique, I think. Not many industries have people who were so successful and so dynamically grounded in doing what's right. I think every decision he ever made was based around what he thought was right as opposed to what he thought was best for him. Not that he wasn't tough! Everything he approached was grounded to the standpoint that your word is your bond and you didn't cheat."

Over the years Maxwell and his publications wrote a lot of things about the cable industry and its players that Daniels took exception to. When it came to business, he was never reluctant to make his feelings known.

"I used to hear from Bill all the time," says Maxwell, "and not necessarily to the good. He would call up and say, 'Paul, I think you're dead wrong and here's why.' He would listen, then give his point of view, and I didn't always agree with him, but he was always thinking of what was best for the industry, from his standpoint. Of course, when you're in a business like mine, you don't always write the nicest things because that's not what your job is. He'd get upset about that and he'd get upset if he weren't portrayed how he thought he should be portrayed. I must say he loved being known as the father of cable.

"He challenged me about dozens of things over the years. I don't remember them now, because everything would blow over real fast. It would be 'yesterday was yesterday' as long as you were straight with him. There was no grudge, no latent disapproval or anything like that. He would get over it right away, and sometimes he would call back and say, 'You know, I think you were really wrong.' A couple of times he would call back and say, 'You know, that's a better way of looking at it.' He wasn't ever afraid to change his mind.

"One time I got fired over something, and before I got home, he'd already

Bill Daniels with Olympic gold medalist Florence Griffith-Joyner, her husband, and Dr. John McMullen, owner of the Houston Astros, at a launch party for Prime Sports Network in 1988.

called my house. I don't know how he found out—I asked him, but he wouldn't tell me and I never did know. But as I drove into my garage, he was on the phone with my wife! I walk in and she said, 'Hey, it's Bill.' He was disappointed and he was ready to help, which was the main thing. I didn't need help then, but when I needed help, he was the first guy I called and he was the first guy to help."

A Daniels close friend and political adviser, Bob Lee, once gave an interview to a local periodical, and after reading in print what he'd said about Daniels, he was afraid that the man was going to be very upset with him (Lee stated that Daniels was a brilliant businessman but when it came to his relationships with women, "the SOB had a lot of problems"). Expecting the worst, he went into Daniels office and confessed his sins, thinking it was better to confront the mess directly instead of waiting for Daniels to hear about the remarks from another source. As it turned out, Daniels (as usual) had already read the comments himself. After listening to Lee's apology, Daniels looked up at him over his glasses and gave him that penetrating stare, while holding his silence.

"I thought you would be unhappy with me," Lee said.

"No," Daniels replied. "As long as you told the truth, that's all that matters."

Nineteen

If Daniels was changing and expanding in the 1970s, cable TV was also going through a major transformation. Back in the mid-sixties, Chuck Dolan and Irving Kahn had taken on the massive task of wiring one of the world's largest cities. Dolan's company, Sterling, had contracted to bring cable to the southern half of Manhattan, while Kahn's TelePrompTer wired the northern half. The process had been slow, difficult, and very expensive. New York's skyscrapers blocked or distorted signals, many apartment owners didn't want cable installed in their buildings, and some tenants were known for breaking into cable boxes and pirating the TV shows for themselves without paying a cent. It was a logistical nightmare, costing an estimated $100,000 per mile of strung cable, but Dolan and Kahn persisted in the teeth of every obstacle. When the cost of laying more cable became prohibitive for Dolan, he went in search of a partner with deep pockets and found one in Time-Life Pictures, a subsidiary of Time Inc. The parent company already owned numerous TV stations and cable systems, so it seemed like a natural ally for what Dolan had in mind.

He immediately began negotiating with New York's Madison Square Garden so that he could show New York Knick basketball games, New York Ranger hockey games, and other events taking place at the Garden. He soon had the deal in place and the games on the air, but this was hardly the extent of his ambition. For a long time he'd been thinking about another endeavor, and when he presented the concept to the brass at Time Inc., he called it the "Green Channel." He wanted to show sports and films to cable subscribers in New York and around the country, and he needed $300,000 to get started.

At a meeting of Time Inc. executives, Dolan carefully laid out his idea to the corporate chairman, Andrew Heiskell, who listened patiently and then sat for a while in silence, giving no response at all. With the silence growing more uncomfortable by the moment for Dolan, he assumed that he'd just bombed in front of the most important people in the company. Then the chairman scribbled something on a piece of paper, folded the paper up, and gave it to another executive, Time president James Shepley. The meeting continued and Shepley didn't unfold the paper until other matters had been dealt with and Heiskell had excused himself and left the room. By now the tension had become overwhelming for Dolan. He was nearly beside himself when Shepley finally opened the piece of paper and shared the two words that made up the entire message.

"Go ahead," they read.

A milestone in the history of cable television had just been reached, although no one knew that at the time. Three hundred thousand dollars would be allocated to launch what would eventually become the most daring, creative, and innovative TV station ever offered on American airwaves. But it wouldn't be called the Green Channel.

Following this meeting, Dolan was ecstatic and went to work assembling a team to help him move forward. He didn't want to sell the new station on a program-by-program basis, but as a monthly subscription, just as one would subscribe to a magazine (this was a concept that Time Inc. understood because it was one that the company had perfected).

Daniels had also been pushing the cable subscription idea for a long time, but until now he'd been working against the grain.

"Bill was certainly one of architects of the cable industry," says John Malone, "and he may have been the prime architect on its capital structure—the whole way in which the cable industry decided to make money, which was subscription-based. You have to remember in the very early days, the theory was that you charged people a lot to hook them up and then you wouldn't charge them hardly anything after that. Bill took it the other way, which was we'll have much higher revenues and much more success if we treat it as an ongoing revenue stream. But the guys who started the industry didn't think it would last very long or amount to anything."

With Green Channel in place, Dolan set about finding a better name for the service. A group of people kicked around ideas, but none of them was very satisfactory. The best they could come up with was Home Box Office, which nobody really liked. The three letters HBO—and particularly the last two of them—seemed off-putting because of their long association with the idea of offensive body odor. But they decided to use the handle until they could figure out something better. The honchos at Time Inc. weren't much bothered by the name because they didn't think the experiment would last more than a few months.

When Dolan asked Hollywood to provide him with motion pictures to show on the new channel, all the studios turned them down except for one. Universal was at least willing to try the novel idea and offered a package of movies that featured *Sometimes a Great Notion*, starring Paul Newman. With this in place, Dolan's first lieutenant, a young man named Gerald Levin, went looking for venues that might be interested in the new product. In keeping with cable's roots, he found a microwave system in Pennsylvania that could transmit HBO to operators around the state, and after searching some more, he finally found an outfit in Wilkes-Barre what was willing to put the channel on the air. When it came time for HBO's very modest grand opening, Wilkes-Barre was recovering from a flood. Debris and mud were everywhere in the town—and had even seeped inside the small HBO office. Wilkes-Barre resembled a disaster area, but was about to give birth to a show that would start to fulfill Daniels' longstanding dream of cable TV providing content to American homes.

On November 8, 1972, HBO began broadcasting. Less than four hundred subscribers had signed up, and they were lucky to see anything at all on the new channel. The weather was bad and high winds had knocked down the microwave dish. Technicians had to go out into a cold, driving rain to repair it for transmission. When at last it was ready, Gerald Levin appeared on the screen, made a brief speech telling viewers what to expect from HBO, and then christened the service with a live hockey game from New York. Movies soon followed. A new era had arrived in broadcast communications, yet it was anything but an overnight success.

For months and even years it appeared the cable outlet would not survive. It had financial problems, technical problems, more resistance from movie studios and theater owners, and content problems (the channel kept showing the same few films over and over again, to an increasingly bored audience).

There were also customer problems. Some patrons were upset with the risqué movies HBO was bringing to television and others were annoyed by the cost. Cable subscribers who'd been paying $6 to $8 for the entire service were now being billed roughly the same amount just for HBO. A lot of people dropped the channel not long after signing up, and HBO teetered on the edge of extinction. Time Inc. did not pull the plug, though. It continued underwriting the experiment, and under Levin's guidance the business gradually stabilized and more subscriptions were sold to other cable systems. HBO began to spread into the suburbs and across the country. In its first five years the channel enlisted 1.6 million subscribers. The 1977 gross revenues for Home Box Office were $124 million, and in the final quarter of that year, the station finally moved into the black. The experiment was here to stay.

Back then no one could have imagined HBO's long-range future. Ultimately, it was not the airing of sporting events or second-run movies that would launch the channel into the media pantheon, but the presentation of original programming—just as Daniels had predicted several decades earlier. If cable was going to thrive, he'd constantly preached to the industry and regulators, it had to be allowed to create and broadcast its own material. And that material had to be significantly different from what others were offering. In Daniels' mind, that meant appealing to a more adult audience, one that would not turn away from the grit of life. In time, HBO would offer exactly these alternatives and generate significant revenues, but it would do more than that. By the end of the twentieth century, some of the main entertainment events in the United States would be smash HBO hits like *Sex and the City* and *The Sopranos*.

The rise of these two shows signaled not merely the triumph of cable television as an important cultural force, but a shift in the taste of the audience. HBO subscribers wanted more provocative and more challenging material than most of the fare offered by prime-time network TV—they wanted to see the boundaries of television stretched. They wanted shows that reflected their own deeper experience with emotional turmoil, with inner and outer violence, with family conflict or with the relations between the sexes. In earlier decades, the Sunday night airwaves had been filled with variety programs like *The Ed*

Sullivan Show or heartwarming sagas like *Bonanza* or, in later years, with news magazine shows like *60 Minutes* or Disney movies. But television had never created any character as complex and multidimensional as Tony Soprano, the New Jersey mobster and star of the show that carried his name. He was Shakespearean in his richness and in the layers of life he brought to the small screen.

If at times *The Sopranos* or *Sex and the City* became too violent or too vulgar or relied too heavily on brutality or sex to hold their audience, there was something very reassuring about the success of these programs. America had grown up enough to look at itself in the mirror known as television—and to do this without blinking. Our society was confronting its own confusion and pain more honestly through the entertainment medium called TV. Cable's pioneers helped make that possible.

"The bigger an executive is in the business world, the easier he is to talk to. That's why he's there." —Bill Daniels

Twenty

Part of cable's growing success was due to a leap in technology that was being perfected in the 1970s. For years the service had been dependent upon costly and cumbersome microwave links that carried the signals from one location to the next. Throughout the sixties and early seventies, engineers worked on a new system that was not limited to one geographic area but could provide a signal to the entire nation: satellite transmission. In 1958, after the Soviet Union had sent *Sputnik*—the first satellite—into space, the United States immediately set out to create its own satellite technology to compete with and surpass the Soviets. While the government was in the business of launching these so-called birds in the race to conquer space, people in the communications industry realized that satellites could be used to transmit media signals far more efficiently than in the past.

A satellite placed 22,300 miles above the earth could be made to orbit at the same speed as the globe's rotation. Telephone, radio, and TV signals could then be beamed from the satellite to a very large section of the earth, known as a "footprint." One satellite could do the work of a multitude of microwave links. The technology was in place for a great advance, but once again the challenge was the U.S. government and getting it to allow the communications business to use these birds for this purpose.

At the 1972 NCTA convention, Time Inc. introduced the first satellite transmission—and showed the audience a brand-new TV channel called HBO. The receiving stations on earth were very expensive, so cable operators did not rush out and start buying them. Instead they waited for a major corporation to lead the way. Gerald Levin, who'd managed to keep HBO running amidst countless problems, now went back to the Time Inc. brass and asked them to support leasing an orbiting satellite for the next five years, at a cost of $8 million. HBO had yet to show a profit and looked as though it might fold at any moment, but Time's management saw the potential of satellite and underwrote the next phase of Levin's plan. Now he needed operators on the ground to buy his product.

In 1975 Levin convinced cable operator Bob Rosencrans to build an earth station—or "downlink"—to receive HBO's signal from space. With Rosencrans on board, Daniels' old partner Monty Rifkin, who ran ATC, signed up for two more downlinks. Until recently satellite had been looked upon as a futuristic idea whose time might not come for many more years, but the technological future was approaching much faster than most people had expected. An upcoming worldwide televised event was about to herald a new era for cable.

With several birds rotating in the heavens and with several earth stations functioning 22,300 miles below them, HBO had looked for the perfect vehicle to launch its latest service. Boxing, which had long played a role in cable's evolution, was about to do so again. The perfect vehicle arrived with the Muhammad Ali–Joe Frazier fight from the Philippines—the ballyhooed "Thriller in Manila." The men's two previous fights had transcended sports and drawn the attention of people with no interest whatsoever in boxing, including many celebrities. Frazier had won the first fight in 1971 in New York, and three years later Ali had taken the second bout in the same city. Now, in late September 1975, they were moving toward their rubber match on the other side of the globe, where the winner would once again reign as the heavyweight champion of the world. This fight had been years in the making, and the hype surrounding it had been building for months. Ali, unparalleled self-promoter and promoter of boxing, had been pushing the fight everywhere. For one night the Thriller in Manila would be the largest single event on the planet. HBO had found the opportunity it had been seeking. The main challenge was whether it could be ready in time for the opening bell.

HBO contracted to send out the fight through Rosencrans' system in Vero Beach–Fort Pierce, Florida. A satellite dish in Fort Pierce would transmit the signal to other systems around the state. Another downlink was planned in Jackson, Mississippi, and a third one was set up in Atlanta. With the fight scheduled for September 30, technical crews put in the equipment only two days before the bout. As the fighters weighed in, the systems were being tested for glitches, and everything looked like a go. Finally, the boxers came together in the center of the ring, touched gloves, and the great fight was on.

With a symmetry that almost reached the level of the incredible—or the magical—the very thing that had first drawn Daniels to television, a boxing match, was being shown twenty-three years later across America via satellite technology. The action was uplinked from Manila to California and then sent east across the United States through AT&T landlines. Using microwave transmitters, it was sent to New York's HBO headquarters and on down to Pennsylvania. From there it was uplinked once more to the Westar satellite operated by Western Union and fed into the dishes in Florida, Mississippi, and Georgia. The entire transmission route covered 93,000 miles and took less than a second. People across the southern U.S. were essentially able to watch the fight as it occurred. Viewers saw a very dramatic bout, with Ali retaining his heavyweight title with a fourteen-round knockout of Frazier. Within days of the fight's closing bell, other satellite systems were being installed around the country.

The tiny cable operations started less than three decades earlier in rural Arkansas, Pennsylvania, and Oregon had grown into technological wonders that allowed people at home to witness live events on the other side of the globe. The world, as prophets in the media had long been predicting, was becoming smaller and smaller, linked together as never before. The global village had arrived. Cable's pioneers were driving this revolution forward, and men like Dolan, Levin, Kahn, and Daniels were helping to wire the earth in an entirely new way.

"Bill had a great rapport with Irving Kahn," says Leonard Tow, who worked with Kahn at TelePrompTer before becoming chairman of Citizens Communications. "Irving was probably the only genius ever in the business. John Malone may have been a financial genius but Irving was a man of vision. Irving always said that his legacy was that his wildest lies all came true. I'm sure that was true with Bill; they oversold a lot. They were passionate and ballsy and committed to a point where they would spend their last dime in pursuit of the objective."

"I always think of Bill as one of the great entrepreneurial spirits that really built the industry," says Chuck Dolan. "He was somebody who was ready to take risks, he had enormous self-confidence, and he understood the profession very, very well. And that's how our industry grew. It didn't grow because of the patronage of the investments of large companies or very wealthy people. It was because of people like Bill who had created their own wealth and brought the industry along. He began the industry in Denver as much as anybody else did. Denver sort of grew around people like Bill and Bob Magness. Denver was the birthplace of the industry. There were other beginnings elsewhere, but the real industry began in Denver."

The triumph of satellite technology was particularly gratifying to Daniels because it accomplished one of his original goals in cable. It brought the medium to people who did not have many choices of entertainment. It helped those in isolated regions and out-of-the-way towns, the same kinds of towns that he'd grown up in. He'd moved a long way from his roots in terms of the connections he'd made, the traveling he'd done, and the money that had passed through his hands. But he'd never forgotten that one of cable's two best friends had always been, as he put it, "Main Street"—the average man or woman out there looking for a little humor or drama or a sporting event to enjoy at the end of a working day, something that would bring them pleasure.

Satellites, he once told The Cable Center, "eliminated the need for expensive and hard-to-get-in-place microwave. Overnight, it made it possible to distribute a television signal from one point to a satellite in space and cover the entire country, far cheaper than we could have ever done with microwave, but more important, instantaneously. If we had to microwave all over the country…it would have taken forever…."

"It made us a better business overnight…. It provided farmers, ranches, uncabled areas with a way to receive additional programming not in the usual broadcast manner."

Twenty-one

As Daniels grew older and more successful—despite the ups and downs of the cable business—he made a point of helping others within his company succeed. His policy had long been to treat them as associates or partners, not as employees, and he gave many people stock when they went to work for him, even when they didn't ask for it. In time, these investments made some of his associates millionaires. In return for his generosity, he expected punctuality, dedication to the company, neatness around the office, and a certain style in how one presented oneself to the world. If he didn't like your shoes, he wouldn't just tell you that, he'd send someone out to get you a new and better-looking pair. He hated it when those he worked with drove any cars that were not American made, and he was not quiet about his opinion. Occasionally, this issue would make him so angry that he'd buy someone a new car without telling the person and then insist they get rid of the old one.

He also demanded high energy and high performance.

"The number one thing that was most impressive about Bill," says Zelbie Trogden, a Security Pacific Bank officer who worked with the Daniels staff for decades, "was his ability to attract excellent executives to work for him. He had the best, and they were totally loyal. We dealt mostly with those people. Bill would come in after the deal was finished, shake hands, and we'd go have a drink. But we had to deal with his financial people, and they were tough: John Saeman, Tom Marinkovich, Buzz Mitchell. They were all tough and had his interests at heart. Again, they were honest and we could depend on what they told us. You couldn't work with Bill if you didn't have integrity. And he didn't like you to wear brown shoes, either. Or a tie that didn't match."

When one is young and just starting out in a profession, nearly everybody has a fantasy of meeting an older and powerful person who sees just how much value and potential you really have. Everyone wants to be "discovered" and then given the chance to grow and shine. In the fantasy, the older individual takes the neophyte under his wing and provides him or her with support and opportunities to fulfill that potential. Daniels not only wanted to play the role of nurturing young men and women in cable, but he had an uncanny instinct for being able to spot talent and pluck it out of the crowd. He also had the confidence in his intuition. He seemed to know ahead of time that this person or that one would eventually became a star in his firm. Down through the years he made a lot of fantasies come true.

In 1973, during his first ever business trip, Steve Halstedt met Daniels in Denver. After graduating from Dartmouth's renowned Tuck School of Business Administration, Halstedt went to the East Coast to work for Travelers Insurance as an analyst. Travelers had a venture-capital investment in Daniels & Associates and sent the young man out West to oversee the deal. Like many others from the East, when Halstedt flew into the Mile High City for his initial visit, he had the impression of entering a desolate wasteland bereft of culture and short on trees. It looked like cowboy country and would probably hold cowboy businessmen as well. Civilization had apparently not crossed the Mississippi River just yet.

He went to the Daniels office and was introduced to the boss. The older man had a presence that Halstedt hadn't expected—and Denver itself didn't look quite so bad from ground level. There were some trees lining the side streets and the parkways. The duo went to lunch at the Cherry Hills Country Club, the site of several nationally famous golf matches, including the 1960 U.S. Open, which was won by Arnold Palmer in dramatic fashion. The town was starting to look better still. While eating, Halstedt gazed out the window at the Rocky Mountains rising up on the western edge of Denver, filling the sky with their majesty and beauty. Like many easterners, he was taken aback by their sheer size and grandeur. There wasn't any view like this back in New England.

After returning to the East Coast, he began receiving notes from Daniels. The notes were mostly about Halstedt himself. Daniels remembered how many children he had and where the young executive had gone to school, and he mentioned these and other parts of his life. The letters enclosed articles from newspapers and magazines that Daniels had read and felt Halstedt should know about. The younger man was amazed at all the attention he was receiving. The letters made him feel important. Someone with clout and real reputation in the cable world, really cared about him in ways that included business but went beyond that. And what had he accomplished in his short career? Halstedt was keenly aware that at the moment he was, as he would later put it, "simply a lowly analyst at Travelers."

He eventually became dissatisfied with his position at the insurance company and began looking for other employment. He studied the world of American business from top to bottom and discovered that in the last half of the 1970s, the two most intriguing industries were cable television and independent oil firms. Then he put together a map of the cities where these two industries were prominent and came up with Denver and New York. Having spent time in the former with Bill Daniels, he decided that Colorado was the more attractive place, so he sent a note to Daniels indicating that he was seeking work. The older man quickly boarded a plane, flew out to Hartford, and hired him to be a vice president of Daniels & Associates, with an emphasis on investment banking. In the process, the boss confided to the new hire that there were several reasons he was bringing him in.

"One reason," recalls Halstedt, "was that I was a royal pain in the ass and he wanted me to be his pain in the ass. Bill was really too nice a guy, and he needed to hire people that had talents he didn't have. Second, I had been a structural iron worker, and he figured anybody crazy enough to get up on a skyscraper and walk out onto those beams was the kind of guy he wanted involved with him. If you look at Bill's background as a Golden Gloves boxer, as a fighter pilot, and as head of the Blue Angels, he had a certain level of risk-taking in his life that he liked to generalize to others.

"And finally, I had been in the military, and if you look at the people Bill surrounded himself with, there were a whole lot of people that had served their country. He appreciated that and remembered it. Not too many years later, I was in my office one day and I received a replica of the Vietnam Memorial with a note from Bill Daniels thanking me for serving my country. Having been ostracized by my peers when I came back from Vietnam, I realized that was the first time anyone had ever said thank you. I was very touched by that. That was the kind of guy he was. He was thoughtful and remembered things. I didn't realize when I was receiving my notes from Bill that he kept up that kind of correspondence with probably five hundred people. He had essentially a machine in place whereby he could remain in contact with a large number of people in such a way that they would feel special. Frankly, in Bill's mind, they were."

Like many other people, Halstedt was amazed by Daniels' selling ability and was particularly struck by a negotiating technique known as the "negative sell." One time Halstedt and his boss were in Los Angeles, where Daniels was trying to get a listing on a cable property that he was eager to sell. The property had been developed by a large real estate company that had installed an extensive cable system into its tract housing. Thousands of homes had already been wired, so this was a very lucrative potential sale for Daniels. The first thing the man running the company told Daniels was that he really didn't think he wanted to let the property go. This was exactly what Daniels did not want to hear, but instead of arguing with him or putting up any resistance, he looked the man right in the eye and said that he was absolutely right to feel this way. He explained how he'd been an advocate of the cable business since 1952 and that it was a great business and during all that time he'd seen the industry do nothing but grow. The man was doing the best possible thing by holding on to his property and waiting to see what the future might bring.

After letting these comments sink in, Daniels went on to say that if the owner should ever change his mind and decide to sell, he should call the Daniels office in Denver because they could get him top price. Then he let the matter rest.

"The guy," recalls Halstedt, "signed immediately with Bill. The guy was trying to negotiate with us so he could get the fee down, but Bill would have none of that. He just told the guy that he shouldn't sell, but the man really wanted to sell. By agreeing with the man, Bill just took the wind right out of his sails in terms of his negotiating. Bill wasn't being negative, but he was negating what the guy was saying to him by coming across and being as straightforward as possible."

The Daniels people got the deal and soon closed it. The old poker player still knew how to play his hand.

Halstedt quickly learned what many other cable executives had discovered about Daniels: he disliked being bothered with the details of many of his operations but much preferred focusing on the big picture. Like any true salesman, the deals he had made were history and the ones that mattered now had not yet been done. He always wanted to do something new—something that had never been created before. The finance people at Daniels & Associates also learned that the boss didn't like to hear too much about dollars and cents that were coming into and going out of their coffers.

"Our chief financial officer," says Halstedt, "wouldn't burden him with our cash position because if you did, he'd spend it! When I joined the company, it was two weeks away from bankruptcy. I knew it because I knew all the numbers. I joined anyway because I thought this was an extraordinary group of people and I absolutely believed we would be able to rescue the situation and turn it into something very positive. Bill and John and the rest of the group did pull together and salvage that situation."

Halstedt recalls another memorable negotiation involving Daniels, where maximum creativity was called for—or at least maximum spontaneity and humor. The ex-combat pilot had always known how to think on his feet, a very useful tool in war and in the world of sales. On this occasion the Daniels team had brought together a buyer and a seller to move them toward a closing, but the talks had reached an impasse. Not only were the negotiations breaking down, the two parties were at one another's throats. Things were getting personal, and yelling and screaming filled the room. Daniels was not supposed to be at this meeting, but he had unexpectedly flown back into town, spent the previous evening with a female friend, and had awakened feeling very optimistic and invigorated. He decided to drop in on the gathering to see if he could offer any assistance. When he arrived, in a chipper mood, he glanced around the room and suddenly understood that things had turned sour—so sour that the deal might collapse.

In a loud voice he made a most unusual announcement:

"Bill," says Halstedt, "looked at both of the parties and said, 'Ain't sex great?'"

Everyone in the room exploded into laughter. The ploy had worked brilliantly.

"He defused the situation," says Halstedt, "and these two guys just

/

broke down because he was right. It was a whole lot better than what they were doing."

Daniels and his staff used humor when they were trying to close a deal or trying to keep the pain of business—and of living—at bay. When Halstedt still worked at Travelers, he received a call from Daniels and his lawyer Bob Nagle, who were in Salt Lake City, staying on the tenth floor of the Hilton Hotel. Daniels had come there to file bankruptcy for the Utah Stars. He'd just lost the primary for governor of Colorado, he was recently separated from Devra, and his business was struggling. The many problems that had been hammering the cable industry for the past half decade had caught up with Daniels & Associates.

Halstedt reconstructs the phone conversation this way: "Bill said, 'I was out on the balcony just a moment ago and looked over the balcony and said to Bob Nagle, 'I think I'm going to jump.' Bob said to him, 'Don't do it! With your luck, you'll live!'

"Bill was fundamentally a positive person. He knew people had faults and shortcomings, and he made allowances for those on a regular basis. People knew that and they knew they could be human around Bill. They didn't have to be perfect, and he would support them. I think that was one of the real key insights Bill had into human nature. Part of the reason for this was because Bill had so many faults himself, but I wouldn't change a thing about him.

"The one theme in his life was 'Was Bill a good boy?' I think his minister at his funeral made the point that he always wanted to be somebody his mother could be proud of. I think he was concerned that some of the very human weaknesses he had would be things she wouldn't be proud of. But I think he was proud of everybody around him."

If Daniels was eager to help ex-military men like Steve Halstedt, he was also quick to recognize the potential women had in business and to give them opportunities. Gail Sermersheim, the senior vice president of affiliate relations at HBO, got her start in cable TV in the mid-sixties working for a small midwestern company called Telesis. At that time she began hearing about a man out in Colorado named Bill Daniels, a name that came up over and over again in conversations about the cable business. He seemed to be everywhere and part of almost every deal. She finally met him at a convention in the early seventies and kept in contact throughout the decade. He watched her progress through the industry and become the chair of the steering committee that founded the organization Women in Cable in 1979. Daniels was one of the first men to take notice of the group and offer it financial support.

Bill Daniels and "Miss Manners," Letitia Baldridge, America's doyenne of social and business etiquette.

"He tried to help us find our way," Sermersheim says, "and encouraged other men in the business to take heed and support this up-and-coming organization. I can't remember how much he gave or contributed, but I know Bill was very supportive. A lot of guys weren't. I always admired his willingness to help others and the unselfish way that he did it. He probably typified, more than any one human being, what made cable such a great industry, and that is both the spirit of entrepreneurship and a willingness to share his thoughts and ideas and help with problems and build something together. Bill personified that spirit and set the tone. I wonder if the industry today could look back with such pride on its history and be able to say, 'We built this together and helped each other,' had it not been for the example that Bill Daniels set from the very beginning."

Pat Thompson, another female pioneer in the cable industry, had worked for Glenn Jones before starting her own company. Several times when she was thinking about quitting the business because it was too hard, Daniels called and encouraged her not to leave.

"I think that in Bill's own perverse way," she says, "he knew how difficult this brokerage business was, and he really did want a woman to succeed in it. I had a fire in my belly to be in this business, and he certainly knew what it was like. I think he had his doubts about me even succeeding because, let's face it— I'm a little bit softer than most of the guys that are in this business. I think in his mind, he was wondering if I could still get the deals done and get the value for your clients, if you had a different manner of doing business than the men. It did work. I don't know how. A man, Bill especially, could get you in doors, get you to meet people, but he really expected you to do everything else on your own."

Women in cable were struck by the dichotomy between Daniels' clear-cut support for their careers and his muddier personal relationships with the opposite sex. In business he strongly promoted women and encouraged them to take risks but in private matters he remained old-fashioned.

"It's not a secret that Bill liked pretty women," says June Travis, who was active in Women in Cable. "After I was widowed, a young man across the street from me took care of my dogs and cats when I was away. When he got a little older, I asked Dan if he would like to go with me to various events. One

Bill Daniels, at his residence "Cableland," sits in front of pictures depicting the aircraft carriers on which he served during World War II.

time I asked him to go to a speech, and I saw Bill there and introduced him to Dan. Later that week we went to another event, and here's Bill again. He says to me 'Good goin', June!' I was so embarrassed that I wouldn't talk to Dan almost all the way home. Only Bill Daniels could assume that I was dating somebody that young!"

Sharon Wilson, an executive at Daniels, was present when someone jokingly asked the boss why he didn't date a managerial-type woman like Sharon. Daniels said, "She's too old, too tall, and too smart!"

Sharon had two adopted children, and the oldest was a boy from Korea. Because Daniels had fought in the Korean War, Wilson worried that he might not accept her son. She took Andrew into Bill's office when the boy was only two. "The next thing I know," says Wilson, "Andrew had walked around the desk and climbed up on Bill's lap. Bill was just in seventh heaven and started showing him all his stuff. He absolutely loved my kids, and one year he sent Andrew a plane to ride around the house for Christmas and another year he got a leather bomber jacket."

When Wilson kiddingly asked Daniels to marry her, he said he would think about it—but wanted a twenty-four-hour trial period!

"He always supported women in the cable industry," says Gail Sermersheim, "which is interesting in a guy who dated around a lot. You might think he had a different opinion of women. It may have been he had so many because he really loved them all!"

He might have loved them all—but that didn't always produce joy in all the women who loved him.

One mid-February day Steve Halstedt was sitting outside the boss's office with Jackie Doty, the secretary for John Saeman, when a woman came in. He could immediately tell from her posture that she wasn't merely irritated or agitated; she was enraged. She rushed up to Jackie's desk and slammed down a heart-shaped box. It was the day after Valentine's—the box still had a corsage tied on it and candy inside. On the outside was written "A Box of Red Hot Love." The woman demanded to see Daniels—right now! Jackie stalled the visitor by asking her what was wrong. While trying to remain calm, she explained that she'd received this nice box of candy for Valentine's and she was quite certain that it was from Daniels, but no card had come with the gift. She wanted to make sure that he'd sent it, so she'd called up the shop and asked them who'd purchased the candy. When they didn't know the answer, she suggested that it might have come from a Bill Daniels.

"At that point," recalls Halstedt, "the shop person told her, 'Oh, yes, it is from Bill Daniels.' The woman said, 'Well, you didn't enclose a card.' The shop person said, 'Look, we sent out twenty-three of them, so you can't expect us to get the card right on all of them.'"

Twenty-two

Cable had created various pioneers and colorful visionaries, but there was a space open for the first person who came along and showed that products could be sold directly through cable television—and sold nationwide. No one had made that breakthrough, until another maverick stepped into this role and expanded the future of cable in exponential ways.

Back in 1970 Ted Turner had bought Channel 17, WTCG in Atlanta, for $2.5 million. At the time WTCG was losing about $1 million a year, but Turner had always liked taking on big challenges and coming from behind to win. His whole life had followed that pattern. A native of Savannah, Georgia, he would claim as an adult that his father had severely beaten him when he was young. Instead of the abuse making him afraid or withdrawn, it instilled in him a bottomless reservoir of risk taking, an outrageous sense that he could do just about anything and never be defeated. In college, he poured this attitude into a love of racing sailboats and became a champion sailor at Brown. A few years later, as he was launching himself into the world of cable television, he won the America's Cup yacht race.

He started his career by taking over his father's outdoor advertising business after he committed suicide when Ted was twenty-four. He was becoming successful in advertising, but he was also bored, so he entered the TV field by purchasing two nearly bankrupt properties, the one in Atlanta and Channel 36 in Charlotte, North Carolina. The stations reached several outlying areas where the reception wasn't very good, until Turner discovered that cable cleared them up. He had a naturally flamboyant personality so he was drawn to the media industry. He liked television and he liked this new technology called cable, and he wanted to become a bigger player in the business.

When he looked around for opportunities, he came to several fundamental conclusions, the same ones Daniels had reached a couple of decades before.

People in the South and the Southeast, just like people throughout America, were eager for more TV programming. These folks liked sports (especially football), but since the TV rights to professional football weren't available, he needed alternatives. Atlanta offered two pro sports teams: the Atlanta Braves baseball team and the NBA's Atlanta Hawks. Neither franchise was much good, but that didn't discourage Turner because he had in mind a novel angle for sports programming. He wanted to offer a major league baseball team's full schedule, via cable TV, not merely to local viewers but to regional viewers through the South, something that had never been attempted before. Would people in small southern towns, who lived thousands of miles away from a major league ballpark, pay a few bucks a month to have this choice?

In 1973 he bought the rights to the Braves games, and two years later he agreed to buy the team. He purchased the right to the Hawks games, putting them on the air locally through his own Channel 17. Using microwave technology he expanded the coverage to the region, and within three years he had 500,000 subscribers. The Hawks never did develop a large fan base outside Atlanta but the Braves were a different story. Perhaps this was because they were often so bad that they generated a kind of sympathy vote from viewers who tuned in to watch their next collapse. Perhaps it was because they were the only baseball to be found on TV during the week in many parts of the country. Or perhaps it was because Turner was a natural-born salesman who would do just about anything to call attention to himself and his product. With characteristic chutzpah, he labeled the Braves "America's Team" and endlessly promoted them. He stationed a mock Indian in the ballpark—named "Chief Noc-a-Homa"—and had him celebrate whenever the Braves hit a home run. Once, after a Braves player hit one out of the park and was rounding the bases, Turner jumped out of his seat and ran out onto the field, accompanying the slugger from third to home plate. This didn't make his team a winner, but it was great publicity. The Braves were slowly building a following that stretched all across the South. Now Turner wondered if he could go national.

Would viewers in places like Waco or Albuquerque or Des Moines be interested in following the Braves? That was only one question that needed to be answered. A second one was technological. The microwave system that supported Channel 17 was awkward, expensive, and limited in reach. Like other cable visionaries, Turner knew there had to be a better way to broadcast over long distances, but it hadn't quite arrived.

With the growing success of Channel 17, he was making a name for himself in cable—the perfect venue for Turner. He positioned himself as the underdog fighting against huge forces of evil (the networks, regulators, and other enemies of the people), and he relished this role. He loved taking verbal jabs at the powers that be, and he quickly became a favorite on the cable speakers' circuit. He was always good for twenty minutes of after-dinner humor and irreverence. In the mid-seventies, he was still largely a regional figure looking for his next break when he learned about satellite broadcasting. He was certain that the bird would allow him to go national in a big way—if

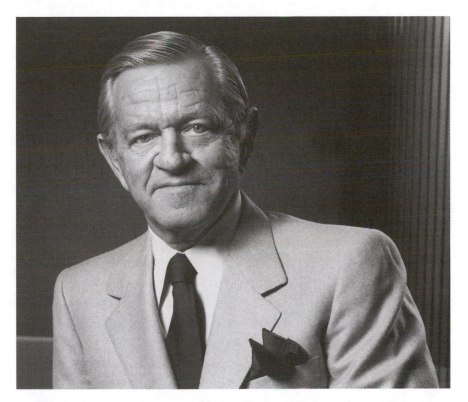

"Give back to the world that gives so much to you. And if it happens to make you feel good to give, that's all right. Feeling good is the one ulterior motive that's acceptable."
—*Bill Daniels*

he could only convince the federal government to give him a shot at selling his system all over the country. While looking for advice and financial backing, he took his salesman's skills to Washington, where he lobbied the FCC.

In 1975, as satellite TV was bringing America the Ali–Frazier fight, Turner made contact with American Television Communications Corp., one of the companies that would broadcast the Thriller in Manila. ATC was run by former Daniels' employee Monty Rifkin, who'd been hearing about Turner and some of his promotional stunts. Hearing about him was one thing, but meeting him in person was something else.

"Shortly after I came to ATC, Ted Turner wanted to come see us," says Tyrgve Myhren. He worked under Rifkin at ATC before becoming the CEO. "We told him that Monty and I would meet him at the TWA club room at Stapleton Airport in Denver. We talked in this private room at the club room, but unfortunately it had louvered doors on each side. Of course, Ted was using the F word every third word—he was really in his prime. When we walked out, we're looking around to see if there was anyone we knew because they'd never have any respect for us again!"

Turner was interested not only in showing Braves ball games across the country but in launching another venture—a twenty-four-hour news network, unlike anything the TV world had ever seen. Until now news programs had come on in the evenings, with the five or six o'clock local and national network shows and then with the local news again at ten or eleven P.M. The news filled a hallowed time slot on American television, and news-gathering teams ran on cycles geared to fit these slots. Everything in television journalism was scheduled to meet the evening deadlines. That was how it had always been done, and most people saw no reason to change it. The notion of showing the news around the clock—or the notion that people would be interested in watching news programs throughout the day—was a radical break from tradition. But then Turner was anything but conventional.

When he met with Rifkin and Myhren at the Denver Airport, he laid out his startling plans for the future, and he wanted ATC to support him by carrying his network on their cable systems. The idea of backing Turner intrigued the men but made them nervous.

"I remember being in the car," Myhren recalls, "and Monty saying, 'God, I just don't know if we should do this thing.' The financial commitment was one thing, and also Ted was such a head case. We talked about it and came to the joint conclusion that we really didn't have a hell of a lot else [to offer the viewing public]. In any event, if he was willing to give it a shot, we would take the risk on our side.

"Before we did it, we visited Ted in Atlanta. We were to meet him at his office at seven-thirty at the stadium, and his office was dark but we thought he would be there shortly. He arrived but he didn't look good. He switched on some lights and he had scabs on the side of his face and his ears were all chewed up and his chin was a mess—caked blood and dirt. I said, 'Ted, what happened?' Natural thing to say. He said, 'Oh well, the Phillies were in last night and the goddamn players don't play hard enough, you pay 'em too much.' He went off on a monologue and finally said he'd decided to run some promotions. One of the promotions they ran was to have a Brave and a Philly, one start from third and one start from first, with a ball right by the bag and without using arms or hands or their feet, get the ball to home plate. The Braves guy lost badly to the guy from the Phillies, and so Ted said, 'I'll go out and beat him.' So Ted came out and raced one of the Phillies and beat him! With his face—on the ground! And who knows what he did after that, rather than getting medical attention! Oh, jeez—Monty and I were saying, 'Oh, my God, we're going to invest with this guy!' But we decided to do it."

The federal government couldn't resist Turner, either. After much persuasion on his part, the feds allowed him to distribute his Atlanta station to cable operators around America. Despite winning this approval, virtually no one thought Turner's grandiose plan of national distribution would work. When he offered a piece of his new business to numerous people across the country, they all said no. But, in the best spirit of cable TV, he persevered, getting ready to make broadcasting history.

On December 17, 1976, after changing the station's name to WTBS—the Turner Broadcasting System—he launched his new service on Satcom I. WTBS was up and running, yet he had no idea if anyone outside Georgia was watching. The only way to find out was to send forth a steady flow of ads for kitschy items like Ginzu knives and K-Tel knitters, and then see if anyone responded. The answer came fast. Turner's office was soon deluged with orders for these products from throughout the South and East Coast to out West. Not only were Americans everywhere tuning in, they were eager to get their hands on this merchandise. Nothing like it had ever happened before: a local TV station, hooked up to the bird and reaching into homes across the nation, was creating a sizable audience that didn't care where the programming originated. It just wanted the chance to watch more shows or more ball games—and to buy the knives and knitters that appeared on their TV screens. Turner had tapped into an audience starving for more stimulation.

He now took his campaign to Madison Avenue, where he wanted to generate expensive ads for more respectable products. This again was a revolutionary idea. Cable had initially been conceived of as a service for which a subscriber paid a monthly fee. The networks sold costly ads for mainstream products through high-powered Madison Avenue firms. These ads offered the public high-end merchandise, but they also broke up the flow of programming. Cable, on the other hand, broadcast shows uninterrupted by advertising. Turner saw no reason why this couldn't be changed. Since cable viewers were responding so well to his spots for Ginzu knives, the world of major advertising would surely fall in line with this concept.

When he first approached the ad moguls, they were hesitant to embrace either the man or his idea. But Ted Turner was impossible to ignore and essentially impossible to resist—and besides, he had the numbers to back up his claims. After six months of pounding on their doors, one ad agency said yes and the barrier fell. Cable was now in the business of competing for ad space with the networks and showing them during programming. Like Monty Rifkin and the federal government, Madison Avenue had been able to hold Turner back for only so long. He had triumphed with an entirely new vision for cable—and he was just getting started.

If Braves baseball games could find a following out there in the hinterlands, weren't people ready to watch the news twenty-four hours a day? Most TV executives thought this idea was preposterous, but one individual was certain that it would work. He was prejudiced in that direction because he himself had been a news junkie for the past several decades. He wanted to know everything that was happening everywhere in America and across the globe—and he wanted to know about it right now. Bill Daniels demanded that his morning papers be delivered by five A.M., but even that wasn't early enough for him. He'd always wished that when he awoke at four or four-thirty and was preparing to drink his first cup of coffee and light his first cigarette that he could sit down in front of a live TV news program and watch the latest reports from New York or Moscow or Hong Kong or Cairo. Then he would really feel that he was informed of the freshest developments in the world as he prepared to take on the day.

Like most people who watched television, he had no technical understanding of how the medium actually worked. And he was hell to deal with when his TV broke down or his channel changer went out at two A.M. He would get on the phone and demand that an employee get out of bed and come to his home and immediately fix the problem. (People who worked for Daniels instantly learned that the worst thing you could say to the boss when he asked you to do something was, "Wait a moment," because he never had a moment to wait.) Despite his mechanical clumsiness, he did know one thing. He understood that his fellow citizens were terribly curious about other people and the globe they were living on. Americans wanted all the media alternatives and viewing options that the communications industry could give to them. Daniels believed that deep down his countrymen and countrywomen were news junkies, just like himself, and they were ready for a twenty-four-hour-a-day news source— regardless of what anyone else said. When he learned that Ted Turner was trying to start a round-the-clock news service called Cable News Network [CNN], Daniels was excited both as a consumer and an investor.

"I started a dialogue with Turner in late '79," says John Saeman, "at which time he identified a need for ten million dollars to launch the Cable News Network. He was very open to what structure that took, because at that point he was desperate for the ten million and his banks were unwilling to advance him the money. Numerous meetings took place in which our colleague Bruce Dickinson was helping us put together the detail we needed to take to the marketplace. Both Bill and I had committed one million dollars to that ten-million-dollar financing which was coming about as a result of the sale of our company called Daniels Properties, Inc."

To facilitate the deal, Bruce Dickinson became more heavily involved. He had been a commercial banker before going to work for Daniels & Associates in April 1980. During his first month on the job, the man in charge asked him to look into the CNN investment, and initially Dickinson was skeptical. Banks were refusing to loan Turner money for his new venture. He'd obviously had some success in cable but he was so unpredictable. He scared off many investors. His company was carrying a lot of debt, and in addition to that he wanted to compete head-to-head with the most sacred cows of the news business: the ABC, CBS, and NBC networks. Each of them was spending a whopping $100 million a year just to put their evening news programs on the air. Turner figured that he could spend less and offer much more: a round-the-clock news service for $30 million annually.

Daniels had known Turner since his days of hanging out with the racing crowd and asking Turner to talk Fidel Castro into letting some of the drivers hunt for treasure near Havana. That adventure had gone nowhere, but Daniels had faith in Turner as a bold entrepreneur. Dickinson, though, was not sold on the concept of twenty-four-hour news.

"I came back the first time after looking at all the numbers," Dickinson recalls, "and said, 'Bill, this is a very, very risky investment. He has a lot of debt already and he's grown very rapidly. If this isn't successful, it's quite possible he'll have to go out of business.' Bill looked me in the eye and said, 'Bruce, I know this is going to be a tremendous success. Find a way to make this happen.'"

With these marching orders, Dickinson went back to the numbers and came up with a plan. Daniels & Associates would effectively help loan Turner $10 million, through what was called a "subordinated debt placement."

"I figured that if everything went to hell in a hand basket," says Dickinson, "Turner could sell his TV stations and pay off his debt. But I also said, 'Let's try and get the debt convertible into equity if it's a real big success.'"

Says John Saeman: "Long story short, we were unsuccessful in putting together the ten-million-dollar offering that Ted needed, but fortunately for him, his banks ultimately agreed to allow him to go ahead and increase the line by ten million to enable him to finance Cable News Network from inside. Bill and I attended the closing of our sale of Daniels Properties, Inc., to the Newhouse family in New York on May 31 and then immediately flew to

Atlanta to be with Ted for the launch of CNN on June 1, 1980. The bottom line was that Bill did not become a shareholder of Cable News Network or of Turner at that point."

In June 1980, CNN debuted with 1.7 million subscribers. By the end of 1981, it had ten million subscribers and was moving in exactly the direction Daniels had predicted it would.

"When CNN came along," says Tyrgve Myhren of American Television Communications, "Bill was a huge supporter of getting it off the ground. We all needed it desperately. On the other hand, we didn't want anything that was an out-and-out bust. We worried a lot about it, along with our worries about Ted, but the financial backers put it together gorgeously."

But before it was gorgeous, CNN nearly died.

Says Julia Sprunt, an executive at Turner in the early eighties, "When we were furiously fighting for survival at Turner, CNN almost bankrupted Ted personally. There were days when we were told not to cash our paychecks. This was 1980 to 1983—we didn't know if we were going to survive. Just when we knew we were going to make it, Westinghouse comes out with Satellite News Channel. That was a bloody battle between our company and this big corporate behemoth. Nobody was winning. It was bleeding both companies, and the industry didn't need two news channels. Something had to give, and it would have been CNN.

"It was Bill Daniels who actually brought Dan Ritchie from Westinghouse and Ted Turner together and actually mediated the settlement. In those last days before Bill stepped in, there were all kinds of business plans going on behind the scenes about shutting down, or paring it down, or changing it because we couldn't exist in that kind of environment. Bill was instrumental in making sure CNN stayed on the table, healthy and strong. It was only Bill Daniels, and he was the only one who could have gotten that done. Ted will tell you how Bill actually introduced Ted around the industry. It took great vision on Ted's part, but it was people like Bill Daniels that continued to support Ted anytime he needed it, and in every way he needed it, that made it possible for Ted to survive.

"Bill made a point of showing me that every person is important and treating every person like they're special. He taught me very early on at our first meeting if you see somebody you want to know, you have to make the effort because you may never get the opportunity again. He tracked me down that way. He didn't know me and didn't know how all this would turn out, and yet he changed my life. He had the most profound influence on my life because he took a chance. If you see somebody, you need to make the effort because you may never get another opportunity. Our lives may have passed and I would never have met him. I think he showed me curiosity and to follow your instincts and to research it—this is what makes him so special."

A few years after launching CNN, Turner bought the MGM film library and consequently needed funds badly. He went looking for backers.

"Turner," says John Saeman, "took the MGM film library and turned it into additional product for television, specifically cable systems, and in this case under the umbrella of Turner Network Television [TNT], his newest venture. The movie library was helpful financially, but Ted had reached consid-

Cable colleague Ted Turner skewers Bill Daniels at a fundraising roast.

erably and put his company at risk. The cable industry became gravely concerned about his economic viability. That viability was critical to our industry because Turner represented a number of products that had become very popular on our cable systems, such as WTBS out of Atlanta, CNN, Headline News, and TNT. The impact of Ted on the cable industry and the cable operator was significant.

"Recognizing this concern, John Malone led an effort to rescue Turner. Bill was an important part of that and became one of the industry cheerleaders to make the investment to save Turner. The bailout effort was complete and Bill was a player. He never hesitated or failed to provide positive comments and encouragement."

"Bill helped make it work," says Turner. "Basically, after he got involved, the major cable operators called around and said they better bail Turner out, so we had a meeting and they bailed me out. They made a strategic investment—they made a lot of money off it. It wasn't like anybody was given charity."

"Bill's judgment," says Bruce Dickinson, "was the overriding factor in Daniels & Associates making this investment. Both his intuition about people and his vision—they were just phenomenal. In my mind, his two strongest characteristics."

With CNN on the airwaves and its funding stabilized, Turner started to round the corner of becoming a media magnate. In time his empire would include the domestic and international arms of the Cable News Network (CNN); the Cartoon Network; Headline News; TBS Superstation; Turner Classic Movies (TCM), after he bought the MGM library of film and television properties; Turner Network Television (TNT); CNN/Sports Illustrated; as well as those he became associated with after Time Inc. bought Turner Broadcasting, HBO, Cinemax, Warner Brothers International Networks, and Time Warner's interests in Comedy Central and Court TV. CNN International, which was launched in 1985, was eventually distributed in more than two hundred countries worldwide.

In 1991, in a gesture that revealed just how large an industry cable had become and how significant its influence now was, Ted Turner was designated *Time* magazine's Man of the Year.

Twenty-three

Once WTBS began generating significant revenues through advertising, other ad-supported cable stations started appearing on the dial. Bob Rosencrans combined with Madison Square Garden to create the MSG Network, which debuted on satellite in April 1977. At first it relied heavily on sporting events for content but would later expand into children's shows and other programming. MSG, like other cable upstarts, now had two income streams, one from subscriptions and one from advertisers. With more shows to offer viewers and more viewers to offer advertisers, cable could charge more for its service and charge advertisers more for their spots. The industry was starting to challenge the networks at their own game and to eat away at their ad revenues and their audience. Although gathering momentum each year throughout the late seventies, cable had yet to establish either a broad market penetration or a clear-cut identity throughout the nation.

One young man—whose path had crossed Bill Daniels' and was about to cross Rosencrans'—was determined to change that. Although no one had realized it when Brian Lamb had been quietly working in the Office of Telecommunications Policy for the Nixon White House, the nondescript fellow from Indiana, who always seemed to ask more questions than deliver opinions himself, was becoming a cable player. In the mid-seventies, he left his federal job and went to work as a reporter for cable trade publisher Bob Titsch and his magazine *Cable Vision*. Ever since meeting Daniels when working for the president, Lamb had remained keenly aware of his activities in the industry. He was again reminded of the cable broker when Daniels took out big ads in the trades—ads explaining to readers his cable philosophy and why they should pay attention to his ideas (the boldness of these advertisements made a great impression on the self-effacing Lamb). The young reporter might have looked retiring, and he may have only been making a thousand dollars a month, but he'd steadfastly studied Daniels and other successful men in the communications industry and he had some large ambitions of his own.

While at the magazine, he saw a void in the cable business that dovetailed perfectly with the lack of information about government that he'd been increasingly aware of during the past decade. When he talked about this with Bob Titsch, his employer told him that he could use part of his time at *Cable Vision* trying to develop a cable network devoted to public affairs. Titsch came up with $15,000 to fund the idea, and Lamb bought a video camera and a tape machine. Bob Rosencrans gave him another $25,000 to keep the project running, and encouraged Lamb by saying that he wanted to put this kind of programming on his satellite. With a morale boost and a little cash behind him, Lamb carried the TV equipment up and down the halls of Congress, looking for politicians to interview. When he found someone who would talk to him, he taped them on camera and then shipped the interview to the cable system in the district in which the congressman or congresswoman served. One day in the fall of 1977, while doing this in the office of U.S. Representative Lionel Van Deerlin, a California Democrat, the ever-observant Lamb noticed that Van Deerlin had installed a camera near his desk—a camera that constantly showed him what was taking place on the floor of the House.

In a burst of inspiration, Lamb had found his calling. He wanted to televise the proceedings of the House and feed it live to several hundred cable outlets around the nation. The people of the United States would no longer have to rely on newspapers or magazines or broadcast networks to tell them what went on inside their own government. They could have direct access to the process of democracy—virtually around the clock—and could keep an eye on their leaders while doing chores at home. The House was soon presented with this revolutionary idea and voted 325–80 to approve it. Before the end of 1977, twenty-two cable companies from across the country pledged nearly half a million dollars to fund the creation of the Cable Satellite Public Affairs Network—or C-SPAN. The service was born on May 19, 1979, and was shown via Rosencrans' MSG satellite network (just as Rosencrans was in the process of changing the MSG name to USA Network).

Initially, Lamb wondered if anyone was watching the new station, but some of his doubts were quelled after C-SPAN featured former Secretary of

State Henry Kissinger at a Republican governors conference in Texas. Before Kissinger went on the air, Lamb got the idea of putting the station's number up on the screen and inviting viewers to phone in and make a comment on his speech. He hoped they would receive at least some response, and he was completely taken aback when the phones began ringing nonstop. He knew he was definitely tapping into the viewers' hunger for more information, so he decided to take the C-SPAN concept a step further. He offered the first call-in TV talk show, in which those who'd been following legislative issues could phone the network and make their views known.

Lamb's doubts were finally laid to rest a few years later when he was on the air interviewing students from an organization called CloseUp. This nonprofit group brought young people to Washington to meet politicians and learn more about government. Some of those on the program that evening had just been speaking with President Reagan. During the show a local call came in from the D.C. area, and Lamb at first ignored it because he always tried to give priority to those who were phoning long distance. He couldn't ignore it after his co-workers held up a sign reading, "TAKE THIS CALL NOW."

President Reagan himself was on the line, wanting to make a comment about CloseUp. Lamb, doing his best to hide his surprise, talked with the president in his unflappable professional mode. When the chief executive hung up, Lamb knew for sure that *somebody* out there was watching the network, and it was having an impact on the viewing public. Until now, cable TV had largely been seen as an outlet for more sports coverage or more entertainment, but Lamb was changing that perception week by week. If a viewer wanted to know what those in power were actually doing on the job, the best place to turn for this coverage was not the broadcast networks but C-SPAN. The station wasn't simply competing with the networks in the news game—it was attracting an audience and making news itself.

C-SPAN (and then later C-SPAN 2) would eventually feature congressional speeches and debates, live coverage of political demonstrations and other events, talk shows about current affairs, in-depth interviews with authors, and a variety of other public-interest shows. It would become the network of record about the inner workings of the House and Senate. Of course, Bill Daniels had been banging the drums for years with this message: if cable TV

"You have to be solid and upstanding in your principles and ideals. You must be strong in the boardroom and shrewd in negotiations. But also make it a point to be compassionate and understanding." —Bill Daniels

could offer politicians an outlet for their views, then Washington, D.C., would be much friendlier to the industry. But it was Brian Lamb who turned this concept into reality. Like many other cable ventures, the new channel would struggle for years on a shoestring budget, but in time it would be firmly established on the dial, with Lamb himself assuming the chairmanship of the C-SPAN network.

By the end of the seventies, the dark ages of cable were beginning to lift, and some light—as well as some profits—were starting to seep through. The 1976 election of Democratic President Jimmy Carter had been a boost for the industry. In the past, Democrats had tended to favor regulation of cable and Republicans had opposed such interference, but Carter was never entirely predictable in any policy area. A former small businessman himself, he understood the entrepreneurial instinct and opposed many governmental restrictions on free enterprise. Competition, he believed, would settle most issues in the marketplace. His rise to power signified a change that in the next few years would bring great benefits to cable.

Since its inception, cable had faced one seemingly irreconcilable conflict. Cable operators and cable brokers—with Bill Daniels first among them—had always believed that they had the right to pull broadcasters' signals out of the air (for nothing) and charge patrons to watch these programs over their systems. Broadcasters had felt just the opposite and with great vehemence: no operator, they felt, should be able to air their programs without paying a copyright fee to both the stations and those who produced the content. When this issue had finally come before the Supreme Court in 1968, the nine justices had thrown it back into the Congress' lap, stating that it was not a judicial dispute, but a congressional one. Congress had spent years trying to resolve the conflict, and throughout this time broadcasters had used the issue as leverage to regulate cable. All of this contributed to the atmosphere of limiting cable in the late sixties and early seventies, until finally Congress reached a compromise solution. Cable operators would pay a fee to copyright holders and in return would have the right to carry the broadcasters' signals.

This was a victory of sorts and was soon followed by another one, when cable operators were granted the right to use phone or utility company poles to string their wire. The operators paid another fee for this privilege. But this ruling helped clarify trouble areas that had destabilized the industry for decades. This in turn made banks and other financial institutions friendlier to operators seeking long-term loans. The man behind the legislation that settled the dispute over the cable wire was a young congressman from Denver, Tim Wirth, a Democrat who'd come to Washington in 1974. Backed by money from local cable businesses, including Daniels & Associates, Wirth had barely won the seat and would never forget who'd helped him. He soon became a member of the House Telecommunications Subcommittee. From there, he would begin the long process of creating legislation that would eventually deregulate cable. "Because of a lot of changes in Congress," says Wirth, "I became chairman of a very influential subcommittee on communications in my third term, which is very unusual. That had a lot to do with the interests in Colorado, particularly the cable television industry, which was headquartered in Denver at the time. It was Bob Magness, Tryg Myhren, Bill Daniels, and John Malone who were the key people in the industry and they were all in Denver, so I got to know them all. I was an advocate for unleashing cable, giving it opportunities, trying to build up the networks, and give cable a chance. Bill was a believer. His politics were a lot different from mine, but he really cared. It wasn't a partisan thing but a deep belief or care for the world. It wasn't false or ideological or brittle but just a deep concern. Couple that with his warmth and that combination I found incredibly appealing."

Cable was not winning every battle, but was making progress in the larger war to establish itself as a permanent—and profitable—segment of the communications business. While these skirmishes were being fought in Washington, the industry itself was undergoing a burst of expansion on the programming side. Chicago's WGN, New York's WOR, and Oakland's KTVU all followed Ted Turner's Atlanta superstation concept and used satellite technology to broadcast their product into homes around the nation. Cable now had five channels featuring uncut movies: HBO, Galavision, Showtime, The Movie Channel, and Home Theater Network. C-SPAN and CNN were offering full-time news broadcasts or educational programming, and children's TV had made its debut on Calliope. The MSG network presented sports, and three other services were devoted to evangelical Christianity: the Trinity Broadcasting Network, PTL (People That Love), and the Christian Broadcasting Network. The original idea of cable's visionaries—that this new medium would succeed by offering genuine alternatives to the three old-line networks—was becoming a reality. At the end of the seventies, nearly 15 million (or 20 percent) of American homes were receiving programming through cable services, and some of these systems were turning a profit. Between 1977 and 1978, cable revenues climbed a whopping 25 percent, to $3.5 billion.

With numbers like this, large American corporations and Wall Street began paying attention to what had been perceived as a minor industry with an uncertain future. From 1979 to 1981, the price of cable shares doubled, and the giants of free enterprise, with names like Time Inc., American Express, Group W, Times Mirror, Warner, Westinghouse, and Hearst began buying into the cable business. Paramount Pictures, MCA, and Time Inc. bought the USA Network. Viacom International launched Showtime. As the head of Warner, Steve Ross wanted to find a TV outlet for his company's movie library, and his executives soon developed Nickelodeon and The Movie Channel. But Ross was looking for something to make a bigger splash.

Two Warner employees, John Lack and Bob Pittman, heard that major record companies were trying out a new way to promote their rock 'n' roll product: they were offering short videos to go along with the most popular songs from albums. Warner began featuring these videos on a show called *Pop Clips*. It wasn't a very catchy name, but young viewers everywhere started tuning in. Warner was on to something. Kids across America devoured the music clips, then went out and bought the songs they'd just heard. They also bought the clothes the performers wore, the cars they drove in the videos, and anything else that was associated with rock stars. The show made instant TV stars out of obscure musicians. It had everything for success except for one thing: it needed a hipper name. The execs put their heads together and came up with another clunky handle—Music Television. Yet when shortened to MTV, it sounded perfect.

On August 1, 1981, MTV entered the world via satellite transmission, and the world would never be quite the same. The baby boom generation (and those born after the boomers), who had made the Beatles and Rolling Stones international superstars, were now altering the look and sound of television. Instead of waiting for a variety show to offer a musical group playing its latest hit, they were flipping on MTV twenty-four hours a day. Instant gratification was becoming a way of life. The early videos were amateurish, but in time rock clips would evolve into a (sometimes scandalous) art form of their own. Church leaders and politicians who found rock music dangerous now had something new to fear. MTV was the devil's handiwork and would only lower America's tumbling moral standards.

Cable TV was not simply offering entertainment but was becoming part of the social, cultural, and political landscape of the United States. It was opening up debate about the role of television—and about freedom of expression itself.

Twenty-four

It soon became very fashionable to attend the MTV Music Awards in Los Angeles, even among older people who didn't like rock 'n' roll. On one occasion Daniels was dating a young woman who greatly desired to go to the ceremony, which always featured the absolutely hippest crowd that L.A. could assemble. The only problem was that the young woman was involved with somebody who had no interest in rock or in those who created it (Daniels was also beginning to experience hearing troubles that would eventually leave him nearly deaf). He came from an earlier generation, where people danced while holding one another and men did not wear ponytails or pierce their ears; one of his deepest convictions was that those who worked for him could not wear facial hair, let alone have strands running down their backs. While he could instantly see the money-making possibilities of MTV, he didn't want to get near the songs the network played. At the same time, he was an open-minded man, a practical and a generous man who didn't want to stand in the way of his paramour having a good time.

"Bill called me and wanted me to take his girlfriend to the MTV awards ceremony," says Julian Quattlebaum, an attorney at Daniels' company. "She was a Marilyn Monroe impersonator. I think she was from Louisiana or something. She had basically browbeaten Bill into taking her out there in the Learjet. He was willing to fly her out there, but that was as far as he was going to go. So he called me and wanted me to take her. I told him there was no favor I wouldn't do for him, but I had already promised my wife that I would take her."

With Quattlebaum bowing out, another Daniels executive, Bob Russo, ended up accompanying the young woman in the jet. The woman made an indelible impression on Quattlebaum.

"She was something else," the lawyer says, "a real sweet gal, but she wasn't wound too tight. We showed up at the Universal Amphitheater, and here's this gal dressed up in some kind of bustier. She had her credit card sticking out of one side of her bustier under her arm. She literally did not have her breasts completely covered by this thing, and she was hanging out of this bustier. Poor Bob Russo."

Besides jumping on a Learjet and taking spur-of-the-moment trips to L.A. with young blondes on their arms, other perks came with working at Daniels & Associates. One was money. The boss liked nothing better than making it, spending it, and spreading it around to those who were in business with him. If he was in many regards a common man who'd stayed close to his humble roots, he also occasionally enjoyed acting the king or the godfather to all of those around him (he never wanted anyone to forget that when push came to shove, he and no one else was the boss). One of his favorite gestures was handing out little pillows to his associates—pillows with several words cross-stitched across the face of them.

"Give me equity," they read, "or give me death."

"In the late seventies," says Julian Quattlebaum, "I'd been practicing at a law firm in Denver for quite some time. One of the earliest matters I worked on was the application before the Alaska Public Utilities Commission for the franchise that served Anchorage, Alaska. Several years later, when Bill sold the Anchorage system, I did quite a bit of work on that too. I woke up the morning after the sale and read in the paper how even the secretaries working for Bill had gotten generous checks—all I got was my salary as an associate at the law firm! I decided right then and there that maybe I really ought to be working for Bill."

He wasn't the only one with that thought. Quattlebaum soon received a call from Bob Nagle, an attorney at Daniels, who asked if he would be interested in changing jobs.

"It took me," he recalls, "about five seconds to say yes. I came over to Daniels, which was by any measure on the face of the planet, the best office in the entire state of Colorado, maybe the entire western United States at the time."

It was a good office in part because of the physical setting—a spectacular new building in Denver's fashionable Cherry Creek neighborhood and shopping district. But it was also a good office because it generated a feeling of optimism and ever-expanding success—the very same qualities that Daniels himself embodied, that he saw in the cable business, and that he most wanted to see in those who worked for him. Why shouldn't they be optimistic? After three decades in cable, Daniels' impact on the industry was reaching its crescendo. His roots in Denver had made the Mile High City the "cable capital of the world." Eight of the largest cable companies in the United States were located in Denver. The three major trade journals were published there as well. Daniels & Associates operated twenty-six cable systems in a dozen states and had arranged the financing for other systems from coast to coast. The company was credited with developing at least half of America's fifty biggest cable operations and with serving as the broker for $3.5 billion worth of property. In 1981 Daniels & Associates participated in an estimated 80 percent of the cable deals closed nationwide. Having achieved this kind of success, Daniels naturally wanted to build a showcase headquarters not just for himself and his employees, but also for the cable industry.

Memories of Bill Daniels "flyboy" days were kept vivid when he acquired the corporate Learjet "Cablevision Tool."

The new Daniels building made a great impression on almost everyone who worked there and perhaps an even greater one on those who visited the company. A big white satellite dish sat out front, where it received TV signals from the thirteen satellites that were orbiting the earth. The receptionist at the Daniels Communication Center, as the building was called, was not quite a human being, but rather a tall beige-colored cylinder standing alone in the middle of the lobby. Instead of a mouth, the cylinder held a blank TV screen. When a visitor pushed a button, an actual human—a woman sitting three floors above the lobby—appeared on the screen and welcomed you to Daniels & Associates and into the cable age. You were invited to come upstairs and make yourself at home in the plush surroundings that represented part of Bill Daniels' philosophy about work. He'd spent a colossal $89,500 on the furnishings and floor space of *each* person who worked for him. He'd decorated the office with very colorful, oddly shaped furniture that one reporter described as looking "strangely edible, like exotic pieces of fruit." One of Daniels' most quoted mottos, which had been chiseled into a column in the lobby, was evident everywhere.

"The best," it read, "is good enough for me."

In the basement of the building was a workout center, complete with weight-training and aerobic equipment. Upstairs, Daniels' office featured pictures of the past six presidents, photos of several astronauts, and a wide variety of elephant figurines (he collected the pachyderms from everywhere, to show his unshakable Republican leanings). The executive suite had a dining room filled with crystal and china and this led into a conference room holding an eight-by-fourteen-foot electronic table. People who did not believe in the magnificence of the future of the communications industry were brought into this room to receive the faith. Push a button and an oval in the center of the table rose like a periscope and offered six mini-Sony TVs that could offer virtually every program being transmitted by satellite anywhere in the world. Push another button and wall panels were removed, video screens dropped from the ceiling, and slide shows or movies, accompanied by stereo sound, filled the room.

The building left some people breathless.

"It had," says Julian Quattlebaum, "a racquetball court and a gym—back then pretty much unheard of—and a sauna, hot tub, and a conference table where the middle popped up with television monitors all the way around, and it had electronic window shades. And a chef and a televised receptionist. There was just nothing like that anywhere else."

Daniels expected his employees to use the gym about an hour a day, working out and interacting there in ways that differed from sluggishly sitting behind a desk for seven or eight hours and never getting their blood flowing or their hearts pumping. He wanted them to vary their routines and to get up and move. He wanted them to relax and spend time daydreaming or fantasizing about the things that he was certain would soon be part of the communications future—even though many others still doubted it. Dreams like five hundred cable channels on the menu rather than the thirty-two or so that were now available; things like being able to shop directly from a TV screen; things like televised up-to-the-second stock market reports from Wall Street; things like video games for kids; and even something called electronic mail, where you could type a message onto a computer monitor and someone connected to you via a telephone line that was connected to another computer could instantly receive the message and send one back to you! That really was daydreaming.

Bill Daniels with pilot Mark Calkins.

Daniels wanted his people to envision a technological future that would make the present look primitive by comparison. If you could imagine it, he believed, there was no reason you couldn't build it and sell it and make money in the process. The past didn't have to control and define what was possible today or tomorrow.

"What I remember the most," says Quattlebaum, "was Bill's enlightened attitude about letting people have fun while they work. Work doesn't have to be miserable, and people could actually be more productive if they felt good about where they were working and how they were working."

The boss's idea of fun included not just exercise and fantasizing about the future, but a large dose of spontaneity.

"In the mid-eighties," says another Daniels employee Chuck Kersch, "we were having a birthday party for Bill on the roof of the new building. He always wore red, white, and blue on his birthday, but that day he had on a pair of blue slacks and a white golf shirt. Someone asked him, 'Where was the red?' Bill stood up on a chair, dropped his pants, and showed his red underwear. At which time Jim Ruybal, who was in charge of human resources, jumped up, turned white, and said, 'Bill, there'll be a sexual harassment lawsuit!' Bill said, 'Hell, there was a time when it used to be a fringe benefit when I dropped my drawers.'"

Before Terry Marinkovich's husband, Tom, became the chief financial officer at Daniels, he'd worked at the staid and very established Price Waterhouse accounting firm. His wife, who had no idea what the cable TV industry was like, was quite apprehensive about her husband leaving such a reputable place for a smaller office in an relatively new and unknown field. At the same time, she wanted to be supportive of her husband's desire for a new business opportunity.

"He took a cut in pay to go to Daniels," she recalls, "but I thought we could still manage. He was going from a very conservative group to something totally different. I remember the opening of the new building, where everybody jumped in the hot tub with no clothes on and I'm thinking, 'Oh, my God! What did Tom get into?' Then I got to know the people and I fell in love with Bill immediately. The thing I always appreciated so much was that Bill encouraged me to be involved in the business as much as I wanted to be involved. He always made me feel a major part of the company."

"Everybody," says Erika Schafer, who started with Daniels as a secretary and became one of Bill's business partners, "remembers that party. We drank and ate and had a wonderful time, and then somebody had the idea to throw Bill into the hot tub. They picked him up and threw him into the water, and Bill had these expensive Gucci shoes on and was wearing a cashmere sweater, but he wasn't really concerned about that. He reached into his pocket and pulled out a bundle of three-by-five cards and held them above the water and yelled at me, 'Save these!' They were Bill's equivalent of a little black book."

If Daniels liked to know everything that was going on in the world at large, he also wanted to know everything that was going on in his office at all times of the day or night. It wasn't so much that he was a busybody, or that he was judgmental; he simply had an insatiable curiosity about his fellow human beings. If he didn't like talking about himself or revealing much of his inner life, he was terribly intrigued by what others were doing.

"At the new building," says Kersch, "there was a security system that used magnetic card readers. Like everything else Bill had, it was fairly high-tech and sophisticated and kept a log of who came and went and at what time. I was told that one of the security guard's responsibilities was to give Bill a daily report of who had come into the building after eleven P.M. every night. I've heard tell on more than one occasion where somebody who had been over at the Bay Wolf [a nightclub in Cherry Creek] managed to find somebody over there who was interested in seeing inside the offices, particularly inside the sauna and hot tub. Bill would make a point of smiling knowingly at that person the next day! He just wanted to let them know he knew."

Despite the fun at night, people were always expected to show up at eight o'clock sharp the following morning—not at 8:04 or 8:05—and to start working immediately. Pleasure did not come at the expense of doing one's job.

"I learned at Daniels that you return every phone call and you always respond to any correspondence you receive, even if it was a solicitation," says Joanne Lintjer, a longtime associate at the company. "You wrote 'thank-you notes,' even if it's to a co-worker. Bill raised the standard and I'm sure each of us had a high work ethic when we came to Daniels, but it grew stronger than I ever had anticipated it would be, which really added to your pride in your work.

"I always loved when Bill was in the office. The hustle and bustle just went up a higher level. You dressed better and I think I even thought sharper."

Although Daniels was encouraging fun in the office, he was involved in a bitter battle over winning the franchise to bring cable TV to his adopted hometown of Denver. One result of all the positive changes that had come to the cable industry in recent years—more programming, a better regulatory mood in Washington, and more available financing—was that cable operators were starting to bring their services to America's major cities. New York had been wired for some time, and in the late seventies and early eighties, cable also arrived in Minneapolis, Milwaukee, Chicago, Boston, New Orleans, Kansas City, Tampa, Pittsburgh, Indianapolis, Houston, Washington, D.C., and other urban settings. But ironically, it had not come to Denver, the capital of the industry and the address of the most successful broker the field had ever seen. The struggle to bring cable to Denver had been very long and hard fought, and the outcome was still uncertain.

Back in 1957, just a couple of years after Daniels had moved to Denver and opened his first brokerage office, he'd gone to the city council and presented its members with a radical idea for the time: he wanted to bring special TV programs into the homes of people who subscribed to a local cable service. For a few dollars a month, the service would give them first-run movies, live sporting events, and Broadway shows. The council was not moved. Many people in Denver still didn't have TV sets and it cost only a quarter to go see a film. Several more years would pass before Denver had its own major league athletic franchise, the Denver Broncos, so why would you want to put more sports on television? The council was polite but firm: thank you, but it had no interest in this new thing called cable television.

In 1968, after Daniels & Associates had been established as *the* powerhouse brokerage firm in cable and with many rural areas of America getting wired, Daniels went back to the council and pitched them again. The local prophet laid out his vision: bringing cable to Denver would not only demonstrate that they were living in a progressive city, but would provide the citizens with far more programming choices. It would also make the pictures offered by network TV much clearer. This was clearly a no-lose proposition. Every other city in the nation was going to be wired soon; why not do it now and get ahead of the rest? The council listened patiently and shrugged again. It turned Daniels down flat, telling him that Denver had enough TV to keep everyone happy and the reception was fine.

Nearly a decade and a half passed—fourteen long years—until February 1982. During those years, Daniels made his pitch several more times to the city council and had been rejected repeatedly.

Finally the council was ready to award the lucrative contract to one of three operators. Competition to wire the city had grown fierce because all the companies vying for the job were based in Denver. United Cable Television Corporation was owned by Gene Schneider, Daniels' ex-partner in Casper. TelePrompTer was headquartered in New York but had a thriving presence in Denver and was aggressively pursuing this contract. The third competitor was an alliance of American Television Communications, Monty Rifkin's company, and Daniels & Associates. It carried the name Mile Hi Cablevision and was 42.5 percent owned by Daniels & Associates. All of them were offering pretty much the same service to Denver—with one notable exception. Daniels had promised viewers that if his group won the franchise, they would receive the new Playboy channel, called Escapade.

A few years before, Daniels had taken a one-third ownership in a group known as Rainbow Cablevision, which was preparing to launch both Playboy's Escapade and the arts channel Bravo. Daniels had also established a personal relationship with Hugh Hefner and his daughter, Christie, who became president of Playboy enterprises in the early eighties and would later become CEO. Since joining the Playboy empire in 1975, Christie had met Daniels a number of times, and he'd always encouraged her, as he had so many others, to develop original programming. Playboy had followed through on this advice and created Escapade.

"There was," says Christie Hefner, "just a handful of people in the very early years—Gene Schneider and Bill Daniels—who were in the elite club of the real visionary pioneers of cable. They were highly entrepreneurial and really brilliant guys. They had built very successful companies but had never become corporate. I remember that Bill was like this godfather to me. I could call him and talk to him about strategy, and he would always listen and he would always have good counsel. He was always willing to extend the considerable goodwill and respect that he had on my behalf, to present me to people through his good auspices.

"This was not universal. There were people in the early years that were kind of disdainful of the programmers. It was like a necessary evil, but Bill wasn't like that at all. He knew the importance of CNN, Playboy, and HBO—the importance of brands."

If controversy over the cable franchise had been building in Denver prior to the Daniels announcement that he was offering the adult fare on Escapade, it reached a frenzy when he went in front of the city council and explained his decision to put this programming on the air. While his rivals were trying to use the Playboy channel against him, Daniels refused to act defensively. He spoke

Bill Daniels poses with his family, including Mitchell, wife Devra, Cindy and their animal menagerie.

about offering Playboy to adult viewers the same way he'd been speaking about the virtues of cable TV for the past thirty years—with enthusiasm, pride, and practicality. If people didn't choose to pay for the service, then it wouldn't come into their home. They made the final decision, not the cable operator. It was their choice to have mature content on TV if they wanted it—and their responsibility to keep it away from kids.

No quarter was given in this highly publicized speech to the council, and no apologies were offered. Bill Daniels had never been one to walk away from a fight. In the 1980s Tom Southwick was a reporter for Multichannel News. He followed the cable competition, and he was struck by Daniels' appearance before the local government concerning the Escapade channel.

"Bill," Southwick told the *Denver Post*, "said to the council, 'Yes, we're going to offer this. We're proud of it. We're not going to lie about it now and then add it later on.'"

In order to win, Daniels needed political allies and had aligned himself with about a dozen of Denver's most powerful Democrats and Republicans. They had influence with the city council, and they used it to promote their friend and longtime business ally.

On February 22, 1982, the city council, apparently grateful for Daniels' candor and respectful of his long record of success in cable, awarded the franchise to Mile Hi. It was worth $78.5 million. Construction would be delayed for another year, following more legal hurdles that tried to prevent Mile Hi from holding a monopoly on the franchise, but in the end Daniels emerged victorious. On a cold day in the winter of 1983, with Mayor Bill McNichols and the city council members standing on a frozen field in southeast Denver, the first strand of copper wire was strung between two old telephone poles and cable TV was at last a reality in Bill Daniels' backyard.

The night he won the franchise, his office held a big party to celebrate the triumph. At the height of it, he excused himself from the crowd and went to the phone. He dialed the number he most wanted to dial, calling his eighty-eight-year-old mother down in Hobbs. When he told Adele what had happened and how long the fight had been and how great this occasion was, she listened quietly, as she always did when her son called with good news. Tonight she heard something more, because he was also crying with joy.

*   *   *

In the early eighties Daniels met a little feisty blond pilot named Betsy Benton. He was fascinated with her work, so fascinated that he had his secretary, Jayne Mitchell, pester her until she agreed to go out to lunch with him. When she initially tried to discourage him by telling him she was married, he shot back, "But you're not dead, goddammit!" They had an on-and-off relationship for the next twenty years, and she was the one who was with him the day he died. She once accompanied him to a White House dinner, and he took delight in watching Betsy pocket matches for a souvenir. He was used to being around powerful people, and was never awestruck by his surroundings. He could be relaxed and playful because he had power of his own. Some people believe that Betsy was the love of his life; others might say it was a relationship based on agendas. His agenda was his desire to control her and he couldn't. Sometimes she wouldn't even return his calls for days—and that was intolerable. Her agenda was to retain her own power and independence. She understood him well enough to know that if she ever gave into him completely, he would be gone.

"I really loved him," Betsy says. "I would have married him, but he was too busy conquering the world. And I wanted to have children, but he couldn't. I went on and got married and had a child and kept in touch with Bill. I think he was happy up until the last five years of his life—when he realized there was more to life than business and he had made so much money but he still was alone, and lonely. I think he really worried about where he was going to go after he died."

Twenty-five

It wasn't always fun working for Daniels—at least not when the boss decided that he'd conquered enough of the cable world and was ready to buy another sports franchise. Rumors that he'd gotten the irrepressible itch to purchase an athletic team sent shakes and tremors through the financial people at the company. They'd seen this before, and it always led to confusion or red ink or something worse. They'd come to believe that Daniels had learned this particularly hard lesson about not mixing business and sports, but he was more unpredictable and unstoppable than that. One Saturday morning Tom Marinkovich thought he would make a special impression on the boss by going in and working on the weekend. He knew that Daniels would be in the office and felt that showing up and putting in some hours alongside him was the thing to do.

He was sitting at his desk looking busy when Daniels walked up and dropped a stack of papers down in front of him.

"Look at this over the weekend," Daniels said, "and we'll talk about it on Monday."

Glancing at the pile, Marinkovich was immediately nervous. He'd heard the stories about car racing, about Ron Lyle and his painful breakup with Daniels, and about the Utah Stars and their bankruptcy out in Salt Lake City. In his first meeting with Daniels, Marinkovich had distinctly heard the man say that he would never deal with sports again. When he took the papers home and read them, they confirmed his worst fears: it was a marketing survey about a new pro league featuring football in the spring—instead of its traditional season in the fall. Marinkovich's nervousness deepened.

In the history of televised athletics, nothing had ever approached the success of the National Football League. Under the leadership of NFL commissioner Pete Rozelle, starting in the 1960s, the league had gone from the second- or third-rated TV sport, behind baseball and basketball, to the top in terms of ratings, advertising, and overall financial clout. The contracts between team owners and the networks ran into the billions. Football was a great sport for television—with the rise of instant replay you could see far more of the action on your home screen than you could see by actually attending the game—and it had also managed to avoid overexposure. The baseball, basketball, and hockey seasons were endless, but football had only fourteen regular season games at the time—just one game per team for every Sunday in the fall. Viewers waited all week to see the next contest. Anticipation and expectations built up during the six off days between games. Each time the teams took the field was an event. By the eighties, football had replaced baseball and basketball as the sport of choice. The NFL was golden and no one had dared to challenge its supremacy—until now.

On Monday morning, Marinkovich went into the office and reminded Daniels that he'd recently said he was avoiding all sports franchises. That was true, the boss replied, but this was different. Hadn't Marinkovich looked at the marketing analysis and read how many people out there wanted to have spring football? Couldn't he see the overwhelming potential? How could anyone deny that this was a winner? Marinkovich did his best to create a counterargument, but eventually Daniels was unable to stay on the sidelines any longer and jumped headlong into the United States Football League, becoming an owner of the Los Angeles Express.

"Bill was a fighter," Marinkovich says. "He was so competitive. Once that got started, he was bound and determined to sign the NFL stars."

Daniels tried everything he could think of to lure college star quarterback Dan Marino to the new league, but Marino would go to the NFL. Then Daniels tried to sign SMU's running back Eric Dickerson—offering him a job for life, an unheard-of proposition at the time—but Dickerson wouldn't come to the new league, either, signing with the Indianapolis Colts. Instead of going to the USFL, the NFL stars mostly used the bids from USFL owners to gain leverage and to boost their salaries in the older league. Once that was accomplished, they turned their backs on the upstarts. Ever the optimist, Daniels kept chasing after big names.

"They were interesting times," says Marinkovich. "Every week or so I had to cut a check and here we would go with the cash-flow issues that we always had."

It soon became apparent that the USFL was costing Daniels vast amounts of money that could not be recouped, so his staff frantically began searching for a partner or a buyer for the Express. Just when it looked as if the investment would be a disaster for Daniels, Marinkovich received a phone call from an attorney who asked if their office had a football team for sale. Marinkovich told him, half-jokingly, that at the moment everything they had was for sale. The caller said that he knew someone in San Francisco who was a real stand-up guy and the USFL would love to have him as an owner. Maybe, Marinkovich told himself, if this "stand-up guy" was really on the level, another ruinous venture into the world of professional sports could be averted at Daniels & Associates.

"I'm shaking in my boots," Marinkovich says about this phone conversation. "I'm so tickled this guy has surfaced."

Within a matter of days the potential buyer and the Daniels people signed a letter of intent for the sale. After the document was inked, the Daniels group went to a bar in Cherry Creek to meet the buyer in person. The group's mood was very good—right up until the moment they made the buyer's acquaintance.

"The guy," says Marinkovich, "turned out to be a slimy individual. He was located in San Francisco and had started this company where they were selling participation in loans with all the savings and loans around the country. They would get a huge fee of like ten to fifteen percent. This was before the S&Ls went down the tubes. The deal [for the Los Angeles Express] was in and out for days and weeks at a time—a horror story for quite a while. But we finally got it done.

"We go to the closing and Bill was with us. They hand us the check and it's a personal check. So we took their lawyer aside and asked what the deal was. He said something to the effect that they didn't have time to get cash. Bill asked what the problem was and we tell him, and this guy is kind of going on a tirade about us not taking his personal check. Bill said to him, 'Let me ask you a question—is this personal check good?' The guy says, 'Yeah.' Bill said, 'Okay, but if it isn't, I'm going to come back and beat the shit out of you.' We deposited it and waited around for a half day or longer for the check to clear before we would hand over the papers. It did finally clear and we handed over the papers. We were out of the football business—thank God!"

"The guy went into debt to the tune of about $20 million and went bankrupt. And he was indicted but not convicted of bilking an S&L he bought. Bill was so happy, he gave me a bonus for getting him out of it."

Daniels was almost done with jumping into athletic investments, but not just yet. He would have a few more colorful adventures with the sporting crowd and would never stop donating money to worthy causes, some of which were connected to intense competition.

In the 1990s, Tim Leiweke ran the Denver Nuggets pro basketball team, before going on to become the president of the Los Angeles Lakers. While working in Colorado, he oversaw the Olympic Festival in Colorado Springs, where athletes lived and trained for the upcoming games. The Olympic Festival brought prestige to the Springs and to the entire state, but it was a serious money drain. In order to keep the festival afloat, Leiweke had to scramble for funds, and more than once that meant calling the closest thing he knew to a sure bet: Bill Daniels. Like hundreds of other people who'd come in contact with the man, Leiweke understood that Daniels did not simply talk about doing charity work. He did not wait for others to make the first move. Daniels put his money where his heart and his convictions were, and he expected other to do the same.

One year, Leiweke recalls, "there was no government funding, and we had to pay for the whole thing privately. At the end of the day, we were about $500,000 in debt and I picked up the phone. Bill had already given to the event generously, and I said, 'Bill, I hate to do this, but I have to go back on the streets and raise money.' He said, 'Timmy, you tell anybody who gives you a dollar, I'll match it with another dollar. You go raise $250,000 and I'll give you $250,000.' "I'm like, 'God, how many times is this guy going to be a safety net for me?' He didn't have to do that, but Bill wouldn't want me or anybody else to be like that. Bill would want us to feel better that we knew him."

It wasn't always fun to try to keep on top of Daniels' estate planning. Susan Goddard was the attorney in charge of this for the last eighteen years of his life. Just as he managed the cable industry through a stack of three-by-five cards, he also used them to determine which woman was in which position at any given time in relation to his will. Given his endless attraction to the opposite sex, he did a lot of shuffling. And each time he shuffled, Goddard's phone rang.

"It was funny," Susan says, "how his girlfriends would go in and out of his will. There was a certain order in which they would come in at X dollars and go down to Y and then down to Z and then out! He was very consistent about the number, and whenever he would call me, I'd know where a girlfriend was in the scheme of things."

Once, when Goddard was discussing Daniels' will with another lawyer who didn't know Bill, she mentioned that Daniels insisted that his ashes were to be mingled with those of Sydney.

"Which girlfriend was Sydney?" the lawyer asked.

"His beloved cat," Goddard replied.

Twenty-six

Though Daniels was having trouble making his investments in sports teams pay off, in another area his instincts worked much better. He'd long believed that cable needed more programming and that sports could fill a significant portion of this need. In the early eighties, he was fascinated to learn about a new cable station being developed called the Entertainment and Sports Programming Network, or ESPN. In 1979 ESPN was conceived of as the first ever around-the-clock sports outlet, the sports fans' equivalent of CNN. Viewers could get scores and statistics and watch highlights of their athletic heroes twenty-four hours a day. They could also see a wide variety of games broadcast live. Before the network was launched, many people doubted that ESPN could draw a large enough audience to sustain itself. Like many other cable innovations, it was widely perceived as a pipe dream that would never find a lasting place in the American media.

Bill Grimes, who would become the second CEO of ESPN, met Daniels just as the new sports network was being launched. He knew that Daniels not only had a very large vision for cable, but was willing to put his money behind his conviction.

"Bill was a cable operator," Grimes says, "but much more important, he was one of the few pioneer leaders in cable. I remember speaking with him about asking the operators for license fees to help reverse the current economic situation for most programmers. Like other operators, Bill would be initially adversely affected by these fees, but he listened to me and said, 'If we do this and pay a fee, will you make a commitment to improving the programming?' He had the foresight to realize that better programming would increase cable penetration, allow operators to raise prices, and sell local advertising. In contrast, I remember sharing these ideas with other individuals, and they would not acknowledge their future potential. Bill was concerned about the industry as a whole rather than the individual pieces."

A key figure in the creation of ESPN was Roger Werner, who in the summer of 1980 was working as a management consultant at McKinsey & Company in New York. McKinsey had recently been engaged by Getty Oil, which had put up $15 to $20 million to start ESPN. When Getty called the company seeking its help, ESPN had strayed far from its original business plan. The numbers were not doing what anyone had hoped they would do and Getty was thinking of shutting the station down even before it made its debut. Getty wanted McKinsey to do an analysis of the cable industry and the potential market for an all-sports television channel, then advise them on how to proceed.

"Basically," says Werner, "our job was to give them a decision—go or no go. Help them to figure out to liquidate it or build it into a company."

When Werner began working on the ESPN analysis, he wasn't very familiar with cable TV or the people who'd been building the industry for the past three decades. He really wasn't sure if cable had a future or not. During his first half year as a consultant on the project, Werner met Daniels at the Western Cable Show in Anaheim, California. Daniels was a good friend of Stuart Evey, president of the diversified operations division of Getty and the executive in charge of Getty's ESPN investment. Just as Daniels had encouraged Ted Turner to start CNN, he now played a similar role in the creation of the world's first all-sports network. In part because of his meeting Daniels and listening to the man's unlimited faith in cable, Werner himself became a believer in the cable industry—and in ESPN's potential.

"Ultimately," he says, "we recommended that Getty stay in, which they did."

McKinsey created ESPN's first strategic plan. It advised the station in hiring executives, and Werner spent the next year helping the fledgling network implement these plans. In 1982 he joined ESPN full-time as its number two man. The more exposure he had to cable TV, the more he interacted with Daniels.

"My first recollection of Bill," he says, "was that he was a cheerleader for not only the cable industry, but for Getty and for ESPN, for the whole concept of a sports network. He was absolutely in love with it. I remember one meeting that I called of my sales and marketing guys right before the Western Cable Show. It would've been '81 or '82, where Bill came in and joined us and basically exhorted us to go out and buy whatever sports rights we could get our hands on: the NFL, the Olympics, whatever. He was basically telling us he would back us with whatever we needed to go buy the biggest and the best programming. He was absolutely convinced that that was going to drive the growth of the cable business. And of course, he was right. We were ultimately able to acquire all kinds of fantastic programming, including the NFL.

"This was due in large part to the support Bill expressed not just to us and our team, but also to his friends in the cable industry, to other cable operators, and to people in the press and so on. He was really a relentless promoter of the basic idea that cable ought to be creating and acquiring the very best television programming and essentially displacing the broadcasters as America's primary viewing choice. I was delighted that Bill lived to see ESPN blossom into the biggest and most successful television network in the world, meaning the most profitable. He was in on the ground floor of all the major developments in sports programming throughout the eighties and the nineties."

Steve Bornstein took over ESPN after Werner went to work for Daniels. He too had frequent interaction with Daniels and was struck by his idiosyncratic obsession with appearance.

"Bill had his pet issues," says Bornstein, "and one of the things he always despised was how sloppy and messy television sports crews are. Their basic uniform was a T-shirt and blue jeans, and he wanted them in tuxedos."

Daniels wasn't satisfied merely to watch ESPN take off in the TV sports marketplace. He wanted a piece of the action as well. If a national outlet like ESPN could work, why couldn't a regionally based cable operations offer sports programming to viewers who wanted to see more of their local teams on the air? Hadn't Ted Turner successfully done this with his Atlanta Braves broadcasts back in the seventies? Couldn't it be done elsewhere?

When Daniels told one of his financial officers, Bruce Dickinson, that he was eager to start a regional sports network in Southern California, Dickinson balked. He experienced some of the same reservations he'd had when Daniels approached him about investing in CNN. It was just too damn risky. After studying the business plan, Dickinson saw that there was a huge market for televised sporting events in Southern California. But he worried about all the competition from the area's other TV outlets. And people in this part of the country were notorious for not watching sports teams unless they were contending for championships; if they were losing, viewers flipped off their sets and went to the beach. Launching this kind of network would be an expensive proposition, and, as Dickinson saw it, the operation might never turn a profit. Maybe they should pass.

Dickinson shared his thoughts with the boss, who thanked him for his input even though it wasn't what he believed or wanted to hear. Daniels ran on intuition—a gut instinct for what the public was ready to watch and willing to pay for. Because he wanted more choices, he was convinced that millions of other people did as well. Because he loved sports on TV, he knew that others had these same desires. He also believed that televising athletic events would not stop people from coming to the games—a key fear of team owners—but would in fact help market the product to the existing fan base and to new fans. Television was the greatest advertising medium ever invented, and what better way to advertise your team than to let people see what they were missing at the ballpark? Brushing aside Dickinson's recommendations, Daniels moved forward with plans for a regional sports network, which was initially called Box Seat but evolved into Prime Ticket.

The network was to be based in San Diego, but the Daniels people quickly found out there weren't enough pro teams in that city and it wasn't a big enough market. They switched their sites north to Los Angeles, after Tony Acone put them in touch with Jerry Buss, the owner of the National Basketball Association's L.A. Lakers and the National Hockey League's L.A. Kings. Daniels bought a piece of the Lakers, after Buss decided to put both the Lakers and Kings on basic cable service—at the time a breakthrough in sports programming. Prior to this, most athletic events had been offered on a pay channel, not as part of an inexpensive monthly cable package. Buss was aware that showing his product on TV might weaken attendance at the gate, but he was ready to follow Daniels' lead and take this chance. Maybe the broker was right and the exposure that cable brought Buss' teams would help him sell more tickets.

It was a courageous decision—and it worked.

"Jerry was ahead of the rest of the league in terms of generating revenue from television," says Tom Marinkovich. "He was very agreeable to our plan, although his agenda and Bill's were totally different. Jerry's was to generate funds for his team, and Bill's was to make his sports channel bigger and better."

"Once again," says Bruce Dickinson, "Bill knew that there was a very, very large demand for more sports programming in the country. He knew intuitively that that business was going to be a great success."

"Prime Ticket," says cable TV executive Bill Cullen, "became the number one reason that people subscribed to cable. I think what Bill did—with the oversight he provided, the direction, and the encouragement in building this service—became one of the most valuable things to happen to the industry. Also, it became a template from which many other regional sports networks evolved. This may be one of the activities that has been most overlooked in Bill's career. No one had ever tried to penetrate a local area such as that before."

In establishing Prime Ticket, Daniels applied his legendary attention to detail and nitpicking. He drove his executives crazy.

"Bill used to get very involved in production, " says Kitty Cohen, general manager of Prime Ticket in the early nineties. "He would call our production trucks in the middle of games and say, 'I was watching the volleyball game, and I think it would look better if you could make the sand blue.' The crew would tell him, 'Bill, it's at the beach!' "

Daniels was thrilled to be in business with the Los Angeles Lakers, one of the two or three most successful pro sports teams during the 1980s. The kid from Hobbs never cared much for New York City, but at times he was enamored by the glitz of L.A. Once, some friends invited him on a camping trip to the Rocky Mountains, where they were going to cook their own meals, sleep outside in the fresh night air, and enjoy the wonders of nature up close. Daniels declined the offer, much to the disappointment of the others. When they asked him why he turned down the trip, he said that they really didn't understand who he was. He didn't sleep under the stars, he explained; he slept with them.

"Even though Bill owned only a piece of the Lakers," says Brian Deevy, the current CEO of Daniels & Associates, "he used to act like he owned the whole team. He had an opinion on everybody who played on that team. He was very fond of Magic Johnson, and when Magic retired and everyone thought the Lakers wouldn't make it without Magic, Bill gave [Laker general manager] Jerry West all the credit for figuring out how to get Shaquille O'Neal to come to L.A. What was really entertaining was the way Bill got involved and followed it so closely.

"It was a great partnership for us. Jerry Buss was getting divorced and he needed cash. We, being Prime Ticket, were trying to get the rights to the non-network broadcasts. As it turned out, Jerry Buss took a big piece of Prime Ticket and we took a piece of the Lakers, and it was a very good business deal because there were nights when Prime Ticket would outdraw the networks because they had the Lakers on. There was also the psychic value of being a part owner of the Lakers. It was one of the more important things that Bill had."

After years of trying, Daniels had finally found a way to be profitably involved in professional sports.

"Prime Ticket," says Buzz Mitchell, the chief financial officer at the company before becoming the CEO of Daniels Communications, "was one of Bill's biggest business successes. Not that his first love wasn't necessarily cable but Prime Ticket was stepping out. It was a different type of business, but it was one that Bill saw cable needed very badly—to get a corner on as much sports programming as it could. What better way to see that it happens than to do it yourself?

"Bill never asked anybody else to step up and do something financially. He always had the intestinal fortitude to put his own last dollar on the table to get something done. That was clearly the case with Prime Ticket. He used his money right through from start up through its full development and had the guts to do it and the vision to see where it could lead. I think Prime Ticket was by far his most exciting endeavor."

Larry Stewart has covered sports for the *Los Angeles Times* since 1978. He got to know Daniels after the creation of Prime Ticket and would come to refer to him as "the nicest billionaire I ever knew." Stewart was used to executives not giving him information when he asked for it. With Daniels everything was different.

"When the L.A. Kings traded for Wayne Gretzky in 1988," Stewart says,

Bill Daniels with Los Angeles Lakers majority owner Jerry Buss in 1987.

"their owner, Bruce McNall, needed financial support from Bill through Prime Ticket. I got hold of Bill and asked him if he was involved in this and he laid out the whole thing. He helped me write this really good concrete story with this great information. But a better story is when he sold Prime Ticket to John Malone in 1994. As a reporter, on a big sale like this you don't usually get inside information. He gave me so much inside information that a lawyer and his communications officer, Bob Russo, called me from Denver. They explained their confidentiality clause and said that Bill, because he liked me, had given me more information than he should have. They informed me that if I printed that much detail, it could jeopardize the sale. I didn't want to do that, so we compromised and I was glad to do that."

Twenty-seven

When being interviewed about his business career, John Saeman was occasionally asked about the most memorable character he'd ever met. He never had to stop and think about his answer. The first name that always came to mind was Bill Daniels, because no one else made going to work the complete experience of contributing something to society, having fun, and making money.

"The Daniels senior management team," recalls Jerry Maglio, a longtime executive with the company, "was on an executive retreat, and we had been in Florida and gone to Epcot for dinner one night. We had gone to the Italian pavilion around a lake, had a nice leisurely dinner, plenty to eat, plenty to drink, and a lot of good fellowship. Instead of taking a bus or whatever transportation was available, we walked leisurely around the lake and as we got to the monorail station, a Disney employee yelled to us, 'Hurry up, folks, this is the last train of the evening. You don't want to miss it.' So we broke into a trot and Disney has ramps like switchbacks to the platform, and as we were getting into the train, this Disney employee looked back down to the lowest level and Bill was still walking there, hadn't broken stride. He wasn't even on the first ramp.

"The Disney employee yells to Bill to hurry up—he was going to miss the train. So Bill yelled up to John Saeman, 'John! Buy the train!' The Disney employee's eyes popped out of his head and he said, 'Who is this guy?' John said, 'Well, you might not know who he is, but you don't want to let the train leave without him.'"

Saeman wasn't the only person who found Daniels thoroughly unforgettable. For sixteen years Casey Cassetta was Daniels' manicurist in La Costa, California.

"Bill," she says, "was a man who was very, very demanding but the most caring individual I've ever met in my life. He was an era all by himself. When he died, that era ended. He never spoke down to you. He gave you parts of his stability, his knowledge, and he had a great sense of humor. He was just larger than life. I saw him on an average of twice a month for sixteen years, so I got to see him quite a bit. He hated every minute that he had to sit still. He was not the kind of man that could sit still for anything. He would yell at me, 'Aren't you finished yet?' And he would always say, 'Aren't you done yet, goddammit?' That was his favorite expression. I told Bill one time, 'You know, you make me extremely tolerant of other people because you want everything right now!' And he would give you that little look over his glasses and say, 'Yeah, you're right.' And giggle.

"It's amazing how he is still such a part of my life. A day doesn't go by that I don't think of something that reminds me of Bill. There isn't a time that I'm not doing something that I think of what he spoke about. If it's sports, I think of Bill. I have tried to pattern my work habits after Bill—what would Bill think of this, would he be proud of me in this situation? I try to conduct my working life as if Bill is standing over my shoulder. If he wouldn't be happy doing this, then I better not be doing it."

Scott Hamilton won the Olympic Gold for ice skating at the 1984 Games in Sarajevo. Upon his return to America, Daniels put together a celebration and victory parade for him in Denver. The men became friends and stayed close through the unpredictable years that lay ahead for the champion.

"When I got sick with cancer," Hamilton says, "Bill was one of the first ones to call. He said that he was sending his jet to bring me back to Denver and I said that it was way too generous of an offer and I can't accept it, I will make my way back. He said, 'No. It is available to you, and I will be offended if you do not use it.' As I looked at everything, going through my first run of chemo, and having everything from when I was on tour in bags all over the place—the only way for me to get home properly was through him. So he sent his plane out to bring me home, and I will never forget that.

"I don't want to get emotional, but the thought that went behind that— here I was going through something emotionally devastating and he wanted to help in any way that he could. He did. After the first round of chemo, it shakes your image of immortality. You realize that you are vulnerable and when he sent his plane I realized just how difficult it would have been to fly home. He really anticipated my needs, and for that I will always be grateful."

After his recovery from the disease, Hamilton started his own cancer fund to assist other victims. Like so many people who'd come in contact with Daniels, he'd learned the value of helping others, even when they didn't ask for it.

"I also help friends that have charitable aspirations that need help," he says. "I want to put it into something that will continue to give and give, long after I am gone. I learned a lot from Bill. The people that I love and respect the most are the ones that have taken what they have been given and turned it into something beyond success. Bill was one of the greatest examples of that."

And he was a great example of the richness and idiosyncrasy of human experience. The legacy he was building was based on his success in the cable business and on his charity work, but it was also based on the individual lives he touched and the stories that people told about him. They talked about Daniels as if he were not just a man, but an eccentric and powerfully creative spirit, an ongoing inspiration that would never leave their lives, not even after he was dead.

"Everything in his kitchen," says Frieda Cowan, Daniels' housekeeper and caregiver in California, "every label on every can had to face toward the front. Every item had to be exactly the same, the towels had to be folded exactly so. The best girl I had working for me could never get that one down. She said, 'What does it matter—he's only going to dry his body.' I said, 'It matters because it is for who it is.' I never met anyone like Bill in that way."

Says Jim Watson, a Daniels pal from California: "If Bill left one impression upon me in the business world, it's 'Pick the people you do business with—not the business.' He was just so focused on people who do the right thing and who are honest. The thing about Bill was his great self-confidence. There's not a lot of guys who go around kissing and hugging each other, and it's humorous to think about this now, but I'd get a note from Bill in the mail and it would say, 'Love, Bill.' I'd have a new secretary and they'd say, 'What was this all about?' But that was just him. You'd be in front of the Ritz Carlton, and he'd give you a hug and say, 'I love ya, Watty.' And the parking attendants are looking at you oddly."

Says Susan Goddard, Daniels' estate-planning attorney: "I think the reason Bill Daniels made money is because he was one of the few people in the world that listened—he really listened to people."

"I found it terribly fascinating that Bill loved to do laundry," says Andrew Gerhard, Daniels' interior designer. "He just loved it. I put the laundry in the garage [in his beach house], and everyone has heard the story about him locking himself in there. He got moved in to this new little beach house and we've all warned him, 'Bill, be sure to fix the lock on the door going into the house, if the garage doors are down.' So he gets up at his usual three A.M. and goes out to get the paper and opens the garage door with the clicker, goes back in the house and leaves the clicker in the house, and goes back to the garage and shuts the door without fixing the lock.

"Bill gets stuck in the garage for about two to three hours. No phone, no clicker, no key. After that, we had a phone installed in the garage. Did you hear about the fire he set at the house in the desert? Jayne Mitchell [Daniels' secretary in Denver] calls and tells me to drive to the desert, because he did a little bit of damage cooking chicken and it caught on fire. He threw chicken, grease and all, into a wicker wastebasket, which burst into flames and turns on the sprinkler system. Water damage everywhere. We had a major re-do there.

"Within six months, I get another phone call from Jayne. This time he left the water on in the bar that is in the living room. Luckily, it was in a pit with a door going outside so the water was just leaking out the door. I fixed that real quickly. The things he did—pushing the wrong button and water goes off and garage doors open up and one day he fell in the pool, clothes and all. Then I get another phone call, 'Get a goddamn cover on this pool, it's your fault I fell in.' 'Yes, Bill, it's my fault.' He really was a joy, though. And I miss him."

"Bill had a proclivity to give girls cars, but they weren't gifts," says Daniels' friend Don Hyder. "The girls could use them because they were all leased. And at the end of the relationship, they had to pick up the lease or buy it or whatever they wanted. This one girl got so mad, she was going to steal the car, so Bill had to bring it down to my garage and left it there for about a week. When it stopped, it stopped. When enough is enough, it's over and he was that way about a lot of things.

"One girl he went with is now selling real estate here in Southern California. She was considerably younger. He helped her get a condo, got her a nose job and all this stuff. One day he just vanished."

For years Jayne Mitchell was Daniels' secretary. She remembers an occasion when the women at work challenged the boss on his political views—which was the equivalent of an uprising in the office.

Jackie O'Brien, executive secretary to John Saeman, recalls, "He used to send out memos concerning elections. It used to be a sensitive thing because Bill was a true Republican. But he didn't tell people how to vote—he just recommended and let them know how he was voting so they could think about it. In this particular election, there was an issue concerning pro-choice and abortion. He was taking the Republican stand on it and it was a negative vote on it. I am very much pro-choice. Jayne [Mitchell] came down to my desk and told me what he was doing and I said we need to talk to him—he can't send that out and tell people to follow the party line. It was very personal and controversial. So we went and sat down with him and he listened very patiently and we really hit him hard on it. And he changed it. We just said it's a personal, private choice and everybody has to look at their own conscience. And he did. I was so flattered that he took our opinion on that.

"After political correctness came in, Bill stopped by my desk and said, 'I understand I'm not to call you honey anymore and it's offensive to women nowadays.' I assured him he could call me honey any day, and I would be more offended if he ever stopped. I liked those days, I think we all have lost a lot with political correctness. We all can take care of ourselves and the ladies could. You just laughed it off. I like strong men and strong men like strong women, and if you couldn't handle it, maybe you suffered. But I don't think any of us suffered."

Says Daniels friend Chuck Reiff: "One time Bill went to Florida, and he called me from there and wanted to know the address and phone number of my parents. I gave it to him and he called them and said, 'I'm taking you both to dinner tonight, but I don't know where to go.' Well, he picked them up and they took him to a restaurant called Wolfie's, which in those days was a big restaurant in the South Florida beach area. They had a nice dinner and he takes them home.

"They live in a dumpy boardinghouse with rocking chairs outside. They had maybe two rooms, one bedroom, and that was it. They go into the lobby and there's all these people sitting there arguing about what program to watch on TV. There's only one television set in the whole place. So he said, 'I don't believe this.' The next morning, a color TV set was delivered to my parents.

Then he used it against me! Bill would say, 'Did Mom call us? I'm their new son.'"

"Bill," says Chuck's wife, Barbara, "wanted to impress some girl he was dating with his ability to do a crossword puzzle. So he used to call me on Sunday mornings for me to tell him all the answers to the puzzle and he would write them all in *The New York Times* puzzle."

"Bill was nomadic," says Mitchell Fox, Daniels' stepson from his marriage to Devra. "He was incapable of settling down. He had wanderlust in his personal life and his professional life. But what was really interesting is how my relationship seemed to endure to the very end. From before he and my mother were married, until many years after they were divorced. It probably is not unusual at all for a stepparent to become divorced and lose touch with those kids, but in my experience with Bill, we actually started getting along much better after the divorce. It was fun watching him enjoy his life. He was a mixture of cockiness, impatience, kindness, caring, loving, and a self-effacing guy. He was total charisma."

Mitchell's sister, Cindy, remembers an alligator briefcase that Daniels owned when she was a child.

"I used to listen for him to drive up at night," she says. "I would run out to the car to get the briefcase, and it was always so heavy. I would take it out, run upstairs, and make him a scotch and water. He would take the drink, and I would go out of the room until he got done. Then he would sit in his black leather chair and watch the news or talk on the phone. I would sit in between the closets and just watch him. He would look over and smile at me, then ask me how my day was and I would just sit in there and watch him until dinner. I don't know what it sounds like, but he was my knight in shining armor. He was the only father that I really remember. He was home a lot at first, but once the business took off he was gone a lot, which was upsetting. When you are attached to someone and they are traveling a lot, you look forward to when they are home.

"I remember my English teacher, an old lady named Mrs. Shaker. I was maybe a sophomore in high school. I remember Bill going to class and she was very stiff and quite serious, and she talked about teaching eighteenth-century British literature, and everything else that would be taught throughout the year. All of a sudden Bill raised his hand and said, 'Mrs. Shaker, I am Bill

Daniels, and I just want to know what the hell this will do for my daughter in the real world.'

"Of course, I was just about purple, and meanwhile all of the other parents were commenting on how wonderful the curriculum was. She said, 'This will help Cindy with her maturing language and all this other stuff.' He raised his hand again and said, 'What the hell will this do for her life? It will have no impact,' or something like that. She said, 'Mr. Daniels, you are not going to ever be invited back to parents' night.' He sat there with his arms crossed, and the only thing on his mind was how would this benefit me in the real world. He could see no importance at all in any of this."

In time, Cindy went to work for Daniels. "The other investment bankers at the office," she says, "had a male stripper come in for my thirtieth birthday. Everyone came on to the floor for this, and I looked up and Bill was standing there with his arms crossed at the doorway. He looked at me and just walked away. That was the father in him. Like he didn't really care for me seeing another man undressing, or something. Like he was saying, 'I'm not real happy with this situation.' He told me that he would give me a hundred thousand dollars if I stayed a virgin until I was forty. He didn't like that part. He scared people away all the time. I would have one date. It was terrible. He just was so awesome—he really was."

Cindy eventually left Daniels & Associates and went on to become a veterinarian. Her stepfather's influence followed her everywhere.

"Bill seriously contributed to my life," she says, "and I have emulated him to a T. I have set up an equity plan at my hospital. I set up an emergency fund at the hospital to take care of stray animals that need medical care, and I remember him saying that he had done the same thing for people that I was doing for animals and he thought it was terrific. But no matter what I have done, it has been to please him or to follow almost everything that he has done. He was my idol and he meant everything to me."

Jerry Maglio was a longtime executive at Daniels & Associates who went to his first cable convention, known as the Western Show, soon after joining the company.

"It was June of 1980," he says, "and I remember sitting in a cocktail lounge with some of my friends and colleagues. Bill Daniels arrived a little breathlessly, sat down at the table and somehow, some way, he'd lost his money or had his money clip stolen. He didn't have any money. Now Bill Daniels without money is an oxymoron. So he asked me if I had any money. I looked in my wallet and I had about four hundred dollars and this was supposed to last me for the entire show. Bill took it all. Without batting an eyelash. It was as if to say if one of us isn't going to have money for the cable show, it's going to be you. Bill certainly repaid me after the show, but all I remember was that I was going to this show and I didn't have any money. Bill had it."

Daniels liked to give people nicknames, and he eventually started calling Maglio "Shoes" because of his choice of footwear.

"I got tremendous support from Bill when I was getting a divorce," Maglio says. "He would always ask how I was doing and I would say I was doing fine. But one day he threw a new dimension into it, he said, 'Shoes, how you doing financially?' And I said, 'Bill, I've probably got about forty-eight bucks.' That was pretty close to true and I said, 'But don't worry, I'll be fine.'

"So I went out to lunch—I think I was surviving on supplier lunches at the time, and this lunch happened to be with HBO. I came back from lunch and there was an envelope on my desk. There was a note in the envelope and it said, 'Shoes, I wasn't sure if you were kidding about the forty-eight bucks, but in case you weren't, this ought to help. Just let me know what you do, for my records. Go get 'em.' It was signed by Bill and it was a blank check. It wasn't a loan—it was Bill saying, 'You're one of my guys and my people are always going to get themselves in a jam, but when they do, I want you to know I am there for you.' I'm sitting there at my desk with tears in my eyes. Now, I never cashed the check, but it was really wonderful to know if there ever was a need, Bill was there for you."

One person to whom Daniels gave a special name was J. J. Ingalls who worked in customer service at Combs Aviation, where Daniels kept his private jet: Cablevision Tool. Although well under five feet, Ingalls possessed a huge heart, which Bill was drawn to. Daniels invited Ingalls on some of his flights, and whenever Ingalls was facing a tough decision, he called up the older man and sought his advice. When Ingalls retired in 1989, Daniels brought two hundred of J. J.'s friends together for a party at his mansion, Cableland. An invitation to this event was the talk of Denver's aviation community. As a retirement gift to his friend, Daniels commissioned a bronze in Ingalls' image by renowned sculptor Kenneth Bunn. But it wasn't these things that made the friendship unique.

"Bill is the only person," says Ingalls, "I ever allowed to call me 'Shorty.' He called me Shorty out of respect. He called me J. J. around his business associates but one on one, it was always Shorty. The things Bill did for me were overwhelming and I was very fortunate to be a part of what he accomplished. They say that if you make one great friend in a lifetime you can feel very lucky. My friend was Bill Daniels."

"You have to make decisions. But you don't have to be tough to succeed in business. All you have to do is treat people decently and you'll be amazed how they'll respond."
—Bill Daniels

*   *   *

Because people knew that Daniels was so generous, they constantly approached him for money. Requests came over the phone and through the mail, a steady stream of individuals asking him for help.

"Bill had a very hard time saying no," says Sharon Green, Daniels' secretary for the last decade of his life. "It was easier for him to say yes. Some of the requests were off the wall, and some were from people who were not struggling but pretended they were. We only gave him half of his mail and half of his phone messages because it was not practical to give him all of them. I think he was more touched by people he read about in the newspaper who were down on their luck than by those who approached him. He was a softie. He was tough as nails but as soft as anything too."

Ralph Clark was a former Daniels lawyer and consultant: "In the mid-seventies there were a lot of years when Bill was broke, and during a lot of those years we were his attorneys. It bothered him greatly, but I sat in his office and heard him do something every week. He would go through his creditor list and call each one of them. He would call every creditor, give them a report, and tell them what was going on, and because of this they had so much confidence in him that he never had any overwhelming financial problems. He was always in control. A confident man does this and his creditors always respect it and cut him more slack."

Alan Gerry was another pioneer in the cable industry. "Bill's life shows that someone with ambition and guts—or you could call it soul—can rise above where he came from, rise out of the dust and climb the ladder and do something. Basically, it showed that you can do anything you set your heart on."

"About two or three years ago," says Daniels' friend Jim Watson, "my fourteen-year-old black Lab named Stoly died—a total tearjerker and heartbreaker. My kids are sad and I'm a train wreck. The kids are just starting to school, Catholic school, and my wife was telling them that Stoly went to heaven and heaven is up in the sky. Bill and I were on the phone talking and he asked me what we were doing in the next couple of weeks, and I said we were going up to Aspen, taking the kids. So he said, 'Well, goddammit, I want you to bring them to Denver, spend a night or two. I'll send the plane and I'll have a car.' I said, No, Bill, I don't want the car or the plane. We'll come by and see you.'

"A few hours later I get a phone call from the Daniels office, and they said that Bill had called and he wants the plane to take your family to Denver and when do you want to go. I told them I already had airline tickets, and they said, 'Absolutely not—he won't hear of it.' Anyway, the plane comes, my daughter is nervous and doesn't want to get on this small plane, but we get on board, and as we're climbing out of John Wayne Airport [in Southern California], there's this huge white puffy cloud. We had spent weeks talking about Stoly being up in heaven. As we go up through these huge puffy clouds, my daughter lets out this huge scream and glues her face to the window. I said, 'Honey, what's the matter?' She said, 'We're in heaven—I see Stoly out there!' The other kids leap up and smash their faces against the window.

"The beauty of this is that all three kids thought they saw Stoly out there in heaven. Now I'm thinking, 'Only my friend Bill Daniels could make some crazy fantasy like this come true. I looked over at my wife and she's got big tears streaming down her face and I'm crying. You know kids of that age—we spent two hours flying there and they were absolutely confident they saw Stoly out there. No one could have pulled this off but Bill Daniels. When we landed, I told him, 'You can't believe what you did.'"

Some people thought that although Daniels talked and voted like a staunch Republican, he had the heart of a deeply compassionate Democrat, always fighting for the underdog.

Jim worked for Carlsbad Cablevision, one of the Daniels properties. "I remember when they asked me to say something at Bill's memorial. I thought of the ants and the LifeSavers™. In the last six months of Bill's life, he thought a lot about life and God, and he was taking looks at the little things in life. I came in one day and he had LifeSavers all lined up across his driveway. I thought, 'This is it, Bill's losing it.' I said to him, 'What are you doing?' He said, 'I'm feeding the ants. If I don't feed them, who's going to feed them?' He was out there with LifeSavers. It was the silliest thing you ever saw, but when he'd leave the house, he'd call me and say, 'How are my LifeSavers—do I need to put any more out?' He cared about every little thing."

"Bill," says Daniels executive Phil Hogue, "called me on a Saturday morning in December and asked me to meet him at the office, and we headed down to Holy Ghost Church. He was talking about Father Woody and this was the day of the Christmas dinner for the poor. We sat in Father Woody's office and he gave me an envelope to give to Father Woody, which I guess was my duty for the day. So we went out to the hall where the dinner was being held, and Bill was introducing himself to kids in T-shirts in December and people who were clearly living on the street. He spent a couple of hours talking to people. When we left, I asked him, 'Was that at all uncomfortable when you have so much and you are talking to people who have nothing?' He looked at me and said, 'I do this as often as I can to remind myself of how lucky I am.'"

"To me," says trade TV publisher Bill McGorry, "Bill exemplified the notion that nice guys can win. Taking the high road, because along the way there are always shortcuts and you can always buy into something that you really don't want to do or you don't think is necessarily right. He lived by example. You know that Robert Kennedy quote about a rich kid that gave a damn? I think it was Jimmy Breslin that said that about Bobby Kennedy. He was a rich kid who cared. I think that holds well for Bill, because he was a guy of means who really gave a damn about people, the little people, the everyday people.

"The industry he built is one thing. But, for me, his legacy is all those people he came in touch with and influenced. Anybody who came in touch with him in the course of their lives was better for it. If he crossed your path, you would be somehow enriched by it and I don't mean by monetary means, but the fact that one would come away with something worth much, much more. You carry that spirit around with you, and it is the spirit of Bill Daniels."

Says former Colorado Governor Dick Lamm: "There was a certain sadness in Bill. When I was around him, I had a sense of *The Great Gatsby*. I am a huge fan of F. Scott Fitzgerald, and one time I went to the University of Wisconsin and we rented this huge mansion right on Lake Geneva, which is where F. Scott Fitzgerald wrote the book. Across the lake there was a red light and a blue light, just like in the novel, and I remember sitting on the dock and staring and thinking about the vividness of this person who had all this money to spend and yet he couldn't get what he really wanted although he could get anything else. To me, Bill Daniels was a Gatsbylike character. He couldn't control his cigarettes or his womanizing, and to me those are very big flaws in an otherwise wonderful person."

Many people, including Governor Lamm, took issue with Daniels on his political stances, but no one argued that he was first and last a patriot and a supporter of his country.

"Bill and I had always had one agreement," says Jack Daniels, "and that particularly referred to the presidency. Once an election was over and the president that was elected was *our* president, we weren't going to sit around and take cheap shots and argue about him and say, 'Well, why didn't he do this or why didn't he do that?' We started this probably thirty, forty years ago because I think we had somewhat of a concept of what a big job the presidency is, and we sure as hell didn't want to be disrespectful. We talked about Clinton a little bit—we got into that. And when he'd talk about the womanizing, I'd say, 'Goddamn, Bill, who are you to say anything? It's a good thing you weren't elected governor of Colorado! You know how women migrate to power.'"

Despite his claim to being a hardcore Republican, Daniels' politics were never entirely predictable.

"I always thought he was a closet Democrat," says Gretchen Bunn. "I was fond of teasing him by saying, 'If all Republicans were like you, I'd be one!'"

In the early eighties, Democrat Federico Peña decided to run for the mayor's office in Denver. Daniels' backing of the young man shocked everyone. Recalls Peña, "In the *Rocky Mountain News*, when I first announced my candidacy, its headline actually said, 'Dark Horse Candidate.' Very early in my campaign, when hardly anybody knew I was running, Bill Daniels actually showed up for my fund-raiser. Everybody knew that he was a very strict Republican, with deep roots, and an unabashedly strong Reagan supporter. Why on earth he would ever think of supporting a Democrat was beyond me and everybody else, for that matter. I was actually shocked that he would show up for my fund-raiser, and the people that were there and saw him were equally surprised to see him there.

"Then I got to know him, and what I saw in Bill was a man who minced no words. You always knew exactly how he felt; he didn't hesitate to give you his opinion about things. He was very direct and sometimes assumed something of a tough manner, but frankly, once you got to know him, you really appreciated it. You always knew exactly what his position was, and you knew that if he made a commitment he was going to stick to it. This was a man of his word. I remember that when he finally said that he would support me, it was clear that he would support me and no one was going to tell him otherwise.

"All of his Republican friends would be with him and Bill would say, 'We're going to raise money for Federico. All of you know that I am a staunch Republican and that he is a staunch Democrat, but I don't care. The issues we are dealing with, the airport, convention center, et cetera, are not partisan issues—they are people issues and city issues.' He would just hit them hard. It was never one of these wishy-washy things where some people would say that they were going to support me because I was mayor and they just wanted to be on my side in case I won. I will never forget his support.

"Bill taught me the importance of having a relationship with the business community. He taught me in a time when people questioned having relationships with the business community. There was a school of thought that said you could not have a positive relationship with the business community because they were the evil empire. Here was a Republican, very successful businessman, a tough guy who taught me that there is really a way to work this and you can work that relationship in a way that is beneficial for a lot of people.

"The other thing that he taught me was that you have to stick to your guns, and if you really believe in something, stake a course and don't hesitate. You may get knocked down here and there, but pick yourself up and keep going. I think that he taught people how to have a spine and not to be so wishy-washy about things and to be willing to stand up to your principles whether they are popular or not and to be your own person. Those were terrific lessons, and the other thing that Bill taught me over time was how wonderful it is to be generous with your money. I don't have as much as he did, but he was a wonder to observe, primarily because his generosity would come out of nowhere. There are some people that when they give their money, they have to spend weeks and weeks telling everybody about it, and finally when they make the announcement you think, 'Well, finally you made the donation.' With Bill it was like a lightning bolt."

Neil Bush, the third son of former President George H. W. Bush, was on the board of Denver's Silverado Savings and Loan in the early nineties when it collapsed in a scandal. Everyone associated with the company, including Bush, was tainted. Many people who had previously been close to him suddenly distanced themselves. But not Daniels.

"Bill was my one true friend in Denver," says Bush, "despite the fact that I was going through a horrible public relations crisis. He stood by my side and held out a helping hand."

Daniels got Bush a job at a company he partly owned, Transmedia Communications in Houston. Never one to back away from controversy or to refuse to help someone when he was down, Daniels was instrumental in helping Bush rebuild his reputation and his life.

"I would go to his office and solicit advice," Bush says. "What was special about this is that his advice came from his heart and he cared about me as a human being. It was never professorial or in a tone that was diminishing or demeaning to me, but rather as a father to his son. I just loved his demeanor, his humbleness, and his caring. You could just tell that he was a loving human being."

He was also a human being who inspired comparisons with some notable historical figures. "Bill," says Professor James Quinn of Dartmouth, "was a classic guy in the same way that Alexander the Great was. That may seem like a strange analogy, but it is true. The way Alexander conquered the world was that immediately after the battle, when the surrender was present, he would identify a few people from the local area that had very high prestige and give them the opportunity to run the conquered area. Mind you, this was always under the very careful eye of Alexander, but he left them very autonomous. He believed that they would operate his provinces well, and he knew that if he had to put Macedonia on all those provinces it would never work. So, he left them highly autonomous. He was the first conqueror in history to do this, and the result was that he established this enormous empire with relatively few resources and it held together as long as Alexander lived. This is how I believe that you run a successful enterprise. You find good people, let them know what your expectations are, then you leave them alone and gently prod them with visions and the feeling of what success is. You let them run the enterprise, and you multiply your capacity by a thousand.

"I remember Bill in terms of images. The wonderful big smile on his face, the challenging glint in his eye, and the capacity to say something a little outrageous that would make you start talking. What always fascinated me is how he would sit there and listen. Even with his dominating presence in a room, he was a listener. Other people could say things directly and he never interfered with the conversation or insisted that it be his way, but yet, in the end, you knew he was the guy that was going to pull everything together. It is a fascinating talent and is one that few people have. It is the combination of high energy, risk taking, and the willingness to get in the pits and do the work themselves, yet to have the capacity to step back and listen and to trust people. Those are the things that stand out in my mind, along with that glittering eye and his big grin."

Says Gretchen Bunn: "There was an amazing combination of charisma and kindness in Bill. With some powerful executives you got the feeling people were dispensable—that they would only take themselves and their inner circle on a journey up the ladder. With Bill, you knew he intended to take you with him—he left no one behind."

"The one thing I learned from Bill," says his longtime friend Dick Robinson, "is that you don't play games with people. If you have something to say, say it. One day I said to him, 'How do you get away with saying what you do?' He said, 'I just tell people the truth. If I tell the truth, I never have to remember what I told anyone.' So just tell people what you mean."

Dale Bradley is the CEO of Greater Than Technologies. When he was fifteen, he walked into the Young Americans Bank, which Daniels had founded in order to educate young people about the use of money and the free enterprise system (which Daniels always called the eighth wonder of the world). The day that Bradley came into the bank as a customer, he was hired on the spot to set up the bank's computers. He ended up training the staff and assisting customers with educational software. Getting hired at Daniels' bank like this told him that he had entered a new world.

"My first impression of Bill was twofold," he says. "One was that he had an incredible physical presence. You could almost reach out and touch it. The second thing I remember is that if I bring my hand to my nose, I can still smell Bill. He wore some cologne that was wonderful, and he shook your hand and it was the softest hand, and for hours afterward you could smell Bill. What I miss the most about him was his sense of invincibility. When Bill was here, we could do *anything*. There are a few people in your world that, standing next to them, you feel you can do anything. You can walk off a cliff and fly. The feeling I got when he was at the table was that anything was possible."

Twenty-eight

For three decades, going back to the 1950s, the issue of regulating cable had been a hotly contested subject on Capitol Hill. The networks, phone companies, local political groups, and Hollywood's movie moguls had all fought to give Congress some control over the growth and economics of the cable industry. On the other side of the struggle, cable operators and brokers like Daniels had battled to free their business from the constraints of Washington. The tug-of-war had tilted one way and then another ever since cable had begun. In the sixties, cable operators had won a round in Congress, but in the early seventies, they'd lost some gains they'd made in earlier years. By the eighties, the pro-regulation mood that had been prevalent for the past decade or more was starting to change. Cable had risen from being TV's poor cousin to becoming a permanent and respected player on the television dial. It was creating more and more programming and finding a wider audience every week. But the issue of who controlled its rates and who decided which franchises got renewed and which didn't had never been resolved.

Congressman Tim Wirth, the young Colorado Democrat who by 1984 was the chairman of the House Telecommunications Subcommittee, was determined to change the situation. As a friend and political ally of Daniels and Denver's other cable powerhouses, he'd gone to Congress a decade earlier with the notion of deregulating the industry. Ten years later, he was ready to make his move, and conditions for deregulation looked good. In 1980 Ronald Reagan, a free-market Republican with a long record of opposing government intervention in business, had captured the White House. Historically, Republicans had supported deregulating cable while Democrats had often taken the opposite stance. Following the 1980 election, Republicans won control of the Senate for the first time since Harry Truman's presidency. If deregulation passed, it would be the greatest boon to cable in the industry's history.

In 1983, after months of work, the Senate passed a version of a cable deregulation bill. Then it went to the House, and throughout 1984 compromises flew back and forth, until it appeared that the bill would become law in October—just before the session came to an end. Because 1984 was an election year, it was critical that the legislation take effect now or be subject to all the political vagaries that elections bring. If the bill didn't pass in this session, the entire process would return to step one. At the last moment, a snag arose that threatened to kill the entire legislation.

Late at night on October 10, the chief counsel on Wirth's subcommittee, a California lawyer named Tom Rogers, contacted the congressman with a possible solution. California had already adopted an innovative deregulation bill that essentially allowed cable operators to make the deregulation decision for themselves: if they didn't want to deregulate, they didn't have to, but if they did, then they were required to contribute a percentage of their gross revenues to public service programming. With the support of Governor Jerry Brown, the measure had become law. The effect of the bill was to allow for gradual cable rate hikes and the generating monies to be used for homegrown programming. This plan had served the Golden State well, and Tom Rogers believed it might help salvage the current legislation.

Wirth and Rogers worked very late into the night of October 10, putting together a compromise solution based on the California legislation. The following day, both the Senate and House passed the bill only hours before ending the session and heading back home. Deregulation had finally come, and it was a great victory for Daniels and his side. Thirty years after he'd begun preaching the gospel of letting free market forces determine cable's economic fate, the United States Congress officially had accepted his position.

In the next few years, the unshackled cable industry took off and began to fulfill its potential. Cable systems could now set their own rates, which in turn generated much more stability. Because of this, franchises were more assured of being renewed in cities around the country. Cash flow increased and debts were serviced more easily. The entire system was healthier. In 1988 Daniels & Associates sold its cable systems to United Artists and achieved a level of financial solidity it had never known before. The company that had often edged toward bankruptcy because of the boss's unpredictable desires to buy up sports teams had turned a significant corner. Daniels was rich and his business was increasingly lucrative. Decades of uncertainty were over—and not just at his firm.

Wall Street now looked favorably upon the whole industry, investors followed their lead, money flowed heavily toward cable, and it was growing into a multibillion-dollar enterprise. The major cable players—Comcast, ATC, and Telecommunications, Inc.—were on their way to becoming household names. More battles lay ahead for cable, because every shift in the political wind brought forces that would challenge its power in the marketplace, but the biggest battles had been won. Cable TV was here to stay, and in the 1990s it would evolve into a media force that exceeded the imagination of its early pioneers.

While all these changes were unfolding in the industry, Daniels was spending more and more time away from the office, spreading his particular style of business and of living not just across the nation but around the globe. In 1986 he traveled to the Soviet Union with his then-current girlfriend, Catherine Olsen, who had been introduced to Daniels & Associates a few years earlier by performing a Marilyn Monroe impersonation at a company function. She was soon dating Daniels, who was exactly forty years her senior. Even though the age difference was great, the relationship lasted several years.

"I was extremely immature on many different levels when Bill met me," Olsen says, "and there were ways in which I had to grow up very fast. He transformed me."

Julia Sprunt was a Turner executive in the 1980s. Daniels' charity, she noticed, was no different in a communist state from what it had been in Denver.

"Bill went with us, the Turner group, to Moscow, to the Goodwill Games in 1986," she says. "This was before Gorbachev had dissolved the USSR, so we were still in a communist country. Every day we'd get on a bus and these 'in-tourist guides' would direct us. They were all young women, smart as could be, but we all knew they worked for the government and John Malone quickly pointed out to us that they were also spies. So we needed to be careful what we said. The guides were always in the front of the bus on the microphone, and there was always a young man in the very back of the bus and we were told that he was there just in case the bus broke down. We knew both of them were watching each other. And we also knew that the guy on the bus was another spy.

"Bill was with us and we would go to government shops, and there were a few cable executives who just came out with armfuls of gifts and Bill was no exception. He bought and he bought. What was different was that he gave all his gifts away to the in-tourist guides and to women he met in the hotels. Sometimes he would buy a gift in the store and turn around and give it to the women across the counter who had just taken his money for the purchase.

"Everybody at the American embassy, they all knew Bill Daniels because he was such a big supporter of the Republican Party. We went to the ambassador's home, which was pretty special. We walk in and there was Richard Nixon! That was a great surprise. At some point you heard on the other side of the room someone playing 'God Bless America.' We go over, and who is behind the piano but Richard Nixon with Bill Daniels looking on with a smile on his face and an expression that looked like he was about to pop."

When he wasn't traveling around the world helping strangers, Daniels was assisting his friends in America. In the mid-eighties, Marshall Kaplan, the dean of University of Colorado Graduate School of Public Affairs, received a call from Bob Russo of Daniels & Associates. Russo said that Daniels himself would be phoning soon.

"He called," Kaplan says, "and asked if I would help a friend of his, the actress Jane Fonda, get her child into Boulder. I made it clear that I didn't control admissions and there is a process. However, I said I would call and find out. So I called up to Boulder and found out there was no problem. The real problem was that their papers were lost. In any bureaucracy like our own, sometimes people are incompetent. And the papers were lost, but we found them and Jane Fonda's son, who had a different name, finally got accepted into Boulder. I thought that was the end of it.

"A week later, Bill Daniels sent me a check for $75,000 for minority scholarships. I thought that was just beautiful, and it really helped the Graduate School of Public Affairs increase the amount of minorities who could go to the school. It wasn't necessary and Bill didn't have to send me anything. It was something I would do for a friend or a colleague or a respected person like he was. It then became known, apparently, that I was able to help Hollywood people get their kids into Boulder, so Richard Zanuck called me at the suggestion of Bill Daniels! He said, 'My son is applying to Boulder and he hasn't heard anything. Can you help him?' I said the same thing to him: you can't tamper with the admissions process, but I'll find out.

"Sure enough, again the kid's application forms were lost and we found them! Sure enough—again I get a check for $50,000 from Bill for minority scholarships! He did ask me where I wanted to put the money and I said minority scholarships. I really felt good about that because it wasn't a requested amount of funds, it was just spontaneous. It told me what type of guy he was. He didn't have to send me anything. I've done it for other people who hadn't sent me $75,000 or $50,000."

Deregulation had arrived, the cable business was better than it had ever been, and Daniels was feeling exceedingly expansive. He'd recently conceived of and was building a spectacular 24,000-square-foot home in Denver called Cableland on the property where he'd once lived with Devra and her children. Cableland was to be a kind of shrine to the newly arrived success of the industry. The house would feature one wall with sixty-four TV sets, a library of classic movies, a spa, a wide array of elephant sculptures and figurines, a swimming pool, and a fire pole so you could slide down from one floor to the next. Daniels intended to use the grand house to entertain moguls from the communications business and for charity causes. It would be one more asset in his efforts to help other people, but first he had to overcome some local opposition.

"The neighborhood was concerned about it initially because of all Cableland's activities and traffic," says Barry Hirschfeld, who lived next door. "The neighbors formed a coalition to defeat the building of it because it required some variances and things. Bill got through that and even after he moved in, the neighbors formed a group to limit his activities there."

Daniels enlisted Hirschfeld's help in getting past this resistance and Cableland was born. The neighbors, including the kids, grew to like Daniels.

"He was just a really cool guy," says Hayden Hirschfeld, Barry's son. "He was one of the older people that I was around as a little person, but he had this amazing ability to transcend age. I remember shaking his hand and he would have me do this strange, secret handshake that I thought was so neat. He made me feel very comfortable."

Cableland became a mecca for fund-raising activities and many worthwhile causes gained attention and support inside its walls. It was Bill's gift to Denver and the scene of numerous colorful dinner parties. James Riede was the caretaker at Cableland and a witness to both those parties and to the private side of Bill that few others saw. James was a confidant of sorts, and to this day he continues to protect his boss's privacy.

"The first thing Bill Daniels said to me in our initial interview," recalls Riede, "was 'Goddamn, you're tall. Do you play basketball?'"

Riede did not play basketball but he was a gourmet cook, yet he never cooked for Bill, except to make him an occasional grilled cheese sandwich. Daniels rarely had an appetite, preferring his coffee and cigarettes. Riede's main role came into play when Bill entertained.

"The camaraderie with the guests was what Bill cared about," he says. "My job was to make sure everything clicked. It had to be a fun time for the guests, because if the guests weren't happy, Bill wasn't happy."

One such occasion involved twenty women pilots whom he'd kept track of through the years because of their unique profession. He invited them all to lunch at Cableland to celebrate their achievements.

"Here's Bill surrounded by twenty ladies," says Riede, "and he was king of the hill! Each lady had a package that contained a balsa wood airplane. During the meal each person talked about her airline and pilot responsibilities, and then all of a sudden they started opening up their packets. They were sipping a little wine, getting giddy and having fun when one of these planes flies by Bill. He picks it up, throws it across the room, and now there are twenty airplanes flying through the house.

"Bill was very proud of these women. He was seventy-eight years old and he'd watched them grow and was always surprised and happy when someone he knew was flying a 777 and that person was a gal."

One of Daniels' most passionate causes was the United Way fund. He encouraged—and cajoled—every one of his employees to give to this charity every year. He told his people, "You don't have to give what I give, but it's important for *you* that you give." As a result, Daniels & Associates had a 100 percent annual participation. This gave him great pride in his associates.

"I happened to get very involved with United Way only because Bill suggested it," says Brad Busse, president of Daniels & Associates. "I became more and more involved, and United Way started plugging into me as a potential larger giver. I became chairman of the Alexis de Tocqueville Society, which is the top end of leadership giving at United Way. When I first got involved, there were only seventy members of this in Denver as compared to comparable communities with three hundred to four hundred members. I felt a lot of it was due to the fact that people were not getting the message and were not being approached. They just didn't know. So I was doing a lot of things to bring people together, and Cableland was a great venue for that.

"I would always call Bill because I never wanted to take it for granted. I'd say, 'We're having a special event and aiming at leaders in the community and trying to get them involved in the Alexis Society. Would you be willing to let me use Cableland and maybe host this with food and beverage?' He'd always say yes. This went on for several years, and then I asked him again for the use of Cableland. He returned my call and gets me out of a meeting and says, 'Brad, goddammit, if you want to use Cableland, just use it. My house is your house. If you're doing something charitable, just plan on it.' And that was so Bill."

In time Daniels decided to donate Cableland to the city of Denver following his death, in the hopes that the mayor would make it his residence. The house held colorful memories for everyone who attended events within it.

Denver Post sports columnist Woody Paige was once invited to a Thanksgiving dinner at Cableland. "Bill had brought together a wide-ranging group of individuals," Paige says. "It was an eclectic group and different than any other dinner or party that you would go to. He'd hand-picked people from different places and areas and backgrounds so that they could interact. The meal was incredibly prepared by his chef and staff, and he had invited a Native American who got up before we had lunch and explained the traditions and backgrounds and tools that the Native Americans had used to prepare and gather their food. Suddenly, Thanksgiving dinner had a totally different meaning.

"Who sits down at Thanksgiving with a bunch of strangers to get to know each other with a Native American to explain what it used to be like and to explain what it all meant? It was a Thanksgiving dinner that I will always remember because it had a very special meaning."

Paige became a friend of Daniels and was astounded by the wide range of his contacts. He was also amazed at the breadth and depth of the man's influence and legacy.

"Bill," he says, "was very proud of being labeled the father of cable television. He took an idea and gave it to the world. What he did with cable television is establish what we have today. CNN, ESPN, and the proliferation of cable stations is just one aspect of his legacy. He also represented his country in World War II, and I have great respect for people who did what he did during that war. His legacy is in education, in sports, in contributions that have affected tens of thousands of lives, if not more. Just using Cableland as a focus for charity events—and over a period of time there were a thousand different charity events—what is the effect for each one of those on people?

"When you multiply all that he did, it is hard to believe that there is anyone in Denver or Colorado who has not been affected by his generosity. How many people in the country are not affected by cable television? How many people at the University of Denver have been affected by what he has accomplished or his great contributions to that school? Those people who study business and go out into the business world—all those people are affected by his strong belief about business ethics. That has to affect hundreds if not thousands of businesses.

"When you put it all together, it's a pyramid."

One of Daniels' friends in Denver for many years was Police Chief Jerry Kennedy. Bill put up the original seed money—$25,000—to start the Police Athletic League (PAL) in the Mile High City. Daniels insisted on leaving his two California houses to the PAL, which were worth between $3 and $4 million. In his will Daniels instructed that $2 million from the proceeds of the sale of these houses go toward creating a permanent structure for the PAL, named the Chief Jerry Kennedy Memorial.

"This was certainly something I didn't expect," says Kennedy. "Bill did awesome things. There is nobody who's been held in higher regard than Bill Daniels in this community."

Saying he believed Denver needed to recognize the importance of its mayors, Bill Daniels in 1998 donated his $7 million mansion known as "Cableland" to the city of Denver as its official mayoral residence.

Twenty-nine

Ironically, the man who'd pushed for decades to bring cable into the mainstream of American life and who'd believed that it would become both culturally important and a lucrative investment, was not doing very well during the years of cable's great ascent. During the mid-eighties, he was, in fact, going through his worst time ever. Despite building Cableland and opening its doors to many others, Daniels himself was rarely in Denver these days. He stayed in California most of the time, living by himself near the beach and struggling with issues that had tormented him for decades. Demons had always been chasing him and now, perhaps because he was alone or because he was slowing down due to age, they were finally starting to catch up.

Like many people who'd been heavy drinkers or abused other substances over long periods of time, he was approaching a critical choice: he either needed to change his behavior or he was likely going to die. And even if he didn't die, the last part of his life could be dismal and crippled, with the old fighter essentially defeated from within. He'd never allowed that to happen before—pride and strength had always made him straighten himself out and keep moving forward. Maybe he couldn't do that anymore; maybe it was too late for that kind of change. Those around him were disheartened to see him heading inevitably in the direction of no return. His problems hadn't gotten better with age, but worse. Action needed to be taken, but how could you confront someone as bullheaded and strong-willed as Bill Daniels? Would he listen to anyone's advice? And who was going to deliver it? These kinds of questions had surfaced more than once at Daniels & Associates, but a showdown was always postponed.

Then something happened one afternoon in 1986 in a hotel in Scottsdale, Arizona.

"Bill was living at his beach house in California," says John Saeman. "We seldom saw him in Denver. Once in a while he would make a trip to the office, and everybody would clear their desks and get ready for him. I would talk to Bill maybe once a day by phone. All of a sudden, it went quiet, and we didn't hear from Bill for two or three days."

Saeman and Daniels' secretary, Jayne Mitchell, began calling Tony Acone in the Carlsbad office, asking if he'd seen Daniels or knew of his whereabouts. The answer was no. The worry inside Daniels & Associates deepened; even in bad circumstances, the head man had always stayed in touch. Tony looked for the boss's car at the San Diego airport, but it wasn't there. He drove up to Daniels' home at LaCosta, but no one was there, either. He called several other places, including the Desert Inn in Las Vegas, but had no luck. He wasn't in Palm Springs, either, so they began looking in Arizona but got nowhere. Daniels had disappeared.

"Now we were really getting concerned," Saeman says. "We were to the point where we thought maybe we should put out an all-points bulletin for Bill."

Saeman needed to attend a board meeting in Baton Rouge, Louisiana, the next day. The office decided that if they didn't find Daniels very soon, they should contact the police or the FBI. At the time they had no idea what Daniels had been going through.

A few days earlier, he'd left his home in Del Mar and started across California headed east. He wrecked his car, and while it was sitting in a ditch a patrolman came but stopped only briefly. The officer had to get to a worse wreck down the road but said he would help Daniels out by calling a tow truck for him. When the truck arrived, Daniels asked the driver to take him to a hotel and get him a rented car. To motivate the man, Daniels gave him a check for $10,000. He spent that night in a hotel and then left the next morning for Phoenix in the rented car. Late that afternoon, he was outside Phoenix when a policeman pulled over Daniels' weaving car. In the front seat were some empty wine bottles and some full ones on ice. The officer booked him and threw him in jail, where he spent the night—in a cell with several other men—dressed only in black silk underwear and long black socks. The following morning, he was released and took a taxi into Scottsdale, where he went looking for another hotel.

That same day John Saeman was down in Baton Rouge, becoming more and more worried about Daniels. He called the Denver office before getting on his flight home, anxious to hear about any developments. There were none. Nobody had any idea where Daniels was. As Saeman's plane was taxiing down the runway, a man ran up to it waving his arms and trying to stop the flight. He succeeded and told Saeman that he had an urgent call.

It was Jayne Mitchell telling Saeman that Daniels had just phoned from the Scottsdale Hilton in Arizona. He didn't say why he was there or what he'd been doing, and he sounded very bad. Saeman told her to contact the most important person in Daniels' life—his younger brother in Albuquerque—because they were going to have to go to Scottsdale to confront Bill and Jack needed to be there. Saeman said that he would fly to Scottsdale and be waiting for Jack at the local airport. For the past several days, Tom Marinkovich had also been a part of trying to locate Daniels, and he felt he should be at the showdown as well. He jumped on a plane and flew to Phoenix. Tyler Johnson, the caretaker of Daniels' home in Denver, went along with him as backup.

They all met at the Scottsdale airport, drove to the hotel, got Daniels' room number, and the four men gathered in front of it. Jack knocked on the door. There was no answer. He knocked again, this time harder.

"Who is it?" a weak voice came from the other side.

Jack told him that it was his brother.

"Who?" the weak voice asked.

Jack told him again.

Very slowly, Daniels opened the door. He was a ghastly sight. He was standing in front of them—"weaving" is a better word—in knee-length black nylon socks and a pair of black underwear, with nothing else on. The room was pitch black at four in the afternoon and reeked of booze and other stale odors. The floor was a mess and so was the man.

"He just looked like death warmed over," recalls Saeman. "The room looked like a den of iniquity."

"What are you guys doing here?" Daniels wanted to know, as he stumbled around making a feeble effort to pick up some of the trash.

Before they answered him, the men walked around the room, opening up the curtains to let in some light and the windows to let in fresh air.

For several awkward moments there was silence. Then Daniels' brother took the lead.

"He'd been drinking and taking Valium," Jack says. "I asked him a question and he started blubbering to me, crying, saying, 'My sweetheart left me.' It was about a woman. About a week earlier, he'd told me that he was going to dump her, but she dumped him first and that's what got to him. I said, 'Goddamn, man, you've dumped more women than anyone. What are you doing to yourself?' He said, 'You don't understand. I lost my sweetheart and I've had a little bit too much to drink.' I said, 'Let's make some coffee. We're gonna take you to the Betty Ford clinic and get you some help.'"

This was not what Daniels had been expecting to hear and it clearly took him by surprise. He wasn't sure if they were serious. He looked at Saeman and asked what he thought about this suggestion. Saeman said that he was fully behind taking him to Betty Ford.

"Then," says Jack, "he turned to Tom and said, 'What about you?' Tom hadn't been with the company too long and he began stuttering around. So John said, 'He's with us.' Bill looked at all of us and said, 'I've never had three better friends in my life. Let's do it.'"

They dumped out all the booze stashed in his room and made plans to go to dinner that night at the hotel restaurant.

Because Bill had a prior relationship with the Fords that went back to his run for governor of Colorado, Jack Daniels and Saeman felt that the Betty Ford clinic was the best choice. The respectability of the organization and its nearby location in Palm Springs were also positive factors. Before the men had flown to Scottsdale, Jayne Mitchell had called Betty Ford and asked if a room could be made available quickly. The ex-first lady's reply was succinct: "You get him there. I'll have a room." Despite this assurance, the men wondered if Daniels would actually follow through and go to the clinic.

Jack had told his brother to meet them at five-thirty the next morning in the Hilton restaurant to start the trip, but Saeman doubted that he would show up. That evening they all rented rooms at the Hilton and ate together. Daniels didn't order a drink with his meal, didn't argue with their mission, and when five-thirty arrived the next morning, he was standing in the lobby of the hotel, ready to leave for Palm Springs.

"He kept telling me that he was afraid to go to Betty Ford, in case he ever slipped up and had a drink," Jack says. "I said, 'Don't worry about that. A lot of people slip up. Just do it.'"

They flew to California, took him to the clinic, and checked him in. The men left him there and went back home, receiving periodic calls from Daniels' counselor at Betty Ford, Jeri Bohanan, who gave them progress reports on the patient. He gave them his own reports on Bohanan, whom he originally described as "tough old lady." She was precisely that when it came to dealing with her charges, cutting them no slack, regardless of how rich or famous or important they felt they were. Daniels' first demand at the clinic was that he be allowed to receive the *New York Times* each morning. This was met with a flat no. When he asked why, Bohanan told him that because no one else got the paper, he wouldn't be getting it, either. He told her to get it for everyone and he'd pay for it. She said no again and that was that.

"My first encounter with Bill," says Bohanan, "was in the unit office, and Bill was sitting there, slouched down with his head hanging down. He was in bad shape; he really had the shakes. I don't know if he was coming off of a drunk or going through withdrawals. Anyway, he decided he wanted to leave. He just didn't think he needed this. I looked at him and said, 'Bill, hold out your hand.' He couldn't hold his hand straight. So I said, 'Look at your hands and how they're shaking. Why don't you give this a try? What do you have to lose?' He looked at me with tears in his eyes and said, 'Well, I guess I will.' That was the beginning for Bill."

Worse days were still to come. When Daniels refused to take part in the swimming pool exercises but just sat and smoked and watched the others work out, the woman in charge of the program, Brie Swift, told him to "put out that goddamn cigarette and get in the pool." He was taken aback by her tone of voice and so embarrassed at being singled out for punishment that he quickly doused the smoke and jumped in the water.

Bohanan and Swift were all over him.

"One time," says Saeman, "Jeri called and said they were having a hard time figuring out what was going on with Bill—he's not telling them everything they need to know. So I said, 'How can I help?' She said, 'Well, he's got to be on something that we don't know about in addition to the things we do know about.' So I went over to his little Denver apartment with a shopping bag and took everything that was a pill and put it in the bag and fedexed it out to her. Couple days later, Bill called me on a Friday night at home. 'You sonofabitch,' he said, 'do you have any idea of what you've done to me?' By then I had kind of forgotten about it, and I said, 'Bill! What's going on?' He said, 'You sent all those fucking pills over here, and now I'm going to have to be here another two weeks!' His stay, instead of being four weeks, ended up being six. I still have no idea what they found in that bag. Whatever it was, it had a compounding effect that didn't do him any good."

Despite Daniels' flare-ups and his reluctance to tell the Betty Ford staff everything he'd been taking, he was gradually undergoing detoxification and showing improvement. When it came time to share his personal story with others at the clinic, he was as hesitant to delve deeply into his private life with these strangers as he'd always been with those in his office, yet he did not run away from the experience. He stayed and endured the rituals that come with stopping drinking, with drying out, and with placing one's life in the control of others.

"I know," says Saeman, "that he was humiliated a great deal out there by having to run a vacuum cleaner and things of that nature. So this was an interesting time. Tom [Marinkovich] made the comment that when he confronted Bill in Scottsdale, he was in fear of losing his job. I was never worried about how Bill would react to these things, because I felt ultimately that if I was right, Bill was a rational guy. He was going to realize he needed help, and he wasn't going to fire me. Maybe I had way more confidence than I should have had, but I didn't feel like my job was on the line. I guess I felt enough confidence in what I was doing because he didn't have anybody else but his brother Jack and me."

After six weeks in the clinic, he was released and returned to his California home. In the future he would struggle with going back to his old habits and would be tempted to drink on a regular basis. He would gulp a lot of coffee and smoke a lot of cigarettes, but the crisis point had passed. He'd made it through detox and wouldn't go on a bad binge again. At the critical moment, when his life might have been on the line, his best friends had bailed him out. Daniels would now return to work as well, something he'd basically been avoiding for a long time, and he would play a significant role in building the

Prime Ticket regional sports network into a huge success. The old warrior was rising once again.

He not only bounced back from his last disastrous love affair, but more girlfriends would come and go. He would never again react as badly to a broken heart. By now Daniels was in his late sixties, and the years were starting to apply some pressure to his brakes. This is not to say that all his adventures were over, but the depths of his self-destructiveness had been reached. After walking out of the Betty Ford Center in Palm Springs, he'd decided to live.

"To Bill's credit," says Bob Russo, "he got that ten thousand dollar cancelled check back that he'd given that tow truck driver in California after he'd wrecked his car. He had the check put in Lucite and he kept it on his desk. If you look at the check, you can tell that it had been written by a person who was drunk. It was barely legible and he wrote over a couple of things twice. But he kept it on his desk in Denver for all of the rest of the time that I knew him, even after he got out of Betty Ford. It was there to remind him of just how low he had gotten."

Thirty

B ecause of his successful stay at the clinic, Betty Ford appointed him to her center's board, and during the next few years he would refer a number of people to her center—people with either drinking or drug problems. Some of them, such as Liz Sterling and Jodi Morrelli, worked at Daniels & Associates and some did not. Not everyone he tried to help got the message the first time. In October 1985, Denver TV sportscaster Mike Nolan called his friend and told Daniels he had a drinking problem. Although the clinic had a considerable waiting list, Daniels got Nolan admitted almost immediately. He was scheduled to arrive at the clinic on a Friday but spent that Thursday night getting drunk. After boarding the plane for Betty Ford, he had a few Bloody Marys and decided to skip the chance to dry out and hopped another plane for Maui, where he stayed drunk for three more days. After a subsequent conversation with Daniels, he got back on another plane and went straight to the clinic. This time the cure took.

"When I entered the clinic," says Nolan, "Bill told me that if I tended to business, he would fly my two boys out to see me. That was Bill. He flew the boys out, and it was just terrific to see them. He was always concerned. After I left Betty Ford and my first-year reunion rolled around, he called and said he was flying some people out to the clinic and asked if I wanted to go along. I said sure. I mean, the guy was a saint."

Mike Kincaid went to work for Daniels at Prime Ticket. Many people perceived Kincaid as a playboy with a drinking problem. He had been a success in advertising at ABC Network and was seen as a golden boy with an unlimited future—until alcohol caught up with him. Bill had been monitoring him and now intervened, sending him to Betty Ford. Kincaid would later credit Daniels with first saving his life and then pointing him toward a new one. Kincaid eventually married and became the senior vice president and general sales manager at KCAL TV in Los Angeles.

"Bill knew that I felt I had a drinking problem," Kincaid says, "so one day he asked for a breakfast meeting with me. At the meeting he brought up the drinking but said it wasn't affecting my job. He told me that if I ever wanted help, he would talk to me about Betty Ford. I went back to the office that day and told my boss I was going to her clinic as soon as they would take me. It was my conversation with Bill that motivated me to do this. This talk took a weight off my shoulders because it showed me that there wouldn't be dire work consequences if I admitted I had a problem. Bill wasn't concerned about my job, but about helping me.

"I haven't had a drink in eleven years, and I'm very vocal about being a recovering alcoholic. I want people to know that if they have a problem, they can come to me and get help. It's a way for me to give back. Bill's whole deal was giving something back to others, and I've tried to follow his example and do that."

Daniels was passionate about getting people help—just as his brother and the other men had been with him back in 1986. The message, even though he'd resisted it from time to time, had sunk into him: if Betty Ford's staff could help him put down the bottle and seal up the pills after more than forty years of dependency, he was convinced they could help others as well. And it was better to live sober than to die too early from chronic substance abuse. He became one of the clinic's biggest supporters, and this only deepened his relationship with the Fords themselves.

"Bill and I got closer after he went to the Betty Ford Center and became a member of the board," says former President Ford. "He was there seven or eight times a year for the meetings. Bill and I always gravitated together before dinner and talked politics. He was a combination of a brilliant businessman and a humanitarian. What did he say all the time? It was 'You don't make your reputation by what you earn but by what you give.' He had that unique balance.

"He was a strong person on the Betty Ford Center board. Thank goodness, his friends intervened and got him to come here because he would have killed himself. He was a great example of how you could turn yourself around and save your life to do all the good things your talents make available."

Daniels insisted that a portrait of Betty Ford be painted and prominently hung in the clinic, and while Mrs. Ford initially turned down the idea, he succeeded in having this done. He also wanted to build a chapel on the grounds, but the organization did not want any religious affiliation, so they declined the offer. With that notion dead, Daniels did what he usually did and found another way to accomplish his goal, by anonymously donating a Serenity Room to the facility.

"I've heard that Bill credited the center with saving his life," says Betty Ford. "Well, a lot of people do that, and I always tell them that we're glad we could be of help, but actually they saved their own lives because they came to the center and made the effort to turn their lives over. We can only do so much. We can offer the program to them, but they have to do the work."

At the end of the nineties, the clinic would add a new structure, the largest one on the campus. It was 35,000 square feet and would carry the name of someone who'd done the work at Betty Ford and whose life had been given back to him. It was called the Bill Daniels Building because of all he had done for the clinic.

"In 1988," says John Schwarzlose, CEO of the Betty Ford Center, "Bill was asked by Mrs. Ford to become the first alumnus member of the Betty Ford Center's Board of Directors. At the time his business was going quite strong and although he didn't serve on boards very often, as part of his love and affection for Mrs. Ford he accepted an appointment. He brought the qualities of a distinguished businessman, a no-nonsense approach, a wonderful problem solver and provider of solutions to the board. Bill taught all of us in the management of the center that there was a right way and a wrong way to run a business. He also talked about why certain businesses were successful and others weren't. The Betty Ford Center is what is called a mission-driven business because it has a distinct mission of treating alcoholics, addicts, and their loved ones, and if it is run with the principles of a good business it will be much more successful. We totally combine the best of business with the idea of being a mission-driven business. Bill was a wonderful teacher. We all learned so much from him, especially the board members.

"I will never forget the first time I visited Bill's office in Carlsbad, California. He had plaques in his office describing how important things such as integrity and consistency were with employees and how did he, as a boss, treat his employees. Did he treat them as if he were better than they were, or did he treat them as if they were assets, the main assets of the company? As Mrs. Ford would often say, 'Without our counselors and without the people that touch the bodies and souls of our patients, we would be nothing.' Bill would take that line and say, 'Those counselors are the assets of the Betty Ford Center.' So, how you treat employees is very important and a matter of ethics. Now, ethics was another principle of Bill's. As a result of Bill, every member of the staff and board of directors all today sign an ethics certificate. I don't think that would have happened without Bill. Ethics was part of his wardrobe.

"Bill would show up at the center at seven-thirty in the morning and, mind you, the board meetings didn't start until nine A.M. He would come looking for me and say, 'Let's go have a cup of coffee.' It was always interesting, because Bill was smoking quite a bit and we have a lot of rules at the center about where you can smoke and where you can't. He was not inclined to pay attention to a lot of those rules, so staff would walk by and here the president was sitting with this distinguished-looking gentleman who was smoking in an area where no one was supposed to smoke. I would get looks from staff like, What the hell are you doing? You just couldn't tell Bill where he could smoke and where he couldn't. So, Bill would come early and say 'John, what are the issues that are going to come up today, and let's decide how we should approach some of them.' He loved to talk about things like that outside of the meeting so he had his mind made up when he went inside.

"When he wanted to meet with you at six-thirty A.M., you couldn't say no because he made sure that you knew that by six-thirty he had already had breakfast and read four papers. You felt so bad that there was no way you could say no and you thought it was a gift to wait until six-thirty. 'You know, Bill, eight o'clock works better for me' was not the right response.

"He sponsored more people at the center than I can count. First, he referred a large number of people that he knew or worked for him. He always made sure that the treatment was covered by health insurance and cost was not an issue. In his much larger network of friends and acquaintances, Bill would always make sure that they got the treatment they needed. For example, a good friend of his from Wyoming came to visit, and the next thing I know, I received a check for ten thousand dollars in the mail. Bill was saying, 'I want to cover Joe Smith's treatment.' He just loved doing that. Invariably, what would happen is that these patients who were so touched by Bill would write him a letter, a thank-you letter, as they got out, saying that they didn't know what they would have done without his sponsorship. Bill would write them a letter back, and he was a great letter writer, very direct and concise. I have kept every letter that he has ever written to me. They are that long and valuable. He would write these people a letter back saying that a thank-you was not necessary and the only appreciation I want is to live your life in sobriety and the way you have always wanted to live your life. 'No thank-you is necessary' was Bill's style.

"He loved to treat people and to take care of people. He would always want to know things about your personal life. He would ask about my three children, and I mentioned one day that my son was a Chicago Bulls fan. He laughed, because he owned part of the L.A. Lakers, and was a huge basketball fan. He said, 'Well, someday we will get him straightened out.' About one week later, in the mail I received a Michael Jordan jersey that Bill had obviously arranged for. You never knew when it was coming and you never had to ask for it. You never had to say, 'Bill, could you do this?' You never had to do anything—it just happened."

Thirty-one

As Daniels approached his seventieth birthday, his role once again expanded in directions that he'd always felt strongly about. In the early nineties, he turned once more to a sporting venture, bringing Grand Prix racing to downtown Denver; this decision would cost him millions of dollars. But in his mind, it was good for the Mile High City and that's what mattered most. *Denver Post* sports columnist Woody Paige remembers watching the event with Daniels.

"We were at the Denver City and County Annex," Paige says, "and it was sort of back away from everyone. Bill had three or four television sets and we sat in there during the race and he didn't even go out and watch. He kept saying, 'Look, you can see the state capitol. Look, you can see the County Building in the background.' He had adopted Denver as his hometown. He wasn't interested in the race. He was interested in how Denver was being portrayed on national television. We talked about how the race would affect the city of Denver. People were used to seeing the mountains, but here was two or three hours of coverage of the downtown area.

"He felt so good about that, although he lost a ton of money. I think he saw it as a donation to presenting downtown Denver. This was the period of time where the economy wasn't so good in Denver, and he wanted to show it in a nice light. Those are the types of stories that people really don't know about Bill. That was a moment that he didn't care about losing the money or being involved. He was sitting there watching the television set saying, 'Oh, that's a nice view of Denver.'"

In 1989 a brash young pilot named Mark Calkins was having trouble finding a job in Denver. He didn't interview for a job with Daniels because he was certain the company would turn him down.

"In January 1990 I finally ran out of money," he says. "I had fifty dollars left, and my wife and I went to church. I put the entire amount in the collection plate because I figured that since it wasn't going to make a house payment, it might as well help someone else. A few days later Don Sellars, Bill's pilot, called me at home. I said to him, 'How did you get my home number, and how do you even know me?' He said that he had been watching me for two years and that his co-pilot was going on vacation for a month. He wondered if I would be interested in flying for him for that month and he would pay me four thousand dollars. This was so unbelievable that it was a miracle."

Calkins asked Sellars if he was kidding. The answer was no. Calkins not only flew that month, but eventually became Daniels' chief pilot and confidant.

Flying for Bill was an exact science. "He would walk into the plane," Calkins says, "and evaluate everything—if his pen was right where he wanted it, was the gum the correct type, and was it where he wanted it. Sometimes he would open up a stick, not even chew it, and just wait to see if it was replaced when he got back on the plane. Coffee was the ultimate test. One of the line guys had offered to fill the coffee container up, and he forgot to bring it back and I forgot to ask, so we took off without it. We were flying from Aspen to Denver, and as soon as we landed, I got in the car and drove back to Aspen to bring it back. Bill told me that he wanted me to write in detail every single thing that I did to get the plane ready. When I got back to Denver, I got my laptop out and spent two and a half days writing everything down. I gave him a fifteen-page report and never heard anything else about it."

On a whim in 1996 he enlisted Calkins to undertake a colossal task— breaking the around-the-world record for a private jet. If Daniels was concerned about the gum replacements on his flights, one can only imagine the kinds of information he wanted for this challenge. In 1983 Brooke Madden had set the record in a Lear 35, circling the world in just under fifty hours. Daniels was determined to beat this mark, if only by seconds. The crew included Calkins, Dan Miller, Daniels' old war buddy, Paul Thayer, and Apollo astronaut Pete Conrad. Daniels followed almost every moment of the flight from the ground. Calkins pursued the task with complete seriousness and dedication—and a lot of worry.

"For me," Calkins says, "this was a pretty big risk. It was the biggest thing that I had ever done, and there was a lot of pressure. I just kept thinking, What if I fail? Especially in front of Bill."

Daniels was not on board, but he might as well have been. He watched tensely as his crew circled the globe and was extraordinarily proud when they beat the old record by one percent.

"In the end," says Calkins, "the trip took 49 hours, 26 minutes, and 8 seconds. Bill was so nervous when we left, and I didn't even know how nervous until I saw some of the videos we were taking. I never thought about it until we got back, but when I saw his reaction, from outside the door when I looked back, it was almost like he was crying. He just let out this sigh and you just knew that he was worried. At that point he wasn't even worried about the flight, he was just worried for the people on the airplane.

"It could have been a dangerous trip, due to the places we were going through, and some of the weather, and quite frankly we were going to push it and we did have a ton of problems. By the time we finished the first leg to the Caribbean, I thought there is no way in the world that we will break this record. We'd just made fools of ourselves and fools of Bill Daniels. But we did it."

In 1995 Denver Mayor Wellington Webb was preparing to close Stapleton Airport and open Denver International Airport. He received a call from Daniels, who requested that his jet be the first ever to land at DIA.

"Bill then said, 'Don't make any big deal out of this, I just want to be the first to land my plane there,'" recalls Mayor Webb. "I said, 'Okay, we'll do that.' Bill's was the first aircraft to land at DIA.

"When he died, I think it was very special that the service held for him in Denver was more like a party and reception. It kind of epitomized his life and the man. Independence, loyalty, integrity, a maverick who was willing to take a chance on people that other people wouldn't take a chance on. Not unwilling to have a good time and let people see that he was having a good time. We elevate people to a status that we expect them to not have warts and to be perfect. With Bill you just took him as he was, and that is the way he was going to take you."

If Daniels' charity work had been important to him before the Betty Ford experience, his recovery made him more determined than ever to give to those in need. This work now carried a sense of urgency because of his advancing age plus a particular desire to help those who were interested in pursuing more education. He'd never let go of his own regrets about not having a college degree, and he dedicated himself to making this possible for countless others. In the nineties, he established the Daniels Foundation, which provided funds to many people but especially to those seeking higher learning. Daniels' early investments in cable content providers such as CNN and the sale of his cable properties to United Artists had made him a very wealthy man. In 1994 he sold Prime Ticket to TCI, which only added to the coffers. His faith in the long-range future of cable TV had paid off in ways that even the visionary found hard to fathom.

The Daniels Foundation would use his money in ways that helped it grow—until it became the first billion-dollar charitable organization in Colorado. He was proud of all of his charitable contributions but he was proudest of the foundation because it would allow many kids to do something Daniels himself had never done.

"In my association with Bill," says Daniels Foundation executive Phil Hogue, "I have never felt so positive about succeeding at anything as I do about succeeding with his foundation. I think of Bill every single day, and I think of Bill every time I make a decision. It wasn't so much what he said about doing all this—it wasn't just 'Let's send some deserving kids to college.' It was 'I want to find these kids that are often throwaways. I want to find the kids that have been knocked down two or three times who keep getting up. I want to find kids who never have an opportunity because their SAT scores are low. These kids are the kids that nobody ever said could go to college.'

"Bill's wishes are the sole basis for the success of this program and the recognition this program has gotten. I really listened to what he was talking about when he said, 'The best is good enough for me.' But it wasn't just about houses and girlfriends and clothes. There was an expectation that when you did something for Bill, it should be the best. So I have an enormous luxury— I don't waste Bill's money but I never do 80 percent of what needs to be done because I am afraid the last 20 percent will cost us to be the best. That's a luxury few people have. I know what he wants, and I know how to get there. It's easy to follow Bill. We wanted to put every single kid whose family made less than $40,000 in a position to make an application. We wanted them to know that these programs were designed for them and the only thing that will keep you from sending in an application is your family income.

"We did some research and came up with more than sixty million dollars of educational charity that Bill had already provided. So you think about all the things he's done. His entire legacy is his foundation and the continuation of this work."

"When these kids graduate," Daniels once said about the foundation's education program, "they will go out and mentor the next group, and it will continue on and on and on. They will graduate with no debt and can go back and help their community."

One thing that made Daniels especially proud was founding the Young Americans Bank in 1987. The bank was created to teach young people how to best use money in a free enterprise society.

Daniels was leaving more behind than this ongoing program, which put a thousand new kids into college every year. The foundation would constantly be searching for new ways to benefit individuals in need.

When Phil Hogue announced he was leaving the foundation early in 2002, an intense search followed to replace him. After considering many other worthy candidates, they found an excellent choice in Hank Brown. A Colorado native and U.S. Navy veteran who was decorated for his service in Vietnam, Brown served in the Colorado Senate from 1972 to 1976 before becoming a U.S. Representative and then a U.S. Senator. In 1998 he became president of the University of Northern Colorado and left that job for the Daniels Foundation because of his great admiration for Bill Daniels and the important challenges of the new job. Because he was a Republican who had served his country in the Navy and in Washington, and because of his deep commitment to education, Brown was exactly the sort of person Daniels would have picked had he still been alive.

"We'll be looking to help people bootstrap themselves up at critical times in their lives," says Brown. "We'll be taking chances with programs that haven't been tried before. For Bill, money was not an end in itself, but a tool to help others, and for him that was a great joy in the world. If he were alive, I'd ask him what we could do to help his endowment do what he most wanted."

Says Peter Barton, former president of Liberty Communications, "Bill's legacy isn't the obvious stuff—it's not cable television. It's not the Cable Center, it's not the Daniels School of Business at Denver University, it's not Daniels & Associates or the thousands of people he made wealthy. It's a style that has come to characterize people of substance in Denver, and by substance, I don't mean money. Bill was a guy who defined how you do business Denver-style and how you do generosity Denver-style. In a very subtle way, everybody in Denver is doing things in a Bill way.

"If there had not been a Bill, I think the cowboyism wouldn't be as refined and it wouldn't be as ethical. I think the philanthropy wouldn't be as sophisticated and generous. I think that's an enormous legacy. The other things are home runs for most normal people, but Bill hit so many home runs, it turned into something else. Bill infected everybody who was lucky enough to come in contact with him with a little voice in their brain saying, 'You know, there's a classy way of doing this.'"

Nobody took pleasure in other people's success the way Daniels did. For several years Daniels & Associates had no real competitors. Then Rick Michaels started Communications Equity Associates and gave Bill a run for his money in the nationwide cable brokerage/investment banking business. On the eve of CEA's twentieth anniversary, Michaels gathered his core executives around him for a celebration. The doors opened and a surprise delivery arrived. It was a huge bottle of champagne with a card that read "Best Wishes and Congratulations. Bill Daniels."

Another part of his legacy sprang from a concept he originated in the mid-eighties to help young people get off to a good start financially. He was always fond of saying that free enterprise was the eighth wonder of the world, yet most folks didn't understand how it worked. What better way to teach them than when they were children? With that in mind, he created the Young Americans Bank in Denver—the nation's only financial institution created solely for those seventeen and under. He wanted small kids and adolescents to learn the value of earning, saving, and investing money from childhood forward, which was precisely what they did at the YAB. One of his favorite sayings was that a turtle never went forward without sticking out his neck, and he wanted young people to understand the nature and value of risk. He was sticking his own neck out again with the YAB.

"In early '87," says Linda Childears, the YAB president, "I was hired to take care of the mechanics of starting a bank, of getting the bank in the checking system in the country and getting all the details set up. I didn't meet Bill until several weeks after that. Frankly, I didn't know Bill Daniels—I didn't know anything about him. But I had read about this kids' bank and thought the guy was nuts! I asked Phil Hogue when he wanted the bank open, and he said Bill wanted it opened on Colorado Day, which was August 3. I said, 'Of what year?' and Phil said this year, 1987. I said, 'I don't know that Jesus Christ could open a bank that fast.' But we got it open on August 3.

"It was one obstacle after another, but every obstacle you would encounter, you'd hear the same thing from Bill, 'So what's your point? Fix it.' We went through one unheard-of obstacle after another and managed to get through them. It became one of those things where you personally get caught up in how exciting it was to conquer these little issues one at a time and make this thing happen.

Cableland, Bill Daniels' house in Denver, boasted a wall of sixty-four television sets. He used the display to demonstrate the diversity of cable television programming to VIP guests.

"It took me a long time to really understand and believe and accept that this just was a big-hearted gesture for Bill because he wanted kids to understand the financial system in this country. He wanted them to know what a privilege and what a gift it is. Bill's tenacity became apparent in the first twenty-four hours of the project when he said, 'We're going to get this done whether or not anybody else believes in it!' Anyone else in banking would hear about his idea for a bank for kids and say, 'This sucker is never going to break even. It's going to require subsidies forever.' Bill knew that and it didn't matter. He didn't start a bank to make money on kids. He started this as a philanthropic educational project. Banking happened to be the vehicle that he chose.

"A lot of us said to him, 'Why don't you just endow a program that does this?' Try anything besides this heavily regulated forever kind of bank, because in banking you're dealing with the public's money and we knew we were going to have layer upon layer of regulatory oversight. He said, 'What part of I-want-a-commercial-bank don't you understand?' He always thought the real world was the best way to teach kids something and let them experience, do it, try it. He wanted all of us to have the option to succeed or fail, because that was a part of who he was.

"The bank certainly exceeded my expectations and I think Bill's too. The one thing he hoped would happen but didn't is that wealthy individuals like himself around the country would look at this and say, 'This is important, this is good, I'm going to do it for this community.' I think that was a disappointment for Bill, but as far as how this community accepted and embraced and got excited about the bank—he was thrilled with it. We've had over forty thousand kids take part in this since the doors opened. When they reach the ripe old age of twenty-two, they get kicked out and a new group comes in and starts over."

Young people come to the bank and apply for loans just as their elders do. Says Phil Hogue: "When a kid asks for a loan, they sit at a desk with a loan officer with the parents off to the side and it takes about an hour and a half. We loaned a kid five hundred dollars or so to start a business painting clothes with acrylic paints. He'd made a running outfit for his mother and gotten rave reviews on it. So his dad made him come to the bank and apply for a loan. We made him write up a business plan and loaned him the money and it was an

Bill Coors and Bill Daniels in 1994 at the renaming of the Daniels College of Business at the University of Denver.

instant success. He went to New York to be on the *Today Show* with his parents—they asked him to explain the whole thing and he was so proud. At the end of the interview they asked if he had learned anything and were there any surprises. He said, 'Well, yeah. Did you know they want more money back than what you borrowed?'"

Artem Gouralev grew up in Siberia and came on a visa to the United States in 1998. While attending Denver's George Washington High School, he visited the Young Americans Bank. Linda Childears invited him to serve on the bank's Youth Advisory Board. Artem had hopes of staying in the United States and receiving a scholarship to continue his education, but his chances appeared slim or worse until Childears suggested that he write a letter to Daniels.

"I sent off the letter and told Bill Daniels about myself," Artem says, "and then they told me that Bill Daniels agrees to pay for education! I was like, Wow! In about two weeks they made everything possible for me to study at D.U. It's like I pulled a lucky ticket—like I win the lottery."

Bo Peretto met Daniels in 1990 through the Young Americans Bank, when Bo was only ten years old. He already had a business plan for selling candy to banks in the area and to his classmates, many of whom found it odd that the fifth-grader carried a briefcase to elementary school. When he met Daniels, he posed some direct questions to the man.

"I asked him," says Peretto, "if anyone ever thought if any of his businesses were stupid and he told me, 'You bet. Some thirty years ago, a lot of people thought that about cable, and I was damned and determined to prove them all wrong.' The most important thing Bill gave to me and gave to his whole community was the sense that you give back to this great world that has given so much to you. It's not just money, it's volunteering and doing whatever you have to do. It's our duty and what Bill stood for."

Not only did Daniels believe that boys and girls should know how to handle money at an early age, he wanted them to understand the importance of ethics in business—and outside business—as they grew older. He had nasty blow-ups, even with people who were close to him, when he felt they were being unethical in business or in their private affairs. He never did forgive one of his top executives and protégés, Alan Harmon, because he believed that Harmon had treated his wife unfairly in a divorce settlement. And he helped another friend, Elizabeth Dick, because he was convinced that her husband had not acted properly during their separation and divorce. Aging did nothing to blunt his conviction that doing the right thing in the marketplace was always going to be more profitable in the long run than doing something wrong.

"Several of us from the Daniels office," says Steve Halstedt, "took Bill back to the Tuck Business School to speak to a class taught by James Brian Quinn. This was probably 1985 or '86."

Daniels had insisted that Halstedt, Brian Deevy, and Jack Tankersly (all Tuck graduates) accompany him on this trip.

"I think Bill was always insecure about his lack of formal education," Tankersly says. "That is why he wouldn't go to give this presentation unless everyone he knew went with him. It was his protection, if you will, in the classroom. That was one of his biggest insecurities that he showed to others. People don't achieve what he achieved that early in life without being driven by things that others don't understand. He was a very achievement-oriented guy, and he wanted people around him that wanted to perform. He had a fabulous sense of humor, and very strong guiding principles about himself, in terms of patriotism and love of country, and those were magnetic doors for Bill. He always knew where that magnetic door was, and that is what attracted so many people to him."

Steve Halstedt introduced Daniels to the students at Dartmouth. "I got up in front of the class," he says, "and this class had previously interviewed other business leaders and absolutely torn them to pieces. It was a very aggressive class. So I get up and introduce Bill and say, 'Bill Daniels was with Pappy Boyington of the Black Sheep Squadron during World War II, he was a Golden Gloves boxer, he was the first leader of the Flying Blue Angels air combat team, and he is the father of cable television.' I told a couple of stories about people that Bill had helped, like Ron Lyle, and then Bill got up to speak.

"He said, 'I just got out of the Betty Ford Center for substance abuse, I've been married and divorced four times, and I have a personal relationship with the California Highway Patrol.' He proceeded to take himself off the pedestal I had put him on and bring himself right down to ground level. When he walked up to the podium, he had a gift with him that had been nicely wrapped. He proceeded to start telling stories about deals he had done. Every story he told had the most outrageous conflict of interest you could imagine. All of us from the Daniels office were listening to this and sinking lower and lower in our chairs.

"Finally, there was a kid in the back of the room who'd worked for Goldman Sachs for three or four years before he went to graduate school. He was an investment banker and understood that everything Bill was talking about was wrong. He stood up and said, 'Stop!' right in the middle of the class. He said to Bill, 'These are the most outrageous conflicts of interest I've ever heard of. They're unethical. How can you possibly conduct your business this way?' Bill goes over and very dramatically picks up the gift he had so carefully wrapped and throws it to the kid. Inside was a pillow that said 'Give me equity or give me death.'

"He looked at the rest of the class and said, 'What the hell is wrong with you people? There's only one person in a classroom of forty people who is ethical?' He then proceeded to retell the stories and explain how with full disclosure and agreement of all the parties that all these deals were perfectly legitimate and perfectly ethical. I didn't know he was going to do this. He didn't share it with me ahead of time.

"We then went to the dean of the school, Colin Blake, and told him that Bill Daniels loves Brian Quinn, and by association, he loves the Tuck School. We said that Bill is going to give ten million dollars to higher education at some point and that ten million could be yours. I told him that Bill had said many times to me that he would give anything to have my MBA. And I told him in return that I would trade him anytime straight up for his fortune. We explained to Colin Blake that what he needed to do was give Bill an honorary MBA, and Colin said that they don't do that; they didn't know how. He had a bunch of diplomas sitting on his windowsill, so one of us went over, picked one up, wrote Bill Daniels' name in the middle of it, and said to the dean, 'This is how you do it and it's worth ten million.'"

Nothing happened with the diploma that day or later on.

"About four years later," says Halstedt, "I was in a position to send Colin Blake the articles about Bill's ten million dollar gift to Denver University. The

Tuck School lost a tremendous opportunity to create a great supporter in Bill Daniels. So all of this shows how Bill influenced me—you don't want to take the last nickel off the table, you want to do full deals with people, and you want to have full disclosure, be honest, ethical, and straightforward. That gets you much further than trying to be tough or chisel people in transactions. I probably had the personality to be a tough negotiator, and I changed that as a consequence of working with Bill. I also recognized that Bill would treat the doorman and the CEO of General Motors exactly the same. I watched this happen frequently. There was something very human about that which I took away, so I try to treat everyone with a great deal of respect."

Pat Bischoff was Daniels' barber in California for more than fifteen years. She was always astounded that Daniels was so interested in her life and asked her so many questions while getting his hair trimmed.

"I remember one time," she says, "when I told him that I had a date that night. He said, 'Well, you'll have to tell me about it next time I'm in.' The next time I saw him, he remembered and said, 'How was your date?' I said, 'Well, you know this guy was really something. We went to LaCosta and he bought me one drink and he was so tight, Bill. We were sitting in the lounge, and when he went to the rest room, I struck up a conversation with the people at the next table and they sent a drink over to me. When he came back, he looked at it like he was really upset, like I had ordered another drink and he was paying for it.' So Bill says, 'Mmm, what's he do for a living?' I said, 'He's a controller.' Bill said, 'Well, he's probably damn good at it.'

"He asked me for a piece of paper and a pencil and wrote something down. He said, 'Here, this is my account number at LaCosta. If you ever want anything, you charge it to my account.' What a sweetheart. At his home in Denver, he had built little condos for the squirrels. At the lake house in California, there was always birdseed out for the ducks and birds. It was like Wild Kingdom out his kitchen window, and he'd just sit and watch all of them."

If Daniels was committed to feeding wildlife, he was also obsessive about human food. He once fell in love with chicken livers and ate them for three months in a row, but like everything else it would run its course and he soon grew sick of them. He also loved Oreos and HoHos, but he really went overboard on white corn. He ate it until the growing season stopped and then convinced two of his cable installers to begin growing the corn. He built them a greenhouse, bought them books, and they became farmers overnight. He insisted on sharing this newfound passion with his friends and soon began loading his jet with bushels of corn for distribution. The farmers could not keep up with the demand and were relieved when he went on to a new interest. Now they could resume their old jobs!

Just as Steve Halstedt had predicted, Daniels gave ten million to the University of Denver—but he handed it over with some strings attached. He'd learned that business ethics were not being taught hardly anywhere in higher education in the United States, so he demanded that the D.U. Business School faculty teach a course in ethics and behavior to every young man and woman going out into the working world. He wanted the course to include guidelines on manners, on being on time for meetings, on how to shake hands and return calls promptly. He insisted on excellent behavior as well as business acumen. He himself had developed many of these traits early on at the New Mexico Military Institute, and he wanted D.U. students to practice them now and in their future dealings in the professional world.

But he didn't stop there in his commitment to help D.U. He also bought a home for the school's chancellor, Dan Ritchie. In 1987 Ritchie had retired from Westinghouse and gone to live on a ranch in the Colorado mountains. He and Daniels had been friends for years, and one day Bill visited the ranch to talk about D.U.

"The university had gotten into some difficulties," Ritchie says, "and Bill asked me about replacing the retiring chancellor, who was going back to teaching. I told him that I didn't feel qualified for this job, and he said, 'Well, nobody's qualified for that.' I thought about that, and I called another friend and sought his advice. Then I decided I could do it for at least a few years. Bill's encouragement was very important to me."

Once Ritchie had decided to accept the position, Daniels was determined to find him a home suitable for the chancellor of such an important university.

"Bill had called me," says Phil Hogue, "and was talking about the chancellor's residence and said that in order to attract and keep a top-flight chancellor, the school needed to provide a very nice house. He wanted me to go buy one. So I went out and enlisted a realtor and started looking at houses that were really close to being mansions. I did this under my name because I didn't want the realtors to know Bill was paying for this. After looking at about six or eight, I found one and called Dan Ritchie and said, 'If you could own a residence that met every requirement you would want, what would it look like?' He came over and looked at this house and said it was absolutely perfect, so we started negotiating for this house."

They paid $1.8 million. Daniels was upset when he learned that the house, which was built in 1926, didn't have air-conditioning. Then he decided that a house this old needed new carpet and paint. He told Hogue to tell the chancellor that he'd toss in another half million dollars to spruce the place up.

"This was typical of Bill," says Hogue. "I told him, 'Bill, why don't I tell Dan to get a list together of things to be done and it may come in at two hundred thousand?' He said, 'Didn't you hear me? You tell him I'll give him another half million dollars and tell him I'm really happy for him.'"

"I think Bill's legacy," says Ritchie, "is his contribution to D.U., his development of the Young Americans Bank, and his foundation, which is going to make a good education possible for thousands of young people. All three of these things address basic questions. How do we bring disadvantaged young people into the mainstream? How do we prepare them to be successful? If you look at who's in the jails, half of them are functionally illiterate, and mostly they are there because they are unable to be successful in today's society. Therefore, they turn to other things out of frustration or need or perceived need. If we can really address the problems of the underprivileged, we can change society radically. It is already having a major impact here, and we in turn are having impacts on other institutions as well.

"People take a look at us and think that maybe these ideas make some sense. And this will grow, not diminish. The success and power of the ideas are demonstrated. You'll find lots of folks joining the bandwagon. It's hard from here to say where this will take us. I have a friend, the actor Eddie Albert, whom I think the world of. He's now in his nineties, and one of his sayings is that 'Love holds the planets in their orbits.' What we're talking about here is love and that's what Bill is all about."

A visionary, Bill Daniels urged University of Denver Chancellor Daniel Ritchie to revamp the college of business' curriculum to include new required courses on ethics, manners, and social involvement. Between 1988 and 1995, Bill donated more than $22 million to the university.

Daniels worked closely with Jim Griesemer, the dean of the Daniels Business College at D.U., and with Joy Burns, the chair of the trustees at the school. He was very hands-on with both of them in the development of the institution that bore his name.

"Bill was very involved," Burns says, "in the creation of some of the business school programs—the Leadership programs and the Emerging Leaders program were very special to Bill. He spent lots of time helping develop these programs. He was very proud to be a part of the university and the business college, and toward the end, I think they helped keep him alive."

In addition to endowing D.U., Daniels was putting the money aside through his foundation that would send a thousand students annually to the college of their choice for four years. He was referring substance-abuse addicts to the Betty Ford Center, and he was also very involved in getting troubled youths enrolled at the New Mexico Military Institute. He believed that the discipline at NMMI had straightened him out for life and that it was the best remedy for kids at a crossroads. His own brother had often said that if it hadn't been for NMMI, Bill could have just as easily ended up in prison. Daniels did not simply refer kids to the institute, but in the late nineties he set up five endowments at NMMI totaling $5 million dollars.

He once helped a young man named Cameron Grey, the son of his girlfriend, Karen Grey, get into the institute.

"Cameron," says Colonel Seth Orell of NMMI, "did a very fine job and ended up being a cadet officer and graduated. Bill called me when Cameron was in his first-class year and said, 'I understand that there's a cadet who's a friend of Cameron's that can't finish school because of financial reasons.' This kid was a black cadet who was there to get a commission. Mr. Daniels said, 'Colonel, I'm going to make sure he gets through. Now, here's what I want you to do. I want you to find out exactly how much money it's going to take for him to complete his year. Every penny. Then you call and give my secretary the dollar amount and she will send a check.' So I said yes, sir.

"This young man came from a single-parent family and was from Georgia, I believe. So I called and found out the amount he would need to complete his year and called back Bill's secretary. I don't remember the amount. I know it was more than a thousand and less than five thousand. But I gave Mr. Daniels' secretary the exact amount, just like he asked. I found out later that the money was there and this young man graduated and went on.

"Bill's legacy," says Bob Russo, "is one of commitment to helping others and to community service. His legacy is about going the extra mile in terms of doing things to make our country a better place in which to live. Others will focus on his role in advancing the cable industry, but I believe Bill's deepest vision was a world where people give of themselves simply because it makes them feel good. His legacy is about the Daniels College of Business, the Daniels Fund, scholarships, the Young Americans Education Foundation. I know he influenced thousands of people in the cable industry, but his commitment to help society in broader ways is going to stand long after we're gone. Imagine the impact of students who graduate from his business school or go to college as a result of his scholarships. It will be truly remarkable forty, fifty, or a hundred years from now.

"I once asked Jack Daniels why Bill was so focused on helping other people. Jack told me that when Bill came back from World War Two, he was a changed man. Something happened in the war—maybe it was him getting shot down and making a bargain with God that said, 'If you get me out of this, I will make this place a better world.' You know, if just half of that story is true, it's still a great story."

Epilogue

For decades Daniels had talked to anyone who would listen about cable's future residing not just in the further development of technology or even in creating favorable legislation for the industry. The real future, he'd been saying since he first started watching boxing matches on TV in the 1950s, lay in providing original content to viewers. Cable's ability to deliver new programming alternatives would ultimately determine if the business was going to grow and thrive. In the 1980s, with cable gradually spreading into millions of homes across America, his words took on greater substance. Cable brand names like CNN, MTV, C-SPAN, BRAVO, ESPN, HBO, USA, and others were challenging the supremacy of the old-line networks and building their identities in the marketplace. Cable was providing more of the content that Daniels had always foreseen it could, but it still hadn't reached its full potential.

As the nineties commenced, Daniels was spending most of his time at his beach house in California. His health was not as robust as it had once been and he was slowly retreating from the day-to-day affairs of running a cable empire. A new generation of leadership had arrived at the Daniels companies. Brian Deevy became chief executive officer of Daniels & Associates in 1991. Buzz Mitchell took over as the head of Daniels Communications, Inc., the entity that directed Daniels Cablevision, Daniels Enterprises, and Sports Programming Ventures. In the final three years of the 1990s, under Deevy's leadership, Daniels & Associates would engineer 154 cable transactions valued at $22.8 billion, making it the dominant cable financial adviser in the world. Bill Daniels was no longer closely involved in all phases of the business, but his essential message had not changed at all. Everyone who dropped by his beach house heard the same sermon that he'd been preaching for most of his adult life: content was king. And as he said this over and over again in the 1990s, his words came true before the eyes of the nation and the entire world. Content on cable TV now fully arrived and changed the nature not just of television but of the society that was watching it.

The first epochal event came in late 1989 and was a harbinger of what to expect in the last ten years of the twentieth century. The Berlin Wall fell, signaling a new geopolitical world—and a new world of television. CNN carried much of the event live, and people everywhere could see the ecstatic German people, so long divided by this Cold War barrier that had been constructed during the Soviet Union's occupation of their country, tear down the wall with their bare hands. As each piece crumbled, they celebrated more of their power and freedom. Human beings around the planet, some of whom were living under the same conditions that the Germans had been living under until now, could see firsthand what had happened when they resisted dictatorship and exerted their own political force. They didn't have to accept tyranny as their only choice. More walls were about to come tumbling down.

Then the Soviet Union fell apart, and the whole world watched the Cold War come to an end. Rebellions sprang up across Eastern Europe as more and more people hungered for the right to determine what kind of government they would have. CNN was there to record the changing of history's guard live and in color—with around-the-clock coverage—something that had never happened before. And then, in the summer of 1990, Iraq's Saddam Hussein marched his troops into neighboring Kuwait, ready to take over the country in defiance of international treaties and law. For several months the United States prepared a military response to drive the Iraqis out of Kuwait, launching Operation Desert Storm in January 1991. When the combat got under way, CNN's cameras were on the scene and broadcasting the action all over the globe. Everyone could see the bombs falling through the night skies and the targets being hit. Early in the battle, a moment occurred that signified not just the astounding triumph of cable TV, but a turning point in the history of communications.

An American general, while being interviewed on CNN, was asked about a strategic development that had just taken place in the war. He stood in front of the camera in full uniform—representing virtually the highest level of military authority in the campaign against Iraq. The viewing public had watched the development live on cable TV, but when the general was questioned about it, he hesitated and appeared stumped. He didn't have an answer because he hadn't yet seen what had happened. Television had outstripped the people who were running the war. Civilians had witnessed something they couldn't have imagined seeing in any previous American military struggle. The public was present on the field of battle in ways no one could have guessed only a few years earlier. All this was possible because of satellite technology and the once outlandish Ted Turner's desire to build a twenty-four-hour-a-day news network. By far the most popular show on the airwaves was the war against Saddam Hussein. People in the United States and people all over the world could not stop watching the action.

What had happened with foreign policy issues and warfare during Desert Storm then repeated itself a few years later with the American legal system, following the arrest of O. J. Simpson for a double homicide in Los Angeles in June 1994. The Friday evening low-speed police chase of Simpson on an L.A. freeway, which ended with his being taken into custody, was watched live by ninety million Americans, most of whom were tuned in to cable television. For the next sixteen months, during Simpson's countless courtroom hearings, his nine-month trial, and his subsequent acquittal, the biggest show on television was cable's almost nonstop coverage of these legal proceedings. For the first time ever, millions of Americans viewed the inner workings of a criminal courtroom and received a profound education about the presentation of evidence, cross-examination, the working of juries, and due process as a whole. Nothing like this had ever occurred before, and it was only possible because cable had the flexibility to follow the trial each day and bring it live into homes all across the nation.

Content—social, political, legal, and cultural—was now being watched on cable almost around the clock. It had become the dominant news medium and talk show medium of the 1990s. Everything that happened in the country was reported on and hashed over most extensively on cable. The adage had once been that newspaper headlines were the first draft of history, but cable had made that saying obsolete. The first draft was now being created on the airwaves of CNN, the Fox News Network, MSNBC, and other cable outlets. Papers and magazines could only scramble in their efforts to keep up. This same phenomenon of massive cable coverage was repeated with all of the major events of the decade, including the JonBenet Ramsey murder case and

President Clinton's impeachment at decade's end, and it continued full steam as the old millennium gave way to the new one. The 2000 post-election chaos, the terrorist attacks on the World Trade Center in New York City in September 2001, and the war in Afghanistan were followed nonstop on the cable outlets.

The greatest show on earth was carried every day and all day long through the piece of wire known as cable. Had Bill Daniels lived past March 2000, he would have seen even more phenomenal events played out in his living room.

In the late nineties, Daniels stayed in his beach house and monitored the world via cable television, while gradually losing his hearing and growing weaker. His long-held view of cable had become the order of the day, yet he was starting to retreat from the world of business and go further within. He called friends around the nation and wrote them notes, sharing a little more than he had in the past, talking more openly about his life and theirs, delving more deeply into the mysteries and wonders of human existence.

Bill Daniels welcomed President George Bush to his residence in 1988 for a Republican Party event that raised more than $300,000 for Bush's presidential campaign.

"When I was young, I used to travel around with Bill," says Cliff Daniels, his stepson by his third marriage. "Back then we would drive from town to town, and he would always talk about cable with people in these places and he was really only interested in building his empire. That's what he cared about and devoted his time to. Near the end of his life, he made contact with me and wanted to talk. I was very surprised by this. We hadn't been close for years, even decades, but he wanted to get back in touch. When we spoke now, it was much more personal and much more about just living life. I think he was very interested in taking care of things and of people before he died. He was far more approachable now and more open."

As he gathered friends around him and gradually withdrew from many of his cable activities, his reputation in the industry—his legend—continued to grow and spread. People everywhere were becoming more aware of the role of the father of cable television

Leo Hindery was working for Chronicle Publishing before he became interested in cable TV. Because of advice he'd received from Daniels, Hindery started his own cable company, called Intermedia. He went on to take over the presidency of TCI, but only after Daniels had again encouraged him to accept the job. Hindery is currently the CEO of Steinbrenner Co.

"Bill's strength," he says, "was mostly ethical. He was very bright and a very powerful presence but he was the ethical foundation of the industry. There are great deal makers out there, great strategists, great operators, and great financiers, but we needed that ethical foundation in our business. I can always find another great financier, or strategist. Bill was the single most important presence to the industry.

"Cable is nothing more than a wire into the house. What's important is what came over that wire—because it did change the world. What's important is the handful of people who were behind it. I always looked at Bill as the moon that orbited around the planet called cable. And yet, who was he? He was the only moon—if he hadn't existed, there wouldn't have been an industry. We can sit here and talk about the great people who ran IBM or GM. Bill Daniels never ran a thing. He was our leader on an emotional level. He conceived of structures and deals but never ran a thing. That's the story. How did this man, who was not without his faults, become so important to an industry and never run anything?

"If you'd plopped Bill down in traditional corporate America, he would have flamed out. But not in cable, because cable was a constant wellspring for him."

In time, Daniels became weaker and more hearing-impaired. Decades of heavy smoking had eaten away at his respiratory system and was now eating away at his life. In order for him to hear people, they had to shout at him, either in person or on the telephone. He was able to stay in his California home, but his loss of hearing kept him confined. Because of the loudness necessary for him to engage in conversations, he was often too embarrassed to go out in public. Daniels had always been an impatient and willful man, and as his health declined, he was sometimes not an easy patient.

"He had a low tolerance for pain," says Frieda Cowan, his housekeeper in California, "and he'd never been sick. I don't know many men that are good patients. On the other hand, he was very cooperative. He couldn't be left alone and he didn't want to be alone. It was in those months that Bill would finally talk about himself. He worked real hard in the last year and a half of his life on his foundation, and that, I think, kept Bill alive. And when that was finished, I remember being at the lake house and he was staring out at the lake and he said to me, 'Frieda, I have everything done. I don't have anything I have to do.' That was a sad day because it was almost like his purpose in life was over. He was done in the true sense of the word."

He was eventually taken to the hospital, where his illness became so intense that the doctors ordered him to see no one. Daniels had never been one to take no for an answer and his most loyal allies kept finding ways to visit him.

"I sneaked into Eisenhower Hospital posing as a doctor," says his longtime California friend Dan Donahue. "Bill was in intensive care. I gave him a speech, the boxing speech about it being the last round and how he needed to keep fighting and stuff like that. He looked up and said, 'What the hell are you doing here?' This was probably a year or so before he died. He was in the hospital for an extended period of time, and I went and stood by his bed and gave him that speech and he recovered!"

In June 1996 Daniels left Eisenhower and was soon able to return to his home in Indian Wells, California. There he hired a nurse, Melissa Rudolph, to take care of him full-time. He had good days and bad, but gradually he was failing and losing control of some aspects of his life. Melissa had to bathe him and walk him—when he was able to walk—and during the last few years of his life, she became not only his caretaker but also his close friend.

"I did things for Bill," she says, "that I didn't think I was capable of doing for anyone. He made me a better nurse because I never wanted to let him down. Sometimes he got very angry because he couldn't do certain things anymore, and he was growing a little fearful. But over time he felt that God had given him an extra bonus of four more years to live after he first went into the hospital. A spiritual side emerged in Bill, and he and I would sit together and pray. He said that he'd never prayed before, but he finally knew that there was something more powerful than he was, and he was content with this. Six months before the end, he told me that he was ready to die, and I'd just sit there and bawl."

With death approaching, he began planning it out as carefully as he'd once planned out his future and the future of the cable business with his three-by-five cards.

"There is a will to live and a will to die," says Susan Goddard, Daniels' estate planner. "At the end Bill had the will to die, so he gathered those few close people around him and started talking to them while he still could."

One of those people was his general surgeon at Eisenhower Medical Center in Rancho Mirage, California, Dr. Carl Schultz. When Dr. Carl first encountered Bill, in the mid-nineties, he was ranting and raving in Room 203, telling everyone that he had to go home and close some deals. He offered his nurse $200,000 to let him leave. When she turned him down, he told her to move his wing of the hospital to his house. When Daniels met Dr. Carl, he offered him $1 million to get him out of there.

"I explained to him how sick he was," says Dr. Carl, "and that he wasn't out of the woods yet. I walked out into the hall and told the nurse this guy was nuts."

Later that day, Daniels failed so badly that he was transferred into the intensive care unit. He had kidney failure, blood poisoning, lung failure, severe malnutrition, and at times was comatose. A breathing machine kept him alive. He fought back and spent three months recovering in the hospital and two more months convalescing at home. As soon as Daniels was well enough to begin complaining, he tried to talk Dr. Carl into reversing his colostomy.

"This," says Dr. Carl, "was a formidable undertaking. To risk his death with another operation, to essentially satisfy a vanity issue, would be very difficult indeed. At this time I got to know Bill better and better. He had a consummate ability as a negotiator, and he worked on me for weeks and weeks to remove the colostomy. The deal was that he had to quit smoking six weeks before surgery. And he stopped. I had to be very upbeat to do this operation, and I got that enthusiastic strength from Bill. No goal was high enough and you can do what you want. That attitude really infected me. So I said Bill was strong enough and could pull through."

And he did pull through. During this time, Dr. Carl and Daniels grew close, the physician calling him "the most remarkable patient I ever had." Dr. Carl came to look upon Daniels as part philosopher and part psychiatrist and when the younger man needed a lift, he went to the older one who was dying. It was only after Daniels was gone that Dr. Carl appreciated the wisdom he'd given him, but that wasn't all Daniels gave. As had been the case throughout his life, he put his money behind his convictions and left the hospital a seven-figure gift. Dr. Carl admired everything about Daniels, maybe even his incredible stubbornness.

As soon as Daniels had pulled through his colostomy reversals, he started smoking again. Naturally, this created more complications for his lungs. He not only wanted cigarettes, but to be close to attractive women, even though he was in such bad shape that he disliked the thought of others seeing him bedridden and dying. The urge to connect was stronger than the urge to hide.

"I went back to California to see him in February of 2000, kind of against his wishes," says Betsy Benton, the airplane pilot and longtime friend of Daniels. "I went into the hospital, and he couldn't talk because he was on the ventilator. He opened his eyes and saw me there and got really alarmed and he was mad! He was clearly mad that I was seeing him. I told him I loved him and that he couldn't keep me away, and he calmed down. Dr. Carl was there and said to Bill, 'Bill, she loves you too much to stay away.' It was like he let go of his pride and it was just love.

"They were trying to wean him off the ventilator, and we had to wear protective gowns when we went in his room. I get in there and he's off the vent and he says, 'Honey, get your ass up here in bed with me like you're supposed to be—get up here!' This is two days before he died! He's in intensive care, he's wired for sound, doctors and nurses are everywhere. I said, 'Bill, you're all wired up here.' He said, 'I don't care, get your ass up here!' I'm looking at Dr. Carl and at Jack Daniels and they are laughing. So I reached up there and just held him. He was so frail. But not his spirit. So I just held him and then he was happy."

"Bill asked that we only keep him alive on a ventilator for two weeks," says his nurse Melissa Rudolph. "After that, if he wasn't better, he was ready to go. We did all we could for two weeks, but then we couldn't do any more. So we took him off that last day. His brother was there with his two daughters, Diane Denish and Dana Reed, along with Betsy Benton, John Saeman, the pilot Mark Calkins, myself, and the doctors and a few other relatives. For six hours Bill was okay, joking and laughing. He said good-bye to everyone and they left, and I helped him get back into bed for the last time. Fifteen minutes later, he started to pass. The family came back in, then he passed. He controlled the whole thing, with just the people he wanted there, to the last few moments. It was a very beautiful thing."

Right up until the end, for as long as he could talk, he kept doing what he'd always done: asking questions and seeking the best information he could find—reaching out for more answers.

"I didn't talk to Bill about business," says Reverend Ed Beck. "He talked to everybody else about that. With me, we talked about life, his hopes, his dreams, his trials and tribulations, his frustrations, and we talked about his faith. That's really where I came in to be not only his confidant, but in a certain sense, his counselor. He shared with me his story about growing up and his father and mother. He shared much more about his mother than his father. He talked to me a great, great deal about his mother. She'd had a profound influence on his life, and he regarded her as a living saint and as a saint upon her departure. He just felt that she was the greatest woman, well, the greatest human being that ever lived.

"I do think that one of his problems with women was that he could never find a woman to measure up to the 'Virgin Mary,' so to speak. He understood that his mother had foibles and challenges, but she had instilled within him values and she nurtured him. On the other side of this deal-making, successful, charming man was this very sensitive, boyish, caring human being.

"The bottom line with Bill was always passion and compassion—and a search for faith. If I had one conversation with him about faith, I probably had five hundred conversations. His struggle was that to get from point A to point B, you have to do certain things. And I talked to him about my understanding of God's love and grace—that you don't have to do anything to receive these things, that they are gifts to you, and when you accept them within your heart and life, then you live a life of gratitude and thanksgiving. Cognitively, he would go back and forth on that, but he always felt that he had to do, do, do. And he did, did, did. I had no problem with that, but he felt that he had to show himself worthy in God's sight because he had all these other challenges, whether it was alcoholism or whatever."

The man who had almost always been more comfortable talking about others did not change very much—not even when death was near.

"Toward the end," says Reverend Beck, "I told him, 'We need to talk about the inevitable, because it's very apparent you are deteriorating.' He said, 'Well,

Bill Daniels poses for a trade advertisement with his team of cable brokers in the late 1970s. Two of his senior executives, Keith Burcham and John Saeman, are seated behind him.

you don't need to tell me that.' I told him that I needed to know what he wanted in his service, and he said, 'You know me well enough and what I want. I will leave instructions that you are to conduct it and all that.' I said, 'Bill, you know I could get up right now and talk an hour or two hours about you. That's not the problem. I really want to hear some of your feelings and philosophies. Whether you write it down or dictate it, it is much more powerful if it comes from you.'

"He looked across to me and said, 'Ed, I can't do that.' I said, 'Bill, I'm not telling you to do it, I'm just asking you to think about it.' He said, 'I'm telling you I can't do it.' I said, 'Well, just think about it.' I wouldn't let him off the hook. I told him he was a very, very important person in the lives of many people, and when you leave this world to go to be with your Lord, there is going to be a lot of loss. I want to be able to say what you want me to say. He said, 'Ed, whatever you say will be fine.'

"The end result of Bill's life was that he was given the graciousness of time to put it all together in what I like to call a very neat package. There are a few individuals who seem to encapsulate what I call 'full humanity,' even with all the foibles and apparent weaknesses. He loved life. We always laughed together and we always had a good time. The very worst thing you could do around Bill was talk about how great he was. So right now, if he could get to me, he would take the fan off my ceiling that's turning around at this moment and he would wrap me up in it.

"But on the other side of it, after everything was done and everything had been said about him, he would be very appreciative of all these expressions and feelings. He'd be very humble and grateful that the things he did had had so much impact on so many different people. He would have liked it, after all."

Following his death, that impact not only carried on but deepened in the lives of some of those who had known him.

"He never told you what to do—not ever," says Penny Nelson, a friend of Daniels' in California. "He would be honest with me and say, 'You may not be very good at this at first but keep at it. Be honest, be truthful, don't tell people something you don't know, always go find out about it, and that has helped me throughout my career. Even now I feel like he is with me. I had that conversation with someone not too long ago, and I said, 'I've just had the strangest feeling.

I've come up against some real big problems now that I never thought I'd have to face. For some reason, I get this calmness over me and I know how to handle it.'"

One part of Bill Daniels was gone—the part that contained the gravelly voice and the quick smile and the stare over his glasses when he was giving you his full attention. The spirit remained and his legacy was still hard at work in his foundation, in the Young Americans Bank, in the offices of Daniels & Associates, in the world of cable television as it stretched around the globe and changed people's lives, and finally in the memories of all who'd known the man. He'd just had his own way of doing everything.

"His last wishes," says Mark Calkins, "were for me to take his ashes and mix them with the ashes of his cat, Sydney, and put them together in one bag and take them in the Learjet out over the Pacific. He even put this in the will. It was just like Bill, with every detail thought out—go out two miles from the beach house and spread the ashes. We spent a week trying to figure out how to do that from the Learjet. We figured out a way to mix the ashes together, put them in a plastic sack, and adhere them to the landing gear of the airplane. Before we took off, no one was saying a word, but I told everyone that we were going to do something that was very unorthodox and will seem unsafe and you will probably never see a jet do this again."

On board the plane were Jack and Peach Daniels and Jack's daughter, Diane Denish, and her husband, Herb. As the jet made a left turn above the water, Jack read the navy prayer for burial at sea. On the beach below were fifty of Bill's employees and friends.

"After five minutes in the air," says Calkins, "we dropped to about fifty feet above the water and retracted the gear and all the contents fell out."

The ashes floated through the air and came down slowly, twirling in the ocean breeze and gleaming in the soft California sunlight, spinning and spinning back toward the earth, before they landed directly in front of his beach house.

"It was wonderful," Jack recalls. "We all felt Bill would have said, 'Good job. Well done!'"

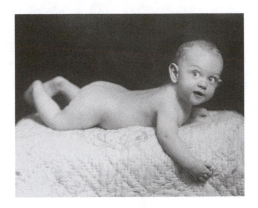

"Yes, I did smell the flowers along the way."

BILL DANIELS'
CABLE TELEVISION ACHIEVEMENTS

FIRST CABLE BROKERAGE BUSINESS

FIRST INVESTMENT BANKING FIRM

FIRST CABLE OPERATIONS MANAGEMENT COMPANY

FIRST MICROWAVE RELAY

FIRST COLOR LOCAL ORIGINATION STUDIO

FIRST TWENTY-FOUR-HOUR NEWS CHANNEL

FIRST REGIONAL SPORTS PROGRAMMING NETWORK

BILL DANIELS' AWARDS AND HONORS

1998
CABLE TELEVISION HALL OF FAME, INDUCTEE

1996
COLORADO BUSINESS HALL OF FAME, INDUCTEE
FEDERATION AERONAUTIQUE INTERNATIONAL,
C-1F CLASS RECORD, GLOBAL BUSINESS JET

1994
BANK OF AMERICA AWARD

1992
NATIONAL ACADEMY OF TELEVISION ARTS AND SCIENCES,
SPECIAL EMMY AWARD

1991
COLORADO ENTREPRENEUR OF THE YEAR
BROADCASTING MAGAZINE,
BROADCASTING HALL OF FAME, INDUCTEE

1989
DENVER ADVERTISING FEDERATION, FAME AND FORTUNE AWARD
WOMEN IN CABLE, ACCOLADE AWARD OF THE YEAR

1986
WALTER KAITZ FOUNDATION, WALTER KAITZ AWARD

1983
UNIVERSITY OF DENVER, HONORARY
DOCTORATE OF HUMANE LETTERS
NEW MEXICO MILITARY INSTITUTE, OUTSTANDING ALUMNUS
CABLE TELEVISION ADMINISTRATION & MARKETING SOCIETY,
GRAND TAM AWARD

1973
HUMANITARIAN OF THE YEAR IN DENVER

1965
NATIONAL CABLE TELEVISION ASSOCIATION, LARRY BOGGS AWARD

Index